There's a sea change sweeping the financial advice business. Anyone contemplating a career in this emerging profession should invest in the new third edition of John De Goey's *Professional Financial Advisor*.

—Jonathan Chevreau, Editor, *MoneySense*

When the minimum requirement to become a licensed financial advisor in Canada, consisting of a self-study course that can be completed in a few months, is coupled with a predominantly commission-based compensation system, consumers clearly need to educate themselves about shortcomings and conflicts of interest. I recommend this book not only for consumers of financial products, but also for financial advisors.

—Preet Banerjee, Personal Finance Commentator and *Globe and Mail* columnist

This book is important because it talks about how advisors can distinguish their services through their standards of evidence and disclosure. It is a refreshing and honest take on how financial advisors can offer genuine value to their clients.

—Tom Hamza, President, Investor Education Fund

John has a unique ability to explain personal finance in a clear and understandable way. He always gives knowledgeable, well-reasoned and practical answers to real-world questions—whether they are about investments, taxation or estate planning. His advice is invaluable.

—Mark Bunting, Anchor, *BNN Market Call*

An engaging chronicle of the progress being made toward professional status for financial advice-givers, *The Professional Financial Advisor III* is a great tool for helping consumers differentiate between product sales and professional advice.

—Cary List, President and CEO, Financial Planning Standards Council

D0249397

The Professional
Financial Advisor III
PUTTING TRANSPARENCY AND INTEGRITY FIRST

John J. De Goey

INSOMNIAC PRESS

Library and Archives Canada Cataloguing in Publication

De Goey, John J., 1963-
    The professional financial advisor III : putting transparency and integrity first / John J. De Goey.

Previous ed. published under title: The professional financial advisor II.
ISBN 978-1-55483-086-2

1. Financial planners--Canada. 2. Investment advisors--Canada.
3. Financial services industry--Canada. I. Title.

HG179.5.D44 2012   332.6'20971   C2012-905395-3

The publisher gratefully acknowledges the support of the Department of Canadian Heritage through the Canada Book Fund.

Printed and bound in Canada

Insomniac Press
192 Spadina Avenue, Suite 403
Toronto, Ontario, Canada, M5T 2C2
www.insomniacpress.com

Disclaimer

The opinions expressed are those of the author and not necessarily those of Burgeonvest Bick Securities Limited. The opinions and generalizations by the author concerning professionalism within the financial services industry reflect the lack of homogeneity among numerous providers of financial services from differing industries (insurance, banking, financial planning, and investment) and with differing standards of conduct based on the fact that each is covered by different enabling legislation and different regulators. For advisors (FSPs) who are regulated by the Investment Industry Regulatory Organization of Canada, certain generalizations about professionalism are not entirely accurate.

With respect to opinions relating to modern portfolio theory and passive versus active management, an attempt has been made to discuss these complex academic issues in simple terms. As such, the discussion does not fully reflect the breadth and depth of opinion and evidence regarding these topics, nor can it be expected to. Everyone's investment and retirement plans must be created to satisfy their particular situation. Therefore, it is recommended that the reader treat the information in this book as general in nature and consider getting advice from lawyers, accountants, financial planners, and other related professionals.

For my parents, Neil and Mary De Goey—
married for 50 years on October 20, 2012

Contents

Introduction

Every book—even subsequent editions of the same book —has an underlying theme. That theme can evolve over time and is often most obvious when considering the subtitle of the book.

The first edition of this book was released in 2003 with the subtitle, "Ethics, unbundling and other things to ask your financial advisor about." The primary idea then was to disturb investors enough to get them to confront their advisors in search of a better deal. Many investors ignored the book, but the financial advisors who read it were often perturbed that I was trying to incite a revolution of sorts in their own backyard.

In 2006, I released a second edition with the subtitle, "How the financial services industry hides the ugly truth." The primary thrust of that edition was that the industry was evolving and certain important elements were not being discussed. This time, instead of encouraging investors to confront their advisors (I have long used the acronym FSP for Financial Service Provider to capture the broad universe of people giving advice), I have tried to empower FSPs by helping them see that the industry has sold them on the idea of stock picking and market timing being value-adding pursuits, even though evidence based on probability suggests that that is not likely to be the case. There seems to have been a modest amount of behaviour change amongst FSPs over the past few years, but many remain unimpressed and firmly rooted in heritage-based value propositions and business models.

This third edition carries the subtitle, "Putting transparency and integrity first." Even as Canada has moved slowly to bring about regulatory reforms and to adopt more professional business models, many other nations in the Western world are forging ahead. Still, there are growing pockets within the Canadian FSP community that are embracing professionalism in a more concrete manner. The practices of more established professions are moving from being mere good ideas and best practices to mandatory preconditions for continuing to provide financial advice. The appetite for change is both clear and exciting.

Every edition has sought to be a bridge between ordinary consumers and mainstream FSPs. Many consumers tell me they don't always get the language of my books because they find the acronyms daunting and the subject matter boring. Meanwhile, many FSPs take exception to suggestions about positive change—perhaps because they have a different concept of progress—even as they find the lingo to be second nature. The idea here is not just to try to forge a consensus, but also to chronicle the process of evolution in the industry.

The financial services industry is going through more change than perhaps any other industry on the planet. As such, it seems only natural that there should be some way of examining where we've come from, where we are going and why. Without a purposeful feedback loop, both consumers and FSPs could be left grumbling to themselves about how the other party "doesn't understand them" and how things would be better if the other side simply "looked at things from our perspective." The third edition is neither pro-consumer nor anti-consumer. It is neither pro-FSP nor anti-FSP. Rather, it is intended as a sounding board to facilitate a purposeful dialogue between two solitudes that have grown alienated from one another. The performance of capital markets over the past decade or so certainly hasn't helped matters, either.

Given how fragmented the financial services industry is, it should come as no surprise that there are almost as many ways to 'run the money' as there are FSPs. It's not only about investing: Financial planning, debt repayment strategies, borrowing, insurance needs and tax integration are all to be considered in the field of comprehensive financial advice-giving. Today's FSPs have the choice between commissions and fees, between discretionary and non-discretionary account relationships and between individual securities, mutual funds, ETFs, wrap accounts, hedge funds, separately managed accounts and structured products as portfolio building blocks. Some 'buy and hold,' some 'trade opportunistically,' some use fundamental and or technical analysis, some rely extensively on their firm's research department—and some do things in an almost ad hoc manner. The point is that trying to be prescriptive in a world where there are so many different strokes for different folks is nearly impossible unless those prescriptions are so basic as be universal to all of the business models and value propositions (and many others!) mentioned above.

I'm also trying to chronicle industry developments while recognizing that there are differences between product licensing and service specialty. There are three primary licences an FSP can have: to sell insurance, to sell mutual funds and to sell securities. Some have more than one licence. Similarly, there are perhaps eight or ten designations that one might have to demonstrate specialized knowledge in a related competency. Since FSPs can have a designation without a licence and a licence without a designation, any discussion about an emerging consensus needs to be taken with a grain of salt. We're talking about a general direction for industry-wide change, but the path is not necessarily linear.

To my mind, the primary unifying element of this evolution is the transparency that comes from purposeful professional disclosure. The acronym STANDUP (Scientific Testing And Necessary Disclosure Underpin Professionalism) still applies as a touchstone for those FSPs who are leading the charge. This simple acronym captures the concept that true professionalism recognizes both real disclosure and evidence-based advice. For the most fundamental considerations, professionals disclose facts. This is in stark contrast to my other acronym of choice: SPANDEX (Sales Pitches and Non-Disclosure Eliminate eXcellence). I use SPANDEX as a way to categorize 'old school' FSPs who still function using a more traditional sales-oriented world view. The intention is to offer an extreme contrast so that readers can clearly differentiate between 'old' (traditional) and 'new' (enlightened) FSPs. In reality, very little is that cut and dried. Most FSPs have at least some elements of both stereotypes in their practices.

The move toward bona fide professional status now seems inevitable. Since the second edition was released, the Financial Planning Standards Council released its own "Vision 2020," which involves a commitment to having all CFPs recognized as full professionals by the year 2020. In addition, the Client Relationship Model (CRM) that was mentioned in passing in 2006 has now finally been enacted. Slowly but surely, the bar of transparency is being raised in terms of FSP compensation, client performance and relationship clarification. In the past few years, both Australia and the United Kingdom have banned embedded compensation as a means of FSP compensation. Meanwhile, the United States is openly musing about forcing all FSPs to adopt the 'fiduciary standard' regarding the primacy of client interests.

Just as those FSPs who moved toward an unbundled practice model have been leaders in the transition, so too are these nearly 18,000 CFPs leaders in education and training, best practices, disclosure (both in regard to compensation and the scope of any engagement) and ethical standards.

Of course, some FSPs use unbundled business models but aren't CFPs. Others are CFPs but use commission-based business models. In short, while there remains an undeniable lack of homogeneity, there is nonetheless a clear way forward in terms of what the business of providing financial advice will look like when it emerges from its transformational cocoon. And emerge it will.

Closer to home, some structural impediments have already been removed, while other elements of professionalism are now becoming mandatory. When the second edition of *TPFA* was released in 2006, there were still a number of firms that didn't have a genuine fee-based platform to accommodate those advisors who wanted to work using a more professional paradigm as part of their business model. Today, all of them have one. In 2006, there were only two firms offering low-cost passive exchange traded funds (ETFs) in Canada. Today there are seven.

Even with all that said, however, there are still some FSPs who simply will not get with the times and there is an emerging consensus that no one will make them do so, either. The historical absence of a forced professional standard that applies to all FSPs is important, because it means consumers need to be vigilant in separating the wheat from the chaff. There will be a few overt tests of professionalism, so consumers will need to understand what it is they are looking for. Professionally oriented (STANDUP) FSPs will be vying for the same business as sales-oriented (SPANDEX) FSPs and members of the public could easily end up working with one when they thought they'd be working with the other—unless they know what specific questions to ask and what specific attributes to seek out. No one will go around saying that a sales orientation is bad, but there will be tests to help the public determine whether the people they are considering hiring use one paradigm or the other. Consumer choice will hinge on the principles of informed consent and evidence-based disclosure.

Looking back on the past decade or so, it seems clear that an unbundled and professional business model was decidedly off the beaten path when the first and second editions of this book were released. Today, those concepts are not only seen as being legitimate, they are also gaining market share— with a large and varied array of available products to help facilitate and legitimize the transition. Almost ironically, the STANDUP trailblazers from the turn of the millennium are now seen as mainstream professional practitioners. Those 'early adopters' have already completed their transition and we are now entering the stage where the 'early majority' of FSPs has begun offering a more purposeful, transparent and client-centred service to clients across the country.

You can almost feel a tsunami of global proportions gathering strength as time goes on.

John J. De Goey
Toronto, August 2012

Part One
Preparing Financial Service Providers

Becoming an Advisor

The past gives us experience and memories; the present gives us challenges and opportunities; the future gives us vision and hope.
—William Arthur Ward

The Chinese word for change is comprised of symbols for risk and opportunity. Many people also like to cite the famous Chinese curse, "May you live in interesting times." There is indeed change going on in the financial services industry and we most certainly do live in "interesting times." So, how do we deal with this, especially since the framework of financial advice rests on rapidly shifting sands? In the past, most people in the financial services industry had titles that described their compartmentalized roles. As the distinctions blurred and everyone became involved in everyone else's business, old titles seemed increasingly inappropriate.

Before looking at how advisors (called 'Financial Service Providers' or FSPs for short) are transforming themselves—some voluntarily; others less so—it is important to consider how people go about becoming FSPs in the first place. There are many examples in life where people do certain things in certain ways simply because they've always done things that way and haven't stopped to consider alternatives. To paraphrase Pogo, "we have seen the enemy, and he is us."

Where Did We Come From?

Until the late 1980s, the dominant model for retail investor portfolio design was one of working with a stockbroker, mutual fund representative or insurance agent who earned commissions while constructing a portfolio of individual securities or selling insurance products. Clients paid handsome commissions for the buying and selling that occurred as a result of that advice. On the investment side, people really had no choice but to work through full-service brokers or mutual fund representatives because discount brokerages were just coming into existence.

The problem with a transaction-oriented business model is that it rewards all transactions—good, bad or otherwise. More trades mean more commissions for the broker. Transaction costs and taxes often correlate negatively to investor performance. The cardinal rule of the industry is that advice should be offered with the best interests of the client in mind.

More recently, many people switched from investing in individual securities to mutual funds. Many of those have since switched again—this time to exchange traded funds (ETFs). A large number of these people, however, still do not know exactly how products like mutual funds and ETFs work, what they cost or how FSPs are compensated. In general, the industry has moved from giving away the advice while charging for the transaction to virtually giving away the transaction while charging for the associated advice. In this age of disintermediation, the only viable value proposition for FSPs is one of superior advising.

Attitudes Constrain Progress

Offering comprehensive financial advice is becoming a profession. Some people reading this might have thought that giving financial advice already was a profession. That's what people in the industry would have us believe. They refer to Financial Service Providers as "trusted advisors" since offering trustworthy advice seems like an entirely professional thing to do.

Old course material used to refer to FSPs as "sales agents" and, frankly, that's what they were. Today, there's an accelerating transition afoot in financial services around the world. This transition recognizes that the best FSPs are far more comprehensive than mere sales representatives, and that they want both the tools necessary to do their jobs and the recognition that goes along with doing it. There are also some old-school FSPs who have not changed and are doing everything in their power to impede progress. Until very recently, corporate infrastructure and incentive frameworks favoured old-school FSPs through their focus on sales. These sorts of 'numbers-driven' metrics are less prevalent in the industry today.

There are still a number of areas where old and new remain in conflict. Fundamentally, we're talking about a progress versus status quo dichotomy. There is a clear trend in favour of constructive and purposeful progress. A number of factors will show the way. Here are three:

1. *Industry Associations and Professional Standards*

Every profession has its own association for individual practitioners and a number of industry trade associations have sprung up, vetting the professional standards and competencies of individual FSPs. This is surely the clearest evidence of a young profession. There is a broad consensus on the general attributes of a professional FSP, but also a whole lot of backbiting about who will monitor those attributes and protect consumers along the way. To make matters worse, FSPs needn't join any of these organizations if they don't want to. In the interim, consumers remain at risk.

2. *Proficiencies and Designations*

How are consumers going to determine which credentials are most appropriate if those in the financial services industry can't even agree amongst themselves? People understand that if they go to see a physician, they should expect to see a diploma displayed prominently in the office, attesting to the fact that the person they are seeing is an MD. The same goes for dentistry, accounting, engineering and architecture. Professions hold themselves to a consistent standard as set by consistent and rigorous training, suitable experience, peer review and ethical conduct. This in turn gives consumers a degree of confidence about a minimum level of competence. There is no such standard regarding financial advice in English-speaking Canada, although there is in Quebec.

At the turn of the twenty-first century, there were about twenty designations available to FSPs who wanted to demonstrate competency in some field of financial advice. Many people in the industry feel the situation is outright embarrassing. What self-respecting profession can't even agree on what is required to join? Today, the industry is coalescing around the Certified Financial Planner (CFP) designation conferred in Canada by the Financial Planning Standards Council (FPSC) as the title that most accurately denotes an FSP qualified to offer advice to the public.

This doesn't mean the other designations are substandard, only that they often convey competence in a more specialized area. The FPSC mandate is to "benefit the public and the financial planning profession by establishing and enforcing uniform professional standards for financial planners."

The many other designations are generally held by relatively fewer (and sometimes substantially fewer) practitioners. In a world where consumers expect to have access to professionals throughout the country, those people representing themselves as practitioners need to offer the size and scope to be available in towns, villages and countryside as well as in the big urban centres. In simple terms, everyone knows what to expect when seeking out a medical professional, but if there are only 1,200 of them in the country and the nearest one is a two-hour drive away from where you live, then ready and personalized access wouldn't likely be considered part of the offering. There are nearly 18,000 CFPs in Canada and fewer practitioners for most other similar designations. As a simple and practical numbers game, therefore, the CFP mark stands the best chance of offering the scope of a national presence that is needed to go along with the more traditional elements of professionalism.

3. *Unbundling*

Simply put, unbundling (the removal of embedded compensation) allows investment products to be made available based on merit and suitability alone. There can be no second-guessing the FSP's motive. Clients no longer have to wonder if their FSP is recommending a product because it's best or simply because it will pay him more. It is doubtful that true product independence could ever be attained without unbundling.

The financial services industry has already gone through a partial transformation. Conventional stockbrokers made (and many continue to make) commissions on both the buy and the sell recommendations that were accepted by their clients. The same holds for many mutual fund representatives. Paying a prescribed fee is likely the best way to eliminate this bias. Ironically, this might involve paying an FSP to "do nothing," but if "nothing" (i.e. deliberately not trading) is the right thing to do, then everyone should hail this as significant progress. The aim here is to develop a framework where the FSP's motive and corresponding advice are aligned with consumer interests and cannot be called into question.

The idea behind unbundling is that FSPs can charge a separate fee for the advice being offered, but the compensation that was previously embedded in the product would no longer be allowed to cloud the issue of suitability. Most investment products today are still sold with embedded compensation going to the FSP for completing the sale. This is especially disappointing for do-it-yourself (DIY) investors who want to use advances in technology to engage in disintermediation. These people often end up paying their discount broker for the (non-existent) 'advice' costs that are built into certain products.

Many FSPs rightly want shelf space as bona fide professionals in the minds of consumers. They position themselves as professionals who can wisely discern suitable options in a sea of complicated financial choices. Without unbundling, however, that claim usually rings hollow. Embedded compensation creates bias, the antithesis of true professionalism.

The financial services industry needs unbundling because unbundling creates trust. However, SPANDEX FSPs generally don't want to have full and frank conversations with their clients about how and how much they are being paid. It's easier to sell things when you don't have to have a discussion about what they cost.

The best FSPs know all about the importance of trust. They know that without trust, FSPs can say whatever they want and their clients still won't likely believe them, even if what they says is measured, appropriate and fundamentally true. There is a clear need to suspend self-interest when offering financial advice, and unbundling does this. There's a certain kind of unimpeachable integrity that comes from being able to say, "There are a few options here; the pros and cons of each are as follows, and no matter which you choose, I'll be paid the same. The best option is the one that works best for you."

Without trust, advice is suspect. It has been said that the fundamental job of the FSP is to create a space where the truth can be spoken, heard and believed. Going forward, there will almost certainly be a premium placed on good governance and transparent business relationships. So far in Canada, FSPs have moved to more transparent and unbundled relationships voluntarily. Other parts of the world have made this transition mandatory. One wonders how much longer Canadian regulators will wait before they, too, make embedded compensation as taboo as smoking during pregnancy.

Where Consumers Fit In

There is a wide range of consumer demand for financial services in the marketplace and it is often difficult for FSPs and their firms to deliver a consistent 'brand experience' when consumer wants and needs are all over the map. Some consumers want more detail on statements, while others would be quite content to get fewer statements altogether since they often don't open them anyway and generally see reporting as a nuisance. Part of the problem is that some consumers find statements too hard to understand.

When considering financial advice, a continuum can be drawn that demonstrates the problem. On one extreme, we have people who want to do everything themselves and find any contact with the financial services industry a nuisance; on the other, we have people who do virtually nothing for themselves, choosing instead to abdicate their responsibilities altogether. Both extremes can be dangerous. Here's a quick glance at this continuum of consumer attributes:

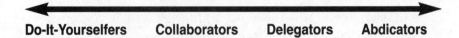

Do-It-Yourselfers   Collaborators   Delegators   Abdicators

Most consumers find themselves somewhere in the middle of the continuum and are generally inclined to some degree of collaboration, with an increasing likelihood of working with an FSP as they move to the right. The challenge for FSPs is that many are trying to be all things to all people, working with whomever comes through the door. They would likely be better off if they focused on one subset of the population: the delegators.

Abdicators are even more likely to do as they are advised, but the best FSPs want their clients to feel a sense of ownership; abdicators don't make for fulfilling client relationships. If FSPs are offering stewardship to clients who appreciate it, everyone feels more fulfilled. Rendering advice is more rewarding when there's a sense that people receiving the advice really want to take destiny in their own hands rather than be prescribed cookie-cutter solutions.

I asked a few prominent industry observers to weigh in on these matters. The first was Tom Hamza of the Ontario Securities Commission's Investor Education Fund. He said:

> There are very few things that are less tangible than investment products and advice. Investors are typically buying products and services where they won't need the results for decades and with the expectation that things will somehow work out. In this environment, clarity can be hard to come by and investor education is a constant need.[1]

John Heinzl, who writes the "Investor Clinic" column for the *Globe and Mail*, seems to agree. He said:

I strongly encourage people to learn as much as they can about investing, whether they work with an advisor or use a self-directed account. Fortunately, investors today are asking more questions about things like costs, compensation, product suitability and such than ever before. Seeing as they also have so much good information available to them, they should be able to find and apply whatever knowledge they need fairly easily.[2]

Former Ontario Securities Commission commissioner and outspoken reform proponent Glorianne Stromberg was perhaps the clearest in her assessment. She said:

No one takes issue with the fact that when they work with a personal trainer, they will have to exert some effort if they are going to benefit from the relationship. Similarly, when you work with a Financial Services Provider, you need to exert some effort. You need to identify your investment objectives, your timelines and your tolerance for risk. You need to understand what you are investing in. This includes obtaining and reading prospectuses and annual reports, reviewing your account statements and reviewing your performance with your FSP in the context of your investment and financial plan.[3]

There's no single best way to determine whether one should work with an FSP or not, but as a general rule, the further right you go on the spectrum above, the greater the likelihood you'll need an FSP.

For people who want to learn more, some website resources might be useful. John has asked me to recommend http://www.theglobeandmail.com/authors/john-heinzl and while Tom invites you to visit www.getsmarteraboutmoney.ca

Preparing FSPs

Men are men before they are lawyers, or physicians, or merchants, or manufacturers; and if you make them capable and sensible men, they will make themselves capable and sensible lawyers or physicians.

—John Stuart Mill

There can be little doubt that we are in the final stages of the creation of a new profession focused on providing financial advice. People have been giving financial advice for years without its being a bona fide profession, just as people built structures before there were professionally certified engineers. Over time, the need to formally train workers and standardize the building work being done moved from being a good idea to being entrenched as a requirement for doing business. What about financial advice? On the surface, it might seem that today's FSPs can be considered professionals…just how rigorous does professional training have to be?

The great number of people who introduce themselves as true professionals despite having met no demonstrable or relevant proficiency requirement underscores the importance of the need for all professionals to have recognized designations.

In the future, formal academic programs will have to be revamped and expanded so that the coursework represents broad exposure to a number of related disciplines. Self-study licensing courses would never be permitted for law, accounting or medicine. The depth and breadth of knowledge simply requires formal classroom training. Besides, the stakes are much too high to consider offering anything less to the public.

At present, there is nothing similar to medical internships, accounting internships or bar exams. As a result, most FSPs hold simple licences to sell a product or two, but no designation. In fact, only a minority have a designation of any kind. As far as anyone can tell, consumers seldom make a decision about whom they will work with based on unambiguous attributes such as a recognized designation. Anyone with a licence to sell a product or products can offer advice—even if they have no dedicated expertise regarding anything other than product sales. Since the industry evolved from the notion that advice is ancillary to a product sale, as opposed to being a necessary pre-condition of assessing suitability before a sale, we've spent generations putting the cart before the horse.

Offering Financial Advice: A Profession for Our Times

The need for qualified financial advice is especially acute for certain segments of society: professionals, corporate executives and business owners. These people often lead busy lives and need to consider a range of options that take into account a wide selection of variables and possible outcomes. There may be multiple objectives where trade-offs between income, security, lifestyle, creditor protection, financial independence, estate planning, tax planning and other matters need to be taken into account.

Let's have a look at what some of the more established professions do:

Doctors and Surgeons

Physicians and surgeons are among the most revered

professionals on the planet. They enjoy a level of implicit trust that most other professionals couldn't even dream about.

Although these medical specialists perform a number of delicate procedures routinely, they still insist on written disclosure and consent before proceeding. It is standard procedure to sit down with the patient and explain, in terms the patient can understand, the risks and limitations of the they are considering. What is the likely outcome for the patient if they do nothing? What is the probability of success? How long is the recovery likely to take if the operation is successful? What is the probability and frequency of failure? What is the worst that can happen? Has the procedure been explained to the patient in clear terms that the patient understands? If yes, has the patient ultimately consented to the procedure?

This is all documented in writing and the patient will be asked to sign a consent form waiver acknowledging these discussions and disclosures before heading to the operating room. The chips will fall where they may, but at least the decision about what to do was made with a clear and purposeful understanding of what the problem was and what the risks, rewards and limitations were before getting started. It should be obvious that this process also protects the professional. There are many who feel those who offer financial advice should be obligated to make similar disclosures before products can be purchased.

There would still be a sales pitch element to many recommendations, but at least the consumer would see some uniformity of disclosure regarding pertinent facts relating to their choices. Other salient points that could be included in the point-of-sale disclosure might be: product cost, FSP fee and portfolio turnover (tax efficiency). Improved disclosure might stifle sales a little in the short run, but it would also add some much-needed trust and transparency.

Some FSPs recommend products based on superior short-term performance, even though there is evidence that short-term performance is not indicative of long-term performance. Over longer time frames, the percentage of products that beat their benchmarks decreases. Very few FSPs disclose these points and few consumers think to ask what might go wrong as well as what might go right. Furthermore, most people's tolerance for (and ability to react to) risk changes over time.

If a surgeon explains every reasonable facet of a procedure to a patient but does not receive written consent to proceed and something goes wrong, there may be a substantial liability. Why should the standard be different for your financial health? Let's take a look at some of the more important aspects of professionalism on display in other established professions.

Dentists

Dentists are reliable and systematized. Say what you will about their operations, but they provide a model of consistency. First, the hygienist does the relatively general spadework, and then the dentist comes in to do whatever specialized procedures are required. At the end of each session, the next appointment is scheduled for about twenty-seven weeks later. How many FSPs do this? Meetings with FSPs are not something people do regularly. Some clients only need to come in once a year, but there are those who may need or wish to come in two or more times a year. There should always be a system in place to ensure meetings are happening in a consistent, predictable and purposeful manner.

Lawyers

Lawyers seem to get much less respect from the general public than other professionals. There are three things that lawyers do, however, that are extremely professional: they use letters of engagement, have a set fee schedule and carry liability insurance. Let's take a look at each and explore how the use of a similar series of documents would raise the bar substantially for those FSPs who wish to present themselves as professionals.

The Law Society of Upper Canada recently took the unusual step of defining professionalism for legal practitioners in Ontario. The Law Society states that:

> As a personal characteristic, professionalism is revealed in an individual's attitude and approach to his or her occupation, and is commonly characterized by intelligence, integrity, maturity and thoughtfulness. There is an expectation among lawyers, whose occupation is defined as a profession, and in the public who receive legal services, that professionalism will inform a lawyer's work and conduct.

The LSUC goes on to itemize the various components of professionalism. These listed are: scholarship, integrity, honour, leadership, independence, pride, spirit, collegiality, service and balanced commercialism. The widely accepted concept of professional practice standards is gaining credence everywhere. One of the most important aspects of such standards is the letter of engagement. Here, both the nature and the scope of the engagement between the client and the lawyer are mutually defined and agreed upon before services are rendered. There are many aspects to this concept, including:

- identifying services to be provided
- disclosing both the nature and amount of remuneration involved
- identifying the responsibilities of both parties
- establishing the duration of the agreement
- disclosing any related ties or potential conflicts of interest (both real and perceived)
- confirming confidentiality

FSPs need to be absolutely clear about how much they charge by using a compensation disclosure document. A separate disclosure document at the point-of-sale would go a long way toward clarifying how and how much FSPs are paid.

All professionals carry liability insurance to cover errors and omissions. Lawyers deserve some credit because they are perhaps the most keenly aware of the liabilities they assume when offering their services to the public. Clients should have some assurance that they will be covered in the unlikely event there should be a major oversight or error on the part of their FSP. After all, their personal fortune is usually at stake.

Lawyers are self-regulating through the use of law societies. Ontario legislation, primarily the Law Society Act, authorizes the LSUC to educate and license lawyers and to regulate their conduct and competence. The society's bylaws set out the professional and ethical obligations of all members of the profession. Those who fail to meet these obligations are subject to the society's complaints and disciplinary process.

The observation that most people make in reviewing these attributes is that they are positive when present, but that they are unenforceable in a world where professionals and sales representatives co-exist and where the latter are not held to the same standards as the former. Later, in the final section, we'll take a look at how to get around this problem. The short answer is to establish clear terms of reference for professional conduct in law (likely provincial) in order to allow professional FSPs to self-regulate (i.e. to set the terms of joining the club and to enforce those same rules for everyone's mutual benefit). The flip side is that it needs to be absolutely clear to consumers whether the person they are considering working with is in the club in the first place or not. They will not be forced to work with one type of FSP or another, but when competency is made to be a clear differentiator, consumers will be able to 'vote with their feet' if there's a recognition that the person who is advising them is ill-equipped to do so properly. In the end, FSPs will be either proud sales representatives or proud professionals. What will end is the abominable practice of having disingenuous sales representatives masquerade as professionals with the broader public being none the wiser about the distinctions that should have always been clear from the outset.

People Don't Care What You Know

Perhaps most tellingly, consumers of professional services often choose their professionals on the basis of relationships and the gut feeling they have at their first meeting. We're all human and no one wants to feel like a number or an account or the living embodiment of a certain number of 'billable hours.' There is a saying that every FSP comes to learn within weeks of starting the job: people don't care what you know until they know that you care. Although a little trite, this is generally good advice.

FSPs are often reminded that they work in a relationship business in which connecting with the client is more than half the battle. Unfortunately, most consumers don't have the wherewithal to make a meaningful assessment of the services provided (or about to be provided) by the professional. They look at the décor of the office, gauge the firmness of the handshake and hope that the person who referred them did not have a uniquely positive experience prior to recommending the services of the advisor in question. All the while thinking: I sure hope I can trust this person.

The client has to presume that the FSP has a certain level of competency and a reasonable degree of personal integrity. Conversations are held, goals are explored and written recommendations are made before most clients embark on a business relationship. As a general rule, the more understanding the FSP seems, the more likely they are to get the business. This represents the triumph of compassion over competency.

The point here is that FSP competency and the best interests of the consumer are paramount. There can be no doubt that competency combined with compassion is preferred, but given the choice, society has clearly chosen competency over compassion. In the professions, it is better to be a brilliant technician with horrible people skills than a horrible technician with brilliant people skills. Imagine a 'nice gal' in medical school whom everyone liked immensely and who had the most pleasant bedside manner in the class. Even if her grades indicate otherwise, should her professors pass her just so that prospective patients could have access to her wonderful demeanour?

Many of the most valuable benefits that accrue to those who work with effective FSPs are emotional rather than logical or intellectual. How can anyone solve human problems if consideration is only given to non-human questions of dollars, tax rates, income levels and pension plans?

On the surface, it seems we're making real progress toward creating a profession. There are a number of problems that continue to persist, however. There's so much that FSPs don't know, largely because they haven't been taught. After all, so much of what FSPs convey to those they work with is predicated on what they were taught in the first place.

Before society can become competent in financial matters, our FSPs need to be properly taught. Most people giving financial advice today were not formally (i.e. academically) trained to do so. Consequently, misinformation, no matter how well-intentioned, can take hold and lead to poor planning decisions down the road.

Many of the most important theories about capital markets that are taught in first-year MBA finance texts are mentioned only as passing footnotes in Canada's securities licensing texts. On top of that, there are a number of sound academic concepts that are never even mentioned in licensing textbooks for insurance.

This is not to suggest that most FSPs have anything less than the best intentions. Rather, many FSPs simply wish to convey what they have been taught to their clients as best they can. But if what the FSPs know comes largely from licensing courses that will allow them to sell products rather than offer competent, professional advice, there are bound to be biases and blind spots.

This gap in the preparation of FSPs could be revealing when considering their predisposition against certain concepts and products. Unwittingly, many FSPs have been co-opted as de facto sales agents for the products offered through their initial point of entry rather than true professionals who are inclined to survey the market for the most suitable products as dispassionate protectors of their clients' collective welfare.

When giving testimony before a court of law, witnesses

are obliged to tell the truth, the whole truth and nothing but the truth. Two out of three ain't bad. Some believe that by not telling FSPs the whole truth when training them to advise retail clients, we only hurt ourselves by doing a major disservice to the clients we aim to protect.

No professional accreditation means no professional status. Of course, people who are licensed to sell products could still do so. They would simply be excluded from being called 'professionals' and be expected to forgo the rights and privileges associated with that status. Such people would simply be called what they are: salespeople.

Presently, most of the FSPs offering advice to retail clients did not go to university to get direct training as financial advisors. Recently, a number of colleges and universities have begun offering a curriculum that leads to the CFP designation. The graduates of these programs are, to my mind, among the effective founders of what will one day be recognized as the world's newest profession. Of course, they're not the only people offering financial advice.

Practical Professional Challenges

There's a lot that goes into creating a profession, and there are a number of technical questions that need to be consistently addressed in the academic training provided before financial advice becomes a truly professional calling. These are matters of preference, training and disclosure. All need to be considered, but here are some of the most notable:

Integrating Suitable Investments with Actual Goals

The objective "to retire at age sixty-five in 2027 with no debts and a retirement income that is equivalent to at least two-thirds of what I averaged in my last five years on the job and lasting for as along as I live" is seldom found anywhere on a 'Know Your Client' application form. This in spite of the fact that such a sentence would demonstrate that the client has succinctly defined financial independence in personal, measurable and practical terms. We're dealing with an industry that is defined and regulated by product choices, not the lifestyle choices that are made as a result of those product choices.

Fee Impact on Calculations and Expectations

Many people believe that true professionals need not only justify their fees but also must account for them when called upon to do so. What rate(s) of return should be used in doing financial independence calculations? In the 1990s, there were some unscrupulous FSPs who were telling their clients they should plan to get long-term returns in the neighbourhood of 12% annually. Some actually used this as a client-acquisition strategy.

Many of the most highly respected academics expect long-term equity returns in the 6% to 8% range for the foreseeable future. That's a far cry from the numbers that many FSPs assume when doing financial independence modelling for clients. Furthermore, everyone should plan for retirement based on real return: the return above inflation. After all, you'll be living your retirement (and paying for it) in inflation-adjusted dollars, not today's dollars. Simple logic demonstrates that the average return for any investment is likely to be the return of the benchmark minus the investment's cost. For example, if the Canadian stock market returned 10% while a mutual fund investing in that market has an MER of 2.4%, the expected long-term return is 7.6%. Over the course of twenty or more years, a difference of 2% or more is gargantuan. The need for meaningful, professional disclosure is evident here, but this is an area where in the past many FSPs have admittedly used some discretion.

Variability of Returns

At present, most illustrations done by FSPs involve assumptions that include a single, unvarying rate of return based on some assumed average. But markets are highly volatile, so the generated results may deviate substantially from actual experience. As a result, modelling that features a probability component is often far more meaningful and informative because it allows for a wider range of possible outcomes.

Time Diversification

Many FSPs encourage investor clients to take a "long-term view." Clients, in turn, often ask their FSP how long "the long term" really is. There's no simple answer. The short answer, however, is that risk (also called 'variability' or 'standard deviation') goes down over time. There's a saying in the portfolio management business that states returns are unknowable in the short term, but in the long term, they are virtually inevitable.

Process, Not Product

Advisory firms tell their FSPs that process is more important than products, but their actions tell a different story. Many even run professional development sessions where they go on and on about the importance of having a process for making investment recommendations. They talk about making recommendations using a consistent, repeatable and unambiguous process, which leads to a more scientific asset allocation that is implemented through an Investment Policy Statement (IPS). If corporate bosses insist that FSPs are better off using wrap accounts (customized portfolios featuring asset mix, reporting, security selection and so forth, 'wrapped' into one product) to calibrate client-specific and risk-adjusted returns, why should they care if they use active investment products, passive investment products, or both, so long as the process is consistent and defensible?

And yet it seems that they care very much. Corporate decision-makers have gone so far as to establish points programs for product sales with quadruple points for these process-driven products. When pressed for a reason, the quadruple weighting is justified in terms of offering a positive incentive for advisors who make the transition from a more transaction-oriented practice to a more process-driven relationship model.

What Next?

As the consensus emerges on how the financial services industry will evolve over time, the next questions revolve around what needs to be done to ensure an honourable and responsible transition. What remains to be decided is how and when this change is going to occur. If everyone understands where we are and agrees on where we're going, then surely the next question must be how to get there from here.

Having come this far, it seems that the best way to understand the disconnect between what many FSPs purport to be (professionals) and what many of them often are (sales representatives) is to look not only at what they are taught but also at how they are taught and by whom.

Inefficient Markets

If a man is offered a fact which goes against his instincts, he will scrutinize it closely, and unless the evidence is overwhelming, he will refuse to believe it. If, on the other hand, he is offered something which affords a reason for acting in accordance to his instincts, he will accept it even on the slightest evidence.

—Bertrand Russell

Having already discussed the mindset of those who work in the business of picking stocks, it should be obvious that the dominant paradigm of the financial services industry is that stock picking is not only valuable but entirely rational. As such, I believe it is safe to say that most industry commentators would agree that the vast majority of all FSPs believe stock picking can be practiced in a manner that is likely to add value more often than not over long time frames. The notion here is to 'outperform' a benchmark through shrewdness, intelligent analysis and a breadth and depth of insight that most individuals could never muster on their own. Not surprisingly, a substantial percentage of individual consumers believe this too. This is presumably why many people use FSPs in the first place.

The idea behind market inefficiency is that a person with reasonable intelligence and diligence can consistently beat the consensus view after accounting for costs. People will gladly pay someone who is thought to be an above average stock picker because no one wants to settle for average when it comes to investment decision-making.

As a result of this perspective, most FSPs recommend that their clients use active management as the predominant and often exclusive way of managing money. They engage in fundamental and technical analysis, do copious amounts of due diligence and generally think of a number of ingenious ways to outsmart their peers in an attempt to get a leg up in determining how much stocks will move, when they will move, the direction they will move and the reasons behind the move. All these people have to do to make money is figure out where the crowd went wrong and then make buy-and-sell decisions to exploit the collective inaccuracy of the market as a whole.

The majority of FSPs are proponents of active management. This is true whether they are licensed to sell mutual funds, a wide range of securities or insurance products. It is true whether the FSP in question has a designation or not. It is true whether that FSP works for a large national institution or a small mom-and-pop shop. It is true whether that FSP is fee based or commission based. In short, no matter how you segment the industry, there is a clear preference among FSPs of all kinds for active management.

The prevailing view within the industry is that active management is the best way to go. Companies have been known to say things like:

We strongly believe consistent outperformance will result from extensive fundamental research on the equity side. You need to have a consistency of approach. We are very focused on the portfolio construction process to ensure we have the right risk controls in place. We feel strongly this philosophy will lead to superior risk-adjusted returns with the consistency and the stability to add value over a long period.

Can't you just feel the conviction? The thing about

conviction, though, is that it can be rational and based on fact, or it can be based on something rather less—an opinion or way of doing things, perhaps. For most people reading quotes like the one above, what comes across is the strong emotional conviction that whatever these people are doing, they sure believe that it works.

In fact, if you just listened to the certainty in what was being said and ignored the content, you'd swear the person doing the talking was a credible, professional practitioner in their field. A good number of industry participants have that kind of conviction when it comes to market inefficiency. Of course, there's a good deal of evidence to the contrary. Still, conviction and proof are different things. Unfortunately, when laypeople are ill-equipped to discern between real insight and practitioner sleight-of-hand, conviction might be the only thing that layperson has to go by.

You'll note that this is by far the shortest chapter in the book. The reason for this brevity is balance. By adding a chapter about active management, I'm offering a counterpoint to an industry that simply refuses to reciprocate in many instances. Short as this chapter is, it likely offers more content about active management than is found in the Canadian Securities Course (CSC) textbook about passive management—and the CSC is the course that all brokerage-based FSPs study before offering advice to retail investors.

Efficient Markets

Great spirits have always encountered violent opposition from mediocre minds.

—Albert Einstein

The large majority of stakeholders (including most FSPs) have come to believe that people can predict how current events can lead to making insightful calls on the impact on security prices. This kind of information and all associated market gyrations are, by definition, unknowable in advance. Random events simply cannot be reliably predicted and exploited. Investing is about markets working properly, whereas stock picking is akin to speculation based on markets not working properly. Making decisions to buy and sell based on random events is speculation masquerading as rational decision-making. The expected return on speculation before costs is zero. Since speculation has an associated cost, the expected net return is actually negative.

The Efficient Market Hypothesis

In the early 1960s, a graduate student at the University of Chicago named Eugene Fama put forward the Efficient Market Hypothesis (EMH). The EMH has three variations (based on the availability of information) and generally suggests that it is exceedingly difficult for active managers to add value in the long run after fees are taken into account because the movement of stock prices cannot be predicted.

Since there is no way to definitively prove or disprove market efficiency or inefficiency, nearly fifty years have gone by without a resolution to this debate. I use the word 'debate' loosely here. Many people in academia have had many a heated discussion about EMH. There's probably not a single finance student who hasn't learned about it. Most FSPs, however, give the idea very little serious consideration.

In the previous chapter, I mentioned that most FSPs are not able to reliably explain market efficiency. This is probably because they were never taught EMH. Given that most FSPs know essentially nothing about EMH, just how likely is it that they will be able to reliably advise their clients about the pros and cons of both the active and passive approaches?

As with the belief in the existence of God, different people may be persuaded or dissuaded by different things. Nonetheless, Dr. Fama, now a world-renowned professor in finance, has made a lasting impact in his field. The concept of market 'efficiency' (now frequently referred to by Dr. Fama and his research associate, Professor Ken French, as market 'equilibrium') is predicated on the notion that everyone has essentially the same information at the same time and that it is therefore impossible for any one manager to consistently exploit that information before anyone else does. Professors Fama and French have come to prefer the term 'equilibrium' because they feel it more accurately depicts the inherent risk/ return relationship in equity markets.

Put another way, it's nearly impossible for any one manager to consistently beat the market by digesting financial information and acting on it. It follows that most pension fund managers, mutual fund managers and discretionary brokers do not add value through security selection in their well-intentioned work. Ironically, their hyper-competitiveness against one another only ensures greater efficiency of the market. In highly efficient markets, active managers generate consistently superior returns that exceed a benchmark only by taking on a similarly high level of risk relative to that benchmark.

Economists have a term that explains the added benefit of each additional unit of a product or service: 'marginal utility.' If you have 50 analysts, markets might be said to be somewhat efficient. If you have 500 analysts, markets might be said to be highly efficient. If you have 5,000 (and the world has far more than 5,000 analysts and researchers), you've probably moved to the point where each additional participant actually does more harm than good. Most people don't suggest capital markets are totally efficient. However, it is probably fair to say that there's a consensus among the world's leading academics that markets are 'sufficiently efficient' and that additional attempts to exploit whatever inefficiencies might remain are largely a waste of time and money.

The industry mentality is that it makes sense to try to beat the market. In spite of this, passive products have been steadily gaining market share over the past decade or so. The best FSPs do what is right for their clients in spite of what their peers, employers or previous product suppliers might want them to do. In a later chapter, we'll take a closer look at how successful active managers have been in trying to deliver on their collective value proposition of 'outperformance.'

Market Eqilibrium and Alchemy

Years ago, I was having a conversation with an industry CEO about the efficiency of capital markets. I mentioned that I believed the balance of empirical evidence shows that markets are highly efficient. To my mind, 'efficient' means 'correct enough that it is difficult to reliably exploit any mispricings.' He said that although he did not agree with my assessment overall, he did concede that the U.S. market is indeed efficient. That conversation has stuck with me. How many other senior management types and product suppliers privately believe that at least some of the world's markets cannot be reliably beaten?

Many believe that 'groupthink' is a powerful motivator of what is said and done in the world in general and the financial services industry in particular. Even as firms try to make a big deal of their 'independent thinking,' most tend to act in a manner that doesn't stray too far from the path of convention. How much longer can this go on? If the weight of the majority of empirical evidence seems to favour the efficient market view, why have opinions been slow to shift? Is market equilibrium a matter of fact or opinion?

Over long time frames, 'beating the market' becomes a finger trap sort of exercise. You've probably seen those little finger traps that can be placed on two opposing digits; the harder you try to get out, the more difficult it becomes. Analysts and money managers are always trying to outwit one another in an attempt to exploit whatever mispricings exist. As some people see it, the problem is that the more they do to exploit mispricings, the less likely it is that those mispricings will exist over time, making the outwitting part increasingly improbable.

If markets do a reasonably precise job of setting prices that accurately reflect all available information about any given security at any given time, then those prices are likely to be pretty accurate. Furthermore, since inaccuracies are just as likely to be positive as negative, it might be futile to attempt exploitation, since the mispricing is equally likely to show up in either direction.

If, for instance, markets are 85% 'correct,' then a stock that trades for $10 might not actually be worth $10. It could be worth as little as $8.50 or as much as $11.50. But since no one can say for sure which side to err on, the consensus best guess of $10 is about as good a proxy for fair market value as you will find anywhere. Making money by picking stocks usually requires that both the degree and the direction of any mispricing be reliably quantified.

Since there's a lot of money to be made in managing other people's money, the industry naturally attracts a lot of bright, hard-working and insightful people. These highly motivated people are constantly competing with one another to determine which stocks are mispriced, by how much and in which direction. The more they compete, the more they are right in identifying mispricings. The more they identify them, the more they can exploit them. The more they exploit them, however, the less likely it is that those mispricings will persist.

Note that the number or percentage of indexers is immaterial in this line of thinking. Market equilibrium is unchanged if the number of market participants changes. Good stock picking exploits mispricings out of existence whether there are a lot or a few people engaging in the exploitation. The critical point is that stock picking is a zero sum game before costs are considered and a negative sum game after costs are considered. Since trades cannot be executed on a cost-free basis, all trading activity can be said to reduce expected returns over time. The question that traders need to ask themselves is: who's on the other side of this trade? By definition, whenever there's a 'winner' in a trade, the person on the 'other side' is 'losing' by an identical amount. Everyone who trades presumably does so because of the belief that the trade adds value. Only half of those people can possibly be correct. This is a metaphysical certainty.

The preceding examples demonstrate the difference of

opinion regarding both the existence and degree of capital market equilibrium between various participants. In Western societies, people cherish their freedom of opinion. My concern is that it is unclear if what is known about capital markets ought to be depicted as fact or opinion. Ratings agencies were asked to explain the bankruptcies of massive institutions in light of the mortgage crisis and misunderstandings regarding credit default swaps of 2007, 2008 and 2009. They took the collective position that many of the defaults in AAA debt should not be too surprising since all they had offered was a mere 'opinion' about their creditworthiness. It seems to me that 'opinions' can be quite convenient in this business— especially when they allow entire organizations to believe things that, in the light of day, are clearly not what they seem. In future chapters, we'll take a look at the factual data regarding attempts to beat the market. I'll leave it to you to decide if the information provided constitutes a series of facts or a series of opinions.

Where's Alpha?

You've probably come across the famous *Where's Waldo?* books where people look at complex illustrations to find a character named Waldo. The corporate stock-picking industry plays a version of this little game, except with a twist: people in the industry are constantly on the lookout for Alpha, the active management equivalent of Waldo.

In short, Alpha is the extent that performance above a certain benchmark can be attributed to superior security selection. Finding Alpha is all about beating the market and is portrayed by industry types as being akin to finding the Holy Grail. There's only one problem: Alpha is sort of like the Loch Ness monster. There have been alleged sightings, but no one has been able to definitively prove that Alpha really exists. People who think they've seen Alpha typically end up admitting that they merely ran into his evil twin, Randomness.

Sighting skills used in this game actually seem to weaken over time. The longer one plays the game, the worse one gets. Over a one-year period, people are tripping over all the Alpha that's out there. Over three to five years, Alpha becomes a little harder to find. Over ten years, finding Alpha becomes downright difficult. Over more than twenty years, it becomes doubtful that Alpha even exists. Like capturing a yeti in a blinding snowstorm, capturing long-term Alpha is a virtually impossible task.

The thing about stock market efficiency is that it's self-correcting. Looking for exploitable market inefficiencies involves looking for ways to exploit market mispricings. The problem is that as soon as the inefficiency is found, it is exploited mercilessly until it no longer exists. In other words, the expedition team effectively causes the thing they are looking for to disappear as a direct consequence of their looking so hard.

Are you confused yet? So are the people who could have sworn they saw Alpha just recently. Let's say someone discovers that stocks with a year-end from January 1 to June 30 consistently outperform stocks with a year-end from July 1 to December 31. As soon as the discovery becomes known and accepted, the price of the stocks with the early year-end will go up and the price for the stocks with the late year-end will go down until the current prices of both sets of stocks fairly and accurately reflect the new information. Even if you could have beaten the market by buying stocks with an early year-end yesterday, that little trick won't work today.

The reason for this is the long-term drag on performance caused by management fees and expenses. If the odds are

48% or 49% in your favour that you'll win any 'Where's Alpha?' contest in the short run, then it becomes nearly certain that you will lose the contest if you play long enough. It's a simple matter of probability. Active managers would never admit to their collective poor track record. It's far more profitable to round up creditors with an appetite for the bragging rights associated with 'bagging the big one.' It leads to more fees to be paid to the search party.

What He Said

When it comes to discussing potentially contentious topics, some people's opinions are just more credible than others. Many of these people have Nobel Prizes to show for their work, while others are revered as investment geniuses. Some of the most intelligent and reputable people in finance have gone on the record with a simple opinion: you can't reliably beat the market unless you take on more risk than the market. Let's look at a number of quotations from some esteemed experts.

William F. Sharpe won the Nobel Prize in Economics in 1990 for his work on the capital asset pricing model (CAPM). In "The Parable of the Money Managers," he asks: "Why pay people to gamble with your money?"[1] Compliance people don't like it when FSPs compare active management to gambling, so I won't do that. Instead, I'll simply point out that a Nobel Laureate thinks the analogy is a fair one. I suspect more people would sooner listen to Sharpe than to me, anyway.

One of the most acclaimed economists of our time is Paul Samuelson, who won the Nobel Prize in Economics in 1970. Here's what Samuelson has to say about the subject:

Ten thousand money managers all look equally good or bad. Each expects to do 3% better than the mob. Each has put together a convincing story. After the fact, hardly 10 out of 10,000 perform in a way that convinces an experienced student of inductive evidence that a long-term edge over indexing is likely... It may be the better part of wisdom to forsake searching for needles that are so very small in haystacks that are so very large.[2]

Of course, these are just academics. What do they know about the real world of investing? It's been said that those who suggest something can't be done should stay out of the way of those who are doing it. If it is all but mathematically impossible to beat the market, then why are there conspicuous examples of people who beat it? What about people such as Peter Lynch and Warren Buffett? It turns out that even 'exceptional' investors have a healthy dose of humility in their work.

Considered by some to be the greatest stock picker of all time, Lynch had the unique opportunity to select and train his own successor—and the guy he chose couldn't beat the market. So, if the "greatest stock picker in history" couldn't pick a good stock picker, what makes people think a less accomplished person can do it? In an interview with *Barron's* magazine in 1990, Lynch was quoted as saying, "Most investors would be better off in an index fund."[3]

Finally, let's see what the Oracle of Omaha has to say. Warren Buffett is perhaps the most revered man in investing today, given his long and laudable track record. Here's what he had to say in his 1996 letter to shareholders:

Most investors, both institutional and individual, will find that the best way to own common stocks is through an index fund that charges minimal fees. Those following this path are sure to beat the net results (after fees and expenses) delivered by a great majority of investment professionals.

Let's assume that 'most' (Lynch) and 'the great majority' (Buffett) of any group is at least 50% + 1. At that rate, over half of all participants should use an indexing strategy. Unfortunately, overconfidence rears its ugly head and most people (i.e. retail and institutional investors as well as virtually all FSPs) think that Lynch and Buffett are referring to someone other than themselves. Well over 50% of the population consider themselves to be above-average drivers, too, but we all know that it is impossible for more than 50% to actually be above average.

Note also that Buffett uses the phrase "investment professionals." But if FSPs are so professional and the evidence in favour of a passive approach is so strong, then why do almost all of them recommend an active approach? Do you think it might be possible that things such as corporate culture, embedded commissions, corporate point programs and the like might be clouding their ability to think and advise clearly?

Here's a short list of the truths that often go unmentioned by FSPs and the firms they work for:

- Most active managers lag their benchmark in the long run
- The handful that outperform cannot be reliably identified before the fact
- Cost is the most reliable determinant of long-term fund performance (as a negative indicator)
- FSPs consistently fail to recommend products that offer

no commissions or trailing commissions, yet continue to hold themselves out as 'independent.'

For a simple understanding of the rationale here, people should review Sharpe's paper entitled "The Arithmetic of Active Management."[4] In a nutshell, Sharpe argues that the average active manager can't possibly beat the market because, collectively, all active (and passive) managers are the market.

One might also note that all passive managers will lag their benchmark over any long time horizon, too, since both active and passive structures have a cost drag that a benchmark doesn't have to deal with. Here's why: passive managers earn the return of the market minus whatever fees are associated with their products (meaning they lag the market net of fees). But since the market is just the sum of all active and passive products and strategies, and since (pre-cost) passive strategies collectively get market-level returns, it follows that (pre-cost) active strategies also get market level returns. Since both active and passive strategies have fees associated with them, the sum of all these strategies is a return that is less than the market return. However, since passive strategies cost less than active ones, the sum of the passive strategies (i.e. the 'average passive investor') must outperform the sum of the active ones (i.e. the 'average active investor').

The only reason why any rational person would want to engage in active management is if that person had a deeply held belief that superior managers could be reliably identified in advance. We'll look at that proposition a little later. For now, let's just recognize that if two people have differing views on where the market is headed, they cannot possibly both be right. Rather, there are three possible explanations:

1. The first is right and the second is wrong
2. The second is right and the first is wrong
3. They are both wrong

A Brief Look at the Theory

The predominant view of market efficiency/equilibrium is that no one can reliably pick stocks, so the most rational thing to do is to buy a series of diversified vehicles with mandates that track particular indexes for the asset classes in question. A more interesting take on market efficiency comes from the father of the EMH himself. Working in concert with his long-time research collaborator Professor Ken French, Eugene Fama has expanded on Sharpe's Capital Asset Pricing Model (CAPM) by developing what he calls the three factor model, which postulates that higher returns can only be achieved by taking higher risk. Since risk and return are related (i.e. since one ought only to expect above-market returns as a result of bearing an above-market level of risk), Fama and French believe that the term 'equilibrium' is more robust and accurate. As an added bonus, it seems to be far less emotionally charged than the original terminology.

In simple terms, they have shown that over long time horizons, stocks have historically produced higher returns than bonds. That's not news, since it's exactly what Sharpe would have predicted. According to Fama and French, the main characterization of risk is increased volatility of returns. As such, low-priced value stocks historically provide higher returns than high-priced growth stocks over the long term. Value stocks outperformed growth stocks over most ten-year periods and almost all twenty-year periods. Value stocks tend to be distressed or out of favour, resulting in a higher cost of capital. A company's cost of capital is equal to an investor's expected return.

The main characterization of the extra risk is deviation or tracking error from the market. According to Dimensional Fund Advisors (DFA), most people don't care much about tracking error and do not use it as a measure of risk. Anyone who does think tracking error is a meaningful measure of risk should be more inclined to use ETFs or index funds. At any rate, by tilting toward value stocks, the volatility is usually about the same as the broad stock market. In a growth market, value stocks may significantly underperform the broad market.

Similarly, it has been shown that over the long term, small company stocks have historically provided higher returns than large company stocks. Over most ten-year periods and almost all twenty-five-year periods, small company stocks outperformed large company stocks. As one might imagine, small companies usually have a higher cost of capital than large companies, resulting in a higher expected long-term return to investors. Risk presents itself as both increased volatility versus the broad market and deviation from the broad market return.

From this perspective, people should 'buy the index' but be smart about it, too. As far as the people at DFA are concerned, strict index funds are largely flawed. Since they are required to buy and sell stocks at the end of the day, stocks are added or removed (index reconstitution). Even in large liquid markets, their research has shown that stock prices are affected and that the indexer incurs this extra cost when it happens. In small or illiquid markets, the effect is even more severe.

Rather than rigidly adhering to an index, DFA will delay or accelerate buys and sells to avoid the excessive prices when the index changes. They will buy at a discount when other sellers are anxious to sell large blocks of illiquid shares and then wait through stock momentum to achieve a better price.

DFA also believes the industry could do a far better job of defining proper indexes to be used for benchmarking. Stocks to be included in DFA funds are based on their research into proper index construction and asset class modelling rather than simply following an externally defined index. It might be said that DFA takes an 'asset class' approach to investing. The DFA philosophy also involves the opinion that:

- the market return is there for the taking
- buying the index will achieve the market return less fees
- all an investor must do is remain invested
- if the market return allows an investor to achieve their goals, then take it
- by intelligently capturing the elements of risk and reward, investors can improve returns

Comparing Paradigms

It should be noted that while there are certainly some large disagreements between the relative merits of active and passive strategies, there are also smaller disagreements in regard to competing passive products and strategies. That said, there's more consensus than dispute on the latter. Differing passive paradigms include: weighting by market capitalization (the most common and traditional way to index), equal weighting, factor weighting and fundamental indexing. Again, the larger discussion revolves around informed consent and making sure investors know what the value proposition of any product is (i.e. how the product or strategy might be expected to behave). The differences between these competing approaches, while more than a little nuanced, are still modest in comparison with the differences between any/all of them and more traditional active strategies. In summarizing equilibrium markets in broad terms, there are four main points to which virtually everyone in that space would agree:

1. Markets work, so stock picking doesn't
2. Diversification is extremely important
3. Costs matter (you get what you don't pay for)
4. FSPs bring discipline and focus to the process of investing

Since everyone is entitled to their own opinion, it seems only fair to examine what the opinions of most FSPs are and, to the extent that this can be determined, examine why it is that FSPs feel the way they do in the first place. Many people formulate their opinons based on what they were taught when they first entered the financial services industry. So what do you suppose we're teaching our newly minted FSPs?

Education or Indoctrination?

People do not know what they do not know...because they do not know what they do not know!

—Benjamin Franklin

Personal beliefs are funny things. Creationists are adamant that their world view is right, while evolutionists are equally convinced that they have it right. Agnostics are the Switzerland of the religious world; they don't take sides. In many ways, agnostics are prudent, since neither the creationists nor the evolutionists can offer incontrovertible proof that their view is correct or that the opposing view is conspicuously wrong. There are precious few FSPs who are indifferent to competing viewpoints when it comes to choosing between active and passive money management. This polarization of FSPs has made it difficult for ordinary investors to get unbiased input regarding their options.

Meanwhile, pension funds have been aware of this for years and have governed themselves accordingly. Most use elements of both active and passive strategies in designing portfolios, so we might call them portfolio agnostics. They're not interested in taking sides and being right so much as in doing whatever they can to avoid being conspicuously wrong.

In spite of the fact that the brightest pension funds act equivocally, the dogmatists in both the active and passive camps act as though they are conspicuously and incontrovertibly right when dealing with retail clients—to the extent that a large number don't even bother telling their clients that alternatives exist. The one thing we should all respect, living in a pluralistic society, is that it is inappropriate for anyone to impose beliefs on others, yet many FSPs do exactly that with respect to how investment portfolios are to be managed.

People have a tendency to believe things based on what they were taught in their formative years. Finance textbooks talk about the various strategies and techniques that portfolio managers might employ in attempting to add value by improving risk-adjusted returns (lowering risk, increasing returns or both). True scientists, of course, are more interested in how things actually work and what is accomplished in practice rather than how things ought to work in theory. Theories are nice, but theories have to hold water in the real world of actual testing. The scientist's mantra is, "Can you prove it?"

There is a further difference between honesty and full disclosure that also needs to be considered, yet practitioners and academics insist that there's nothing wrong. Both sides have managed to make cases for themselves over the years, but the two camps are skeptical of one another—primarily because each is a proponent of a specific doctrine that runs contrary to the views of the other. Academia is mostly for passive management (perhaps due to the examinations of evidence), while portfolio managers are mostly for active management. Perhaps this is due to their desire to protect profit margins. Perhaps it is because they are eternal optimists. Perhaps it is because they are insufferably over-confident in their abilities...and perhaps it's a bit of all these factors.

But aren't FSPs expected to do what is in their clients' best interests at all times? And shouldn't they work to identify the strategies that are the most likely to be successful and then pursue those strategies exclusively? Using a medical analogy, what if your physician said the odds of success were 60% for one procedure and 95% for another? Would you be indifferent regarding the procedure you choose since the odds are in your favour either way?

Proponents of active management point out that various passive strategies need to fully acknowledge that they will never beat their benchmark. This is absolutely true. Of course, the other side of the coin is that in trying to beat their benchmark, most active managers typically fail to do so and often lag by a wider margin than passive options as a direct result of having tried to outperform. Many proponents of active management also fail to explain this part of the story to retail clients.

Purity and turnover are also major concerns in gauging performance. Active funds almost always have cash or other asset classes in their funds. For instance, almost all have some cash component beyond the 5% or so required to meet redemptions and buying opportunities.

In a world where integrated wealth management is the overarching objective, tax efficiency also becomes a primary concern—the higher the portfolio turnover, the higher the tax liability in non-registered accounts. Any FSP who is con-scientious about the delivery of total wealth management needs to give serious consideration to those products that can accommodate this reality. In the U.S., mutual funds are reported not only in absolute returns but also in absolute after-tax returns. Tax considerations often play a major role in the rankings, with the more efficient (i.e. lower turnover) funds often moving up considerably.

Should professionals be taught one way of looking at the world or, if the matter in question is contentious and impossible to either verify or deny, should they be taught all of the possible explanations of how things work? Moreover, should professionals be allowed to think for themselves or should they be essentially told what to think by their educators?

The Canadian Securities Course (CSC) offered by the Canadian Securities Institute (CSI) is a testament to the predominance of the inefficient market viewpoint within the industry. The course is jam-packed with information about understanding and interpreting financial statements, everything you'd ever want to know about bonds and how to judge them, preferred shares, common shares, the factors affecting security prices and various details about stock exchanges, trading and portfolio construction, among other things.

Of course, the CSC isn't the only course available for people who want to learn more about capital markets and how they function. Still, the textbook for the CSC is as revealing for what it omits as for what it includes. It is many hundreds of pages long, yet has less than one page devoted to the concept of market efficiency. In effect, the text acknowledges the existence of the theory but is silent on the evidence that underpins it—and the implications this evidence has for the industry. Taking the concepts presented in the two previous chapters into account, real consideration will need to be a given to the notions of tolerance and acceptance of alternative viewpoints, respect for all evidence and censorship.

I dusted off an old finance textbook to see how the content differed from the CSC. There are considerable similarities, but there are some interesting differences, too. For starters, finance textbooks are far more detailed in working through the theory and practice of portfolio design using the principles of risk-adjusted returns as they pertain to combinations of asset classes. The thing that struck me as being most interesting, however, was the candour with which finance textbooks talk about market efficiency. Here's a quote from the 1997 second edition of *Investments* by Sharpe, Alexander, Bailey and Fowler:

> In Canada and the United States there are thousands of professional security analysts and even more amateurs. Not surprisingly, due to their actions the major U.S. and Canadian security markets appear to be much closer to efficiency than to irrationality. As a result, it is extremely difficult to make abnormal profits by trading securities in these markets.

While the reasoning in the preceding quotation might seem self-evident to many readers, it most assuredly is not self-evident to the army of professional analysts and managers who continue to charge fees in their quest to outperform market returns—on both an absolute and risk-adjusted basis. Note that the textbook does not suggest that markets are perfectly efficient, merely that they are highly efficient. It does not say that it is impossible to beat the market, but merely that it is "extremely difficult." Furthermore, since market efficiency is primarily a function of the number of participants, it should be obvious that irrespective of how true that statement was a decade ago, it is likely even truer today.

When comparing this to the CSC textbook, we see that the industry might not be as forthcoming with information as one might hope. The CSC text makes a brief mention of the existence of EMH and explains what it is. However, it offers no commentary like the "extremely difficult" reference found in university textbooks regarding reliably selecting securities. Instead, it says:

...there have been times when investors have been able to consistently outperform index averages like the S&P/TSX Composite Index. This evidence suggests that capital markets are not entirely efficiently priced.

Is it just me, or does that sound like the educators are making a big deal out of strategies and outcomes that have historically proven to be improbable? The course material for the CSC is set by member firms of the Investment Industry Regulatory Organization of Canada and the course is supposed to be an entry-level 'survey.' Still, this is what new FSPs are taught before getting a brokerage licence. In corresponding with a representative of the CSI, however, I was assured that the organization is "responsible for evaluating current industry trends and requirements and ensuring the curriculum and learning objectives meet or exceed those standards." I might also add that FSPs who are licensed through the other organizations are not given one iota of evidence regarding market efficiency in their course material. The people who designed those courses apparently didn't feel it was important enough.

As a society, we seem to have come to a view that if neither side can be demonstrated with a high degree of confidence, then educators should either remain silent on the matter entirely or teach both and allow students to draw their own conclusions. That may be how it works with the existence of God, but that's certainly not how it works with market efficiency. Ironically, the industry seems smug in portraying those who take a more balanced view (i.e. both active and passive have a place in a portfolio) as 'extremists'—so pervasive is the view that active management is sensible management.

Education or Indoctrination?

I looked up the word 'indoctrinate' and here's what I found: "v: to teach partisan or sectarian dogmas." A simpler definition might be: "teaching people to take your side." Note that this does not mean that your side is either right or wrong, merely that only one side of an issue is being taught.

In universities, students in both the sciences and the humanities are encouraged to take courses that offer competing views of difficult concepts. That way, they will be well-equipped to look at information from varying perspectives in order to make informed decisions. In stark contrast, FSPs are typically allowed to offer advice after having taken one course which is based on gaining a licence to sell products rather than having the dispassionate perspective of multiple points of view from equally valid and reputable sources.

Part of the discussion around unbundling has to focus on the merits of the constituent parts. This is tougher than most people think. For instance, there are many Christians who simultaneously possess a low opinion of organized religions and their weekly services and therefore don't attend. Casual observers might think that this form of Christianity is insincere, based on activity. But this isn't necessarily so. Belief in God and respect for the Church are two different things.

In late May 2002, the U.S. Federal Education Act was interpreted in Ohio through an addendum stipulating that: "Where topics are taught that may generate controversy—such as biological evolution—the curriculum could help students to understand the full range of scientific views that exist."

A similar level of open-mindedness might do FSPs some good regarding active and passive management. At present, virtually all FSPs are strict proponents of the active approach, even though scientific evidence is largely, but certainly not entirely, against them. Not surprisingly, virtually all FSPs have been taught in the 'traditional school' of active management. Least surprising of all, active management features embedded FSP compensation while passive management does not.

Similarly, the media would have many of us believe that consumers can fire their FSPs and pocket the savings, as if the FSPs add no value, only cost. This is a simplistic view that is only sometimes true. Under the current structure, there are some highly qualified FSPs who are actually cheaper than discount brokers. It is equally fair to say that there are some FSPs who, no matter how their services are priced, do more harm than good. Remember that most FSPs recommend active management and that active management generally involves embedded compensation while passive management generally does not. It would be difficult to support the view that these facts are not related.

Prevailing compensation models mean that active management and traditional financial advice are joined at the hip by most FSPs, product manufacturers and product distributors. This connection needn't exist: qualified financial advice and the decision between active and passive approaches can and should be mutually exclusive. As such, FSP recommendations can likely be better explained by prevailing compensation structures than by any form of compelling or overriding logic—including the merit principle. More on that later.

As with any disagreement that cannot be definitively resolved, the perspective one takes might well come down to where one feels the burden of proof lies. The proponents of EMH cannot prove that the active managers who outperform their benchmarks over long time frames are merely lucky.

Conversely, active managers cannot prove that their outperformance is due to insight and intelligence.

What about the FSPs who need to act as intermediaries and sort this all out? It could be said that a major reason why most FSPs don't recommend index-based products for at least part of their clients' portfolios is that they are blissfully unaware of the evidence favouring a more passive approach. They honestly believe active management is always better because that is the only approach they have ever been taught.

I asked Moshe Milevsky, a professor at the Schulich School of Business at York University in Toronto, to offer his thoughts about what is taught to finance students. Here's what he said:

> When finance professors in training (i.e. PhD students) are in graduate school, they are continuously fed a steady diet of efficient market theory using the rigour and language of mathematical economics. And, even though some of the papers and studies they are forced to read contain empirical evidence that violates these assumptions, it is more of the exception than the rule. They graduate to professorship with a very passive (i.e. efficient) view of the world. Then, of course, they come in contact with CFA practitioners and MBA students whose raison d'être is that markets are inefficient and value can be obtained by picking securities. This is why many of the assistant and associate professors of finance you might encounter in graduate school have a schizophrenic attitude to market efficiency and indexing. Some courses might be very dogmatic while others are agnostic about the whole thing.[1]

It may be observed that universities tend to take an 'agnostic' view and teach both sides of the efficient/inefficient debate, while the CSC takes a 'dogmatic' view and teaches one side almost exclusively.

Who Teaches FSPs?

To get a handle on the kinds of recommendations many FSPs make, we first need to examine the kind of training they receive in order to be considered qualified to offer financial advice in the first place. Right away, we have a problem. Until now, the financial services industry has regulated the ability to sell products, while regarding advice as an ancillary function. Only recently has the industry started to come to grips with its own flawed logic.

As a result of the notion of giving advice as an adjunct to selling a product, virtually all FSP educational training has been done by the organizations that grant licences. They are predisposed to portray their products in a favourable light, yet are not regimented like a university. Training courses that grant licences to sell financial products are predictably focused on the narrow attributes of the products themselves. As a result, course graduates might know a lot about stocks, mutual funds or life and disability insurance, but little about the broader context in which these products can be applied, disciplines like economics, law, public policy and ethics.

Virtually all FSPs working in the industry are effectively self-taught, meaning they bought textbooks and studied them for a while and then wrote exams that allowed them to sell financial products if they passed. Unless FSPs take special preparatory courses, there is no formal classroom learning going on at all.

English Canadian regulators have tried to regulate financial advice in the past. The problem with these initiatives, which ultimately failed, was that FSPs had to have a licence to be regulated. If you had a licence to sell stocks, you could refer to yourself as a broker, investment advisor, financial advisor or by a number of similar monikers. If you had no licence to sell stocks, you could call yourself anything you wanted. Regulators are set up solely to oversee product sales. They have no mechanism to monitor advice.

What Are They Taught?

Teachers have a massive responsibility because they collectively shape the opinions, attitudes and competence of their students, who, in turn, make up our future. Students tend to believe much of what they've been taught simply because they trust their teachers. As a result of teachers' presumed expertise, there's an implicit credibility associated with many established teachings, allowing for a certain degree of intellectual imperialism.

When broadly based teaching gives way to more concentrated sales-based training, the perspective that comes from the more formal and often more rigorous approach may be lost. The healthy skepticism that normally comes from a well-rounded university education might well be lacking in the more focused 'curriculum' associated with licensing courses. In these instances, teaching people about an industry can be tantamount to indoctrination regarding product sales.

This might arise through what is implied precisely because it is not taught. For instance, where are the references in licensing textbooks to the fact that the vast majority of money managers fail to beat their benchmarks over long time frames? Evidence to that effect is everywhere for those prepared to be inquisitive and dispassionate, but newly minted securities and mutual fund salespeople are essentially never taught about how rare it is for their kind to actually succeed at beating the market. In short, training for FSPs is presumptive since it teaches FSPs to presume that active management is sensible management.

True professionals would never stoop so low as to withhold relevant information simply in order to perpetuate their own existence. Can you imagine a physician going through medical school oblivious to the principles of basic good health? What if this physician were allowed to practice without ever being told that many ailments can be addressed simply by eating a balanced diet, getting regular sleep and maintaining an active lifestyle? With this fantastic hole in the provided training, the physician would be doing a massive disservice to his patients. Obviously, this could never happen because our society is too knowledgeable about health matters.

Through the ages, people such as Magellan, Galileo, Copernicus and Darwin didn't want to 'stir the pot' so much as they wanted evidence to be fully considered, understood and, if accepted, incorporated into everyday practice. History books are full of examples of ideas that challenged authority being considered radical and their proponents heretics. So there's a pattern where scientific trailblazers say things that are considered inappropriate in their day only to be proven right in the fullness of time. Unfortunately, some ideas take longer to make their way into textbooks than others. This often occurs not because these ideas lack merit or proof but because people in positions of authority actively suppress them. These authority figures often do this while insisting they are fighting for what is right and protecting society (or their industry).

There's an old saying that if you think education is expensive, try ignorance. This is certainly true when it comes to the formal training we offer to financial FSPs in Canada.

The emphasis in licensing courses is on the strategies employed by professional money managers on both the macro and micro level: government fiscal and monetary policy, security valuation techniques and the effects on security prices if they are trading ex-dividend or cum-dividend. There's a little bit about some related planning activities like having retail investors average down their cost base or do some tax-loss selling, but it's a very minor part of the training.

One might go so far as to suggest that many FSPs are unwitting accomplices in what amounts to a massive indoctrination being perpetrated by the industry. In essence, this is how the financial services industry hides the ugly truths of historical motivations and performance. Early in the twenty-first century, the financial services industry still leaves evidence out in plain sight for all to see and then talks endlessly about things that are relatively unimportant, thereby engaging in a de facto bait-and-switch exercise. The industry goes on and on about various micro- and macroeconomic factors, indicators such as earning reports and the like, and people are quickly seduced into thinking that these unimportant things are, in fact, important.

I must stress that I'm not suggesting that the industry engages in deception. Rather, it simply fails to make active disclosures regarding relevant information that would assist investors in making informed decisions about their own welfare. Other professionals (surgeons, for example) would be ashamed of themselves if they acted in a similar manner.

Later on, we'll take a look at concepts such as predictability, probability and persistence and consider the proper role that a conscientious FSP might play in light of those considerations. Choice is vitally important, as is the concept of informed consent. There are unlikely to be any definitive 'right' or 'wrong' answers, but there may nonetheless be options that are superior on a balance of probabilities basis. In spite of this, there are some who perceive the industry's practices as being unduly presumptive about the use of active management to the virtual exclusion of passive options.

Active Management and Intelligent Design

How would you feel if your school board taught only evolution and not creationism? What if it taught only creationism and not evolution? What if it taught neither and let children come up with their own ideas? As fate would have it, most schools throughout the Western world have decided that the best way to deal with this sticky subject is to teach both and advocate neither.

In any decent and progressive society, competing views are allowed to co-exist, yet Bay Street effectively teaches only market inefficiency to FSPs, who in turn offer supposedly unbiased advice to investors. That's the nub of the question of disclosure. Professionals disclose facts.

For surgeons, if evidence of a new drug or new procedure is 'promising,' the limits of the most current research methods and pharmaceuticals will be fully and actively disclosed to those patients who are being asked to consider using or employing them. To many, evidence surrounding the pros and cons of active and passive management is every bit as factual as the evidence showing cigarettes cause cancer. As with that evidence, there are obviously exceptions, but the risks of cigarette consumption are clearly spelled out on the packaging. There are no such disclaimers regarding the nebulous value proposition of security selection anywhere in the investment industry. To date, the industry has consistently dismissed this evidence as being a matter of 'opinion.' We'll take a closer look at what the data shows in the next section.

Before we do that, perhaps you ought to ask yourself about how you would distinguish between fact and opinion regarding questions like the relative merits of active and passive investment approaches.

One of the defining attributes of a decent society is that people are allowed to have their own opinions. Our Charter of Rights and Freedoms has enshrined the right to thought, belief, opinion and expression in Section 2. Is the debate about market efficiency a question of fact or a question of opinion? If it is a question of opinion, then surely everyone ought to be entitled to their own view, provided it is suitably identified as such. Compliance departments routinely insist that advisors offer disclaimers on their written material. Surprisingly, I have read passages written by CEOs of manufacturing and distribution companies that extol the virtues of active management but with no disclaimer about the opinions expressed not necessarily coinciding with the views of others within the organization, such as STANDUP FSPs, for instance. If this were a question of fact, then we wouldn't be considering this right now. One side would have proven itself to be incontrovertibly correct. That obviously hasn't happened—yet.

The prevailing attitudes within the industry offend many people profoundly. Speech is free, but society also demands accountability for the views being expressed. Teaching one approach in great detail while remaining nearly silent on the other is not education, it is indoctrination.

We can learn a great deal about how any society—or industry, for that matter—treats its minorities. In April 2006, two families in Massachusetts filed a lawsuit against the public school system after a teacher read a gay-themed fairy tale called *King & King* to 20 seven-year-olds without offering prior notification. The suit said the school had "begun a process of intentionally indoctrinating very young children to affirm the notion that homosexuality is right and normal in direct denigration of the plaintiffs' deeply held faith." Regardless of where your own sympathies lie, note the similarities: the issues are disclosure, prior consent and respect for both minority views and majority views.

How can FSPs be expected to alert consumers to ensure they make purposeful decisions about competing views of a contentious industry matter if they themselves are oblivious to the contentiousness of that controversy?

We need to stress that some of the most progressive minds in the industry don't even think people need to pick a side, since there's an argument to be made for both approaches. As a result, the real end-game of independent financial advice might bring FSPs to the point where they are indifferent to both sides. Perhaps 'indifferent' isn't the most precise word, either. Perhaps 'sanguine,' 'balanced,' 'adaptive' or 'purposeful' might be better. This is not so much about who is right and who is wrong. Rather, it is a question of professionalism. Irrespective of what anyone believes personally, are personal views being subordinated to the notion that the jury remains out and that, as such, either position may be inappropriate or even incorrect? If one takes the view that neither side is definitively correct, then should consumers (it's their money, after all!) at least be made aware of their options?

Modern Portfolio Theory

So far, we've talked about how likely or unlikely it is to 'beat a market' for any given asset class. Obviously, this is an incomplete discussion, because portfolios consist of multiple investments representing multiple asset classes.

In the late 1950s, Harry Markowitz, another graduate

student at the University of Chicago, theorized that a total portfolio approach was more appropriate than one that looked at a portfolio as a series of discrete parts. This represented a radical breakthrough, since he suggested that portfolios could be created that combine different asset classes in a way that would increase return and/or lower risk when compared to portfolios of individual asset classes. This approach, now known as Modern Portfolio Theory (MPT), took a total portfolio approach to investing. Incidentally, regulators to this day still look at portfolios as being the sum of many disparate parts rather than as a single entity.

Markowitz's big breakthrough was the 'efficient frontier,' a mathematically derived, theoretical continuum of risk/return trade-offs that prescribed a certain mix of asset classes in order to maximize returns for any given amount of risk. Of course, quantifying risk tolerance is an exceedingly difficult thing to do. It is also fraught with varied personal opinions and biases. Still, the mathematical theory became widely accepted. It quantifies the personal tolerance for risk and then maximizes returns within that constraint. Portfolio design began a shift from art to science that is continuing to this day.

A well-thought-out investment strategy naturally serves as the foundation for a properly constructed portfolio. Consumers often focus almost exclusively on security selection (including the extent to which investments should be invested actively or passively), while ignoring other associated risks and underlying asset allocations. It's like being penny-wise and pound foolish.

Relative to EMH, MPT gained acceptance more quickly. But acceptance certainly didn't happen overnight. Again, there are many possible explanations for why it took so long for academic research to enter the mainstream, ranging from healthy skepticism to sloth to hubris to deliberate suppression.

Although it took over a generation for Markowitz's work to be appreciated, it has since become a hallmark of portfolio management.

People are striving to build portfolios that maximize returns but hope to do so by taking on only as much risk as they can personally tolerate. Unfortunately, Markowitz's ideas are still not truly appreciated since virtually all commercial applications of his logic involve the use of actively managed products, something of which Markowitz's co-winners of the 1990 Nobel Prize (Merton Miller and William F. Sharpe) have been particularly disdainful. Markowitz's work is about combining asset classes to improve the theoretical risk-adjusted returns for the portfolio as a whole. It is silent on the question of whether to use active or passive approaches in doing so.

The offshoot of this advance in thinking is that portfolio development now focuses primarily on reducing risk. Recent advances in portfolio design have rested almost entirely in the realm of risk reduction rather than return enhancement. Diversification means not only adding securities within certain asset classes but also including additional asset classes.

There are two primary types of risk within any given asset class: systematic risk and unsystematic risk. The former is simply the risk of being in the market—any market. The latter is the risk associated with individual securities. Unsystematic risk can therefore be diversified away, while systematic risk is inescapable. Simply 'buying the market' is the surest and simplest way to eliminate unsystematic risk.

There might soon come a day when FSPs mix and match these two completing paradigms depending on various considerations. Here's what Michael Nairne, CEO of Tacita Capital Management, has to say about the subject:

One of the emerging trends that will permanently change the landscape of the investment advisory business in Canada will be the widespread adoption of a core (passive) and satellite (active) portfolio structure. Combining a highly diversified core of tax-efficient, low-cost index and enhanced index products that deliver asset class returns with a satellite ring of active managers that seek superior returns or enhanced diversification creates a compelling value proposition to investors—lower taxes, lower volatility, lower costs, lower tracking error, more investment opportunities and superior potential portfolio returns. A core and satellite structure requires unbundled pricing due to the barebones cost of index-based products. Progressive practitioners who construct and customize core and satellite portfolios for their clients on an unbundled fee basis are a tiny minority today—but rising awareness and intense competition will make this an ever-growing and ultimately preferred approach in the coming years.[2]

Note that Nairne refers to a multiplicity of benefits, including the possibility of both lower risk and higher return. Many believe that the questions of purposeful diversification and ethical disclosure must now come together in the pursuit of adding value.

Unfortunately, FSPs are often sucked into discussing what most consumers and the media think is urgent and appropriate. Rather than setting their clients straight about what it is they do, they delude their clients (and themselves) into thinking they have a better sense of where the market is headed, when it will change direction and which stocks and mutual funds will outperform their peer group. Decades ago, Stephen Covey made the important distinction between what is merely urgent and what is genuinely important. When investing, everyone would be well-advised to remember that distinction.

Part 1 has argued for a consistent standard of professionalism—one where there is no confusion between mere sales representatives and true professionals. It has examined the notions of both fairness and respect for competing viewpoints. All of this was done on the assumption that some of the most fundamental matters in question are essentially matters of opinion where intelligent people might properly differ.

However, that may be setting the bar too low. The time has come to examine research and to determine for ourselves whether the matters in question really are mere differences of opinion or something more concrete—verifiable facts. It seems to me that clarity on that matter would greatly assist both consumers and FSPs alike.

Part Two
Scientific Testing

Evidence-Based Research

The reasonable man adapts himself to the world; the unreasonable one persists in trying to adapt the world to himself. Therefore, all progress depends on the unreasonable man.

—George Bernard Shaw

Society generally prides itself on the advances that have been made over the years. Some of these are in political and social fields such as human rights. Perhaps the one area where people feel the most inherent satisfaction is with science. Examples of scientific progress over the past few generations are certainly mind-boggling.

In terms of gadgets and processes, there's a strong interest in the field of technology transfer. That's where ideas that have been commercialized need to make it to the marketplace sooner. It's all well and good to come up with a better mousetrap, but if no one knows about your new product, it won't do you (or them) much good. Similarly, if there's a new production process or management technique that gets more productivity out of a workforce, companies will often be eager to apply it.

What if the better mousetrap was a threat to the status quo? What if a multi-billion-dollar industry had developed surrounding the production and sale of inferior mousetraps? Furthermore, what if there was an army of sales representatives that earned commissions selling these inferior mousetraps? One problem I think everyone would see right off the bat would lie with the motives of the inferior mousetrap sales-people—they would never tell anyone about the existence of a better mousetrap! In turn, they would insist they were doing all they could to help people—even as the vermin-in-fested world they lived in was ready, willing and able to embrace a new solution.

Since dictionaries don't generally deal with two-word terms, I went to Wikipedia to look up the term 'scientific method.' This was defined as:

> The body of techniques for investigating phenomena, acquiring new knowledge, or correcting and integrating previous knowledge…based on gathering observable, empirical and measurable evidence subject to specific principles of reasoning. (It) consists of the collection of data through observation and experimentation, and the formulation and testing of hypotheses. Although procedures vary, identifiable features distinguish scientific inquiry from other methodologies of knowl-edge. Methodological steps must be repeatable in order to dependably predict any future results. Theories that encompass wider domains of inquiry may bind many hypotheses together in a coherent structure. This in turn may help form new hypotheses or place groups of hypotheses into context. Among other facets shared by the various fields of inquiry is the conviction that the process be objective to reduce a biased inter-pretation of the results. Another basic expectation is to document, archive and share all data and method-ology so they are available for careful scrutiny by other scientists, thereby allowing other researchers the opportunity to verify results by attempting to re-produce them. This practice, called full disclosure,

also allows statistical measures of the reliability of these data to be established.

So why all this talk about science and mousetraps in a book about finance and professionalism? Perhaps this chapter should be called 'bankers in lab coats' in honour of the images it might conjure up. Evidence is important, yet it seems certain circles can be rather selective in what constitutes truly reliable evidence. When evidence threatens an income stream and a way of life, it appears there is no end to how far people will go to deny it, or to talk about things that seem relevant but are, in fact, not.

What if there was evidence that showed five ways 'til Friday that cost was a material consideration in product selection, that past performance is an unreliable metric for product selection, that most people who try to beat the market fail as a direct result of trying, that the handful of people who succeed are no more than would be expected by random chance and will not persist in their outperformance at any rate? Books such as *The Quest for Alpha* by Larry Swedroe and *The Big Investment Lie* by Michael Edesess itemize the research on these matters in considerable detail. Of course, the evidence that is known to exist and the means by which the industry functions can be very different things.

Fund Picking in the 1990s

What would you think if you met someone who wrote a book on how to pick winning lottery tickets? I'd wonder why anyone smart enough to devise a system to do something so lucrative would do something so stupid as to share it. Think about it. If you could come up with a way to reliably win even 5% of all lotteries you bought tickets for, you'd be fabulously wealthy if you entered often enough. If you tell everyone else how you do it, they'll go out and do it too... and your winnings would evaporate. Everyone who reads your book will win at the expense of virtually everyone who didn't read the book. Meanwhile, you could have won millions if you had simply kept your idea to yourself.

In the 1990s, something rather similar was going on. It seemed everyone had a take on how to identify top-performing mutual funds. At the time, it seemed no one could get enough information about what mutual funds were, how they worked and how to build portfolios using them. Annual fund-ranking books presumably helped consumers make smart, timeless investment decisions. Today, no one publishes books that rank funds. Why did people lose their appetite for fund picking? Why did most books disagree on what the best funds actually were? If the research was indeed empirical and predictive, shouldn't they all have identified the same funds? And if the books were so committed to a long-term perspective, why did so many of the recommendations change from one year to the next—even from the same authors?

Those authors weren't selling timeless and useful information at all: they were simply selling books. And books that need to be updated annually have the handy attribute of built-in obsolescence, meaning they can be tweaked, repackaged and sold anew twelve months later. From the authors' perspectives, the best thing about these books was their imminent disposability. The second best thing was likely the lack of accountability that the books entailed.

Why would any consumer bother to check the long-term track record of a book from, say, 1996 to see how the recommended funds actually performed by 2006? After all, the thinking goes, whatever was recommended back in 1996 must surely no longer be relevant given all that has happened since. In those days, consumers were always on the lookout for the latest investment idea and could always be counted on to run out and buy the latest version of their favourite rating book the next year.

The whole exercise legitimized the notion of stock and/ or fund picking as a valuable pursuit. None of the books made mention of the fact that there was zero research indicating that this had been done reliably in the past; they simply implied that it could be done—and people believed them. Indeed, in later editions—1998 and beyond—none of them made mention of new research that clearly indicated that what they purported to be doing could not be done reliably and that past winners did not persist.

Whether performed at the micro level (by a hotshot broker in red suspenders) or at the macro level (by a superstar money manager at a mutual fund company), the books lent credence to the notion of security selection as an activity that can be reliably used to outperform the markets. The problem is that past performance is not to be used as an in- dicator of future performance. In other words, between the ubiquitous prospectus disclaimers and the self-professed fund-picking gurus, one group had to be right and the other group had to be wrong.

I took on the challenge of sifting through the most prominent fund-picking books from 1996 (with rankings based on June 30, 1995, results) to see how the ten-year numbers stacked up as of June 30, 2005, and published my findings in the *Globe and Mail*. Just how insightful were these books, really?

The results were stunning. In all four books, the majority of recommended funds lagged their benchmarks over the ten-year time period. A large proportion of the funds weren't even good enough to merely survive the ten-year period. Many studies have shown that 'survivorship bias' causes current performance numbers to look considerably better than they really are. It's easy to have a respectable class average if you don't have to take a massive dropout rate into account. Nonetheless, the funds recommended had a collective performance record that could only be described as awful.

Perhaps even more disconcerting was that the authors generally used only three years' worth of data to make a pronouncement on a fund's relative merit. In their minds, thirty-six monthly data points were the minimum required to make an informed decision regarding performance. Imagine if your favourite polling company used similar methodology.

Of course, having most funds lag their benchmarks would make little difference if people could reliably identify the handful that would ultimately outperform. But can this be done? Once again, contrary to what these books implied, earlier independent research showed that superior funds could not be reliably identified beforehand. I guess there's a first time for everything. I should also add that near the fronts of these books, some authors even included passages saying that they believe good managers can be reliably identified. However, no rationale was ever given for holding this opinion.

Then, near the backs of the books, they sometimes added things like, "research puts the contribution of security selection—that is, choice of specific investments—at only 2% when discussing performance." In other words, "we think superior managers can be reliably identified in advance, but we see only modest evidence at best that it is of any real consequence." That's the gist of it, anyway.

Do you know who particularly loved these books? The companies that had funds ranked as top performers! It was great for business. Corporate Canada has always loved the legitimacy that comes from third-party endorsements—no matter how questionable the research behind those endorsements. By the way, the industry has more recently taken this form of implied legitimacy one step further: setting up the Canadian Investment Awards where a panel of industry experts makes necessarily subjective decisions to bestow 'fund of the year' and 'manager of the year' recognition on select products and individuals—thereby enhancing sales and reputations even more.

But if a high percentage of 'guru-endorsed' funds end up lagging their benchmark by a wide margin, the only truly rational way to justify picking funds at all is if one could have a high degree of confidence that the funds that are chosen had a high probability of outperforming. That's not going to happen. It's the same reason most people should never set foot in a casino. I might add that the word 'guru' means spiritual teacher or guide. What if the thing being taught (i.e. the subject matter) and the guidance being proffered (i.e. picking mutual funds based on past perform-ance) are demonstrably untrue?

Let's look at this from an advisory perspective. It has been suggested by some commentators that the primary role of FSPs is to assist clients in avoiding 'The Big Mistake.' If this is indeed a fair job description, then one could argue that helping consumers avoid funds that lag could be reasonably depicted as a value-adding activity. People could then write books called *Heavy Missers* or *Dumb Funds*. Their mandate would be simple: help consumers avoid underperforming funds. If increasing the likelihood of beating a benchmark could be achieved by weeding out losers, wouldn't it be just as useful to identify those funds that are laggards? Since it's tough to position yourself as an expert if you only help people avoid dogs, that attempt has never been made.

Ironically, all this doesn't necessarily mean the 'gurus' were up to no good. I suspect these people honestly believed what they were writing, just as many FSPs (myself included, once upon a time) honestly thought these guys could do what they said they could. But they were plain wrong, and yet so many people believed them.

We're left with two possible explanations: either the authors knew their recommendations were a load of hooey or they didn't. If they didn't, then they were merely guilty of trying to make a few bucks by preying on society's seemingly insatiable quest for disposable information and professing to be able to do something they could not. On the other hand, if any author actually knew in advance that their books were hogwash, then that person willfully misled people. So which is it? And which is worse? Were these 'gurus' unwitting alchemist wannabes or wily snake-oil salesmen? I believe it is the former. Nonetheless, the 'conspiracy of ignorance' that remains rampant to this day got a huge shot in the arm when these books first came out. Research regarding the lack of persistence of previous top performers had been released prior to these books being published, yet none of them made mention of the academic evidence that disproved their presumptive value proposition.

Since my article appeared, I've had conversations with two of the four 'gurus.' They insisted that their intentions were good. I want to stress that I have always believed them. In my view, these are basically decent, well-intentioned, hard-working people who were genuinely trying to enlighten people. There are three primary stakeholders in this morality play/comedy of misinformation: retail investors, mutual fund companies and FSPs. The gurus helped the fund companies and FSPs—two out of three ain't bad.

Furthermore, since the authors clearly implied that they believed fund picking could be done reliably, shouldn't they have cited a reason for their opinion—and disclaimed the contents as being mere opinion? Had anyone ever picked funds convincingly in the past? If yes, they should have referenced it. If no, then why wasn't the questionable 'pioneering' nature of their work more explicitly disclosed? Even then, shouldn't they at least have cited the work done by a small army of world-renowned economists such as Eugene Fama, Ken French, Paul Samuelson, Robert Merton, Merton Miller, William F. Sharpe, Burton Malkiel, Charles D. Ellis and others who dispute their fundamental thesis?

Quite apart from the 'gurus,' why do so many FSPs depict themselves as being superior fund pickers? Fund picking and stock picking are discredited value propositions in the financial services industry today. Unfortunately, the majority of consumers fail to see it that way, having been bamboozled by all the books, magazines, newsletters and websites dedicated to identifying top performers. These 'resources' are really just perpetuating the myth of stock and fund picking as a reliable activity. Most of the evidence simply does not support that viewpoint.

Benchmarking

The other element of benchmarks is the comparison of funds to one another as opposed to a relevant benchmark. The industry is sneaky that way. Since the vast majority of funds lag their benchmark in the long run, the industry has chosen to score itself against itself. Mutual funds are rated according to their performance relative to other mutual funds rather then in relation to a suitable benchmark.

For instance, if there are one hundred funds in an asset class and sixty lag their benchmark over a five-year period, one might get a false impression when looking at quartile rankings. There would be twenty-five funds in each performance quartile, yet approximately ten funds in the second quartile would have lagged the benchmark. It gets worse. In the very long run, fewer than 25% of all funds beat their benchmark. One could go to a ranking book to find a fund with a ten-year track record that is ranked in the first quartile and, as a result, buy that fund even though it may have lagged its benchmark!

By comparing one product with another, the financial services industry has created the impression of a balanced, apples-to-apples comparison. This comparison is fair in a relative sense (i.e. we can see which funds have been better than the others in the past), but that's as far as it goes. Here's the real challenge: to outperform the portfolio benchmark. That would be far more meaningful to consumers and far more damaging to the mutual fund industry, which, of course, goes a long way toward explaining why it likely isn't used.

If people could identify outperforming managers in advance, those managers would most certainly be worth hiring. Of course, that's sort of like saying if people could identify winning lottery numbers in advance, those numbers would certainly be worth playing. Sadly, outperformers are like lottery numbers—they cannot be reliably identified in advance. Every mutual fund prospectus on the planet says so.

I was once at a conference where a delegate asked a money manager if he thought markets were efficient. "Of course there are inefficiencies!" the manager replied, "I wouldn't be here if that weren't the case!" That was the questioner's point all along. Whether markets were efficient or inefficient, the only way stock pickers or media people get paid is if they can convince enough people that there are inefficiencies. Imagine if you tried this line of thinking on your local clergy:

Parishioner: "How can you be sure that God exists?"
Clergy: "Of course God exists. You wouldn't need me
             if God didn't exist, would you?"
Parishioner: "Exactly. Now please answer my question."
Clergy: "I thought I did."
Parishioner: "No you didn't, you simply validated my con-
             cern."

In contrast, ETFs get market-like returns minus costs while taking on market levels of risk. Since they are concerned with tracking error (performance that deviates from the benchmark) as a primary definition of risk, ETFs are required to buy and sell stocks when they are added to or removed from the index in question. If you define risk as "the extent to which my investments deviate from the market as a whole," then ETFs are for you.

Another consideration is how one might define risk: is it standard deviation (the variance of return outcomes) or tracking error? Again, actively managed funds have all manner of standard deviations relative to the asset classes they invest in. Some are higher and some are lower. There is no way to summarize them other than to say standard deviation can vary considerably and on a case-by-case basis. The easiest products to understand are ETFs. They view risk as tracking error. To ETF investors (and product manufacturers, presumably), risk is defined by how much the investment deviates from the index it is set up to track. Enhanced indexers are more concerned with standard deviation than tracking error. As such, it might also be said that enhanced indexers view risk in absolute terms while traditional indexers view risk in relative terms, that is, relative to a benchmark. Neither is clearly right or wrong, but FSPs should try very hard to ensure that their clients understand the difference so that they use products that reflect their own views.

It might be added that likely the greatest risk of all, market risk, warrants copious disclosure by the FSP irrespective of the strategy chosen. More often than not, an investor will lose money in a falling market and make money in a rising market, and the active/passive decision will make very little difference. Investors should consider their own views regarding risk, reward and the probability of outperformance when making investment decisions. Meanwhile, FSPs should aim to offer dispassionate advice and guidance to assist them. True professionals offer up the details of all salient facts and then let the client make the final decision. The approach ought to involve professional input based on empirical research and addressing material facts. Deliberately remaining silent on those same material facts is, to my mind, a form of manipulation—and there's no room for anything that disingenuous in a professional environment.

Fact or Opinion?

The greatest trick the Devil ever pulled was convincing the world that he didn't exist.

—Beaudelaire

I've asked a number of people I respect about both facts and opinions. I'm interested in when any given idea, process or possible causal relationship makes the transition from being something that is quite possibly true to being something that is demonstrably, verifiably true.

It has long been accepted that smoking cigarettes is linked to the increased likelihood of contracting lung cancer. For years, however, that idea was challenged—even by medical professionals. When, exactly, did it make the transition from being plausible to being probable and ultimately (and this is vitally important) to being verifiably true? I ask because some people tend to get their backs up when others have the temerity to suggest what they have believed all their lives just ain't so.

Essentially every subject known to humanity is either a matter of fact or a matter of opinion. It is important to note that, while both are well-understood concepts, the expectations surrounding them are quite different. In marketing financial services in a manner that is compliant with regulatory requirements, it is expected that all facts contain a reference where the validity of the concept was first established. In matters of opinion, it is required that the person speaking or writing clearly disclaim the position(s) being taken as personal opinions and nothing more.

What about things that are neither definitively proven nor disproven? And what should the standard be when speaking to people one on one? There is obviously no way that regulators can monitor what is said between FSPs and their clients behind closed doors. Still, I have encountered executives in the industry who have expressed their opinons through marketing materials (which is entirely their right) without identifying them as being their personal opinions. This can easily create a dangerous misconception. Since all personal opinions are to be disclaimed, one can easily conclude that, since there was no disclaimer, what was just expressed must therefore be a matter of fact. This, of course, further blurs the line between opinion and fact.

We live in a free and democratic society—a society that values peoples' freedoms of thought, belief, opinion and expression. No one wants to diminish those rights, but pretty much everyone wants to balance them with the concepts of truth and fairness.

For purposes of regulatory compliance, an FSP cannot say something like, "70% of all FSPs prefer a commission-based business model," and leave it at that. Instead, that FSP would either be required to frame his position by saying something like, "I would estimate that..." (an opinion) or he would have to provide a source, like, "A September 2012 Survey by Pollara Research shows that 70% of all Canadian FSPs prefer commissions." Stated somewhat differently, FSPs and industry commentators are allowed to use both (or either) facts and opinions, so long as they are clear to their audience which it is.

Perhaps it's just a matter of time before society catches up. According to a documentary film entitled *The Age of Stupid*, approximately 99% of all research scientists believe climate change is real, yet about 60% of the populace remains skeptical. It seems opinions can persist for some time in spite of factual evidence to the contrary.

In the case of what is considered factual, there are many potential examples: research findings determined through the application of the scientific method (preferably sourced from learned journals), empirical data (market share, average price) that can be provided by reputable firms, public opinion research (statistically significant poll results) and so forth. Note that certain related items (a research report on Canadian large cap stocks from the Royal Bank, for instance) might contain a great deal of professional opinion that is merely supported by factual data. This is an instance where everyone can see what a trend is or what patent protection may have been attained or which market demographic is responding to a new ad campaign, but fair-minded individuals might differ on what that information means. In these instances, we start with facts, but then slide over to opinions both quickly and seamlessly—sometimes almost imperceptibly.

Let's take a look at the respective definitions so that there can be a clearer understanding about the terms of this discussion. According to the *Concise Canadian Oxford Dictionary*, they are as follows:

Fact: n 1. a thing that is known to have occurred, to exist or to be true 2. a thing that is believed or claimed to be true 3. a piece of evidence, an item of verified information or events and circumstances 4. truth, reality

Opinion: n 1. a belief or assessment based on grounds short of proof 2. a view held as probable 3. what one thinks about a particular topic or question 4. a formal statement of professional advice (e.g. get a second opinion)

I believe that it is both fair and factual to suggest that the notion that one can reasonably expect to beat the market is not supported by the weight of the evidence. I reached this position by examining the evidence. This, of course, is all I would expect any fair-minded individual to do.

Let's take a few moments to examine the reasons that have been put forward by various proponents of paying fees for security selection and/or market timing. Before we do, however, consider the earlier examples in context.

How unbiased and accepting would you expect vested interests to be in accepting evidence if it had an impact on their bottom line? You should always consider the evidence on matters that may or may not be verifiable; you should also be careful to take into account the vested interests of those constituencies that might deny that evidence, as they are less than impartial arbiters of truth. Let's take a look at a few positions that are clearly in the domain of those representing the status quo—both in terms of what that position is and what the weight of the evidence suggests.

Position 1: "It is likely (and therefore recommended) that investors use active products and strategies as opposed to passive ones because active products are expected to outperform over time."

Evidence: The logic behind why the average actively managed dollar must underperform the average passively managed dollar was spelled out succinctly by William F. Sharpe in "The Arithmetic of Active Management."

Furthermore, when Sharpe's logic is tested and applied in the real world, what one finds is that for all asset classes and over pretty much every statistically significant time horizon, the average active product lags its benchmark. Every year, Standard and Poor's releases a report to compare the five-year numbers for aggregated funds versus their benchmarks. Every year, the majority of funds lags that benchmark—sometimes by a little; sometimes by a lot. The reason why the folks at Standard and Poor's don't like to go beyond five years in their study is because after that length of time, a large number of funds have historically been merged or closed (presumably due to un-derperformance), thereby biasing the sample. Still, as a general rule, the longer the time horizon studied, the less likely it is that the av-erage product will outperform.

The concept can be simply conveyed with the rhetorical question "Who's on the other side of the trade?" If anyone believes they can add value/outperform/seek Alpha by trading, then surely they must recognize that if they are better off as a result of a trade, then the person they traded with is worse off by an identical amount. There is nothing accretive to trading. As such, trading does not create wealth, but it does redistribute wealth.

Position 2: "It does not matter if the average actively man-aged product lags its benchmark and/or passive counterpart, because I don't recommend average products. I recommend superior products."

Evidence: There is no reliable evidence that anyone

can reliably identify 'outperformers' in advance. There's a reason why every mutual fund prospectus carries a disclaimer to the effect that "past performance may not be repeated and therefore should not be relied upon when making investment decsions": it's true.

Furthermore, this is not the least bit new. Harvard professor Michael Jensen first showed how difficult it is to 'pick winners' in advance in an article entitled, "The Performance of Mutual Funds in the Period 1945-1964." The article was published in the *Journal of Finance* in 1967.

In 1997, Mark Carhart penned what is widely considered to be the most definitive study of the subject to date. In "On Persistence in Mutual Fund Performance," Carhart showed that the likelihood of a top quartile fund remaining in the top quartile for subsequent periods was about what one would expect through random chance. The only kind of performance persistence he could find seems to be on the poor side— lousy funds have a tendency to remain lousy.

What is interesting is what was discussed in the previous chapter. In the late 1990s, there were a number of annual guide books published to 'help' investors make 'informed' decisions about the mutual funds they were looking at purchasing. I own books by at least four of those authors and I cannot find the slightest reference to either the Jensen research or the Carhart research in any of them. What is particularly disconcerting is that one of those books was authored by an FSP who was governed by regulations (then done by the IDA) concerning suitable disclosures for marketing material. No suitable disclosures about the research that contravened the fundamental premise were made and investors were none the wiser.

Position 3: "A sensible way of sorting mutual funds and/or stocks is by looking at their past performance and/or making forecasts about future performance. That is what I do and I do it well. Other considerations, such as cost, are of little or no consequence."

Evidence: Not only is past performance a decidedly unreliable way of picking investment products, but research (done by the famous star-rating service Morningstar, no less) shows that sorting by cost is a more reliable way of making investment decisions.[1]

Position 4: "Passive products and strategies, by definition, cannot 'beat' their benchmarks. Only actively managed products and strategies can outperform."

Evidence: This is largely true, but largely beside the point. It is true if one defines 'passive' as being a cap-weighted approach to investing. Other passive strategies (fundamental indexing, Fama/French three factor model) might beat their benchmark—depending on which benchmark is chosen and the time horizon in question. Many people (myself included) feel that 'beating a benchmark' is an inappropriate way of keeping score because the ability to beat a benchmark is largely a red herring. Is it proper for a felon who committed a moderate crime to cast aspersions on a felon who committed a minor one? Similarly, while it is true that an active approach has a greater chance of outperforming, it is equally true that it has a greater chance of underperforming. How many proponents of an active approach disclose that the likelihood of lagging a bechmark by a significant amount is far greater with active strategies than it is with passive ones?

Let's say you had $100. You have two options in front of you: Option 1 gives you a 15% chance of finishing with more than $100; Option 2 gives you no chance of finishing with more than $100—which do you prefer? If the story ended there, I'm pretty sure most people would choose the first option. But what if those two choices are incomplete? What if, in addition to the information above, you were told that there was a 15% chance you'd end up with less than $80 in Option 1 but were absolutely certain to end with at least $95 in Option 2? This is still a simplification of the choice, but you can see the problem. Risk and reward are related—and they incorporate the competing concepts of variability regarding both frequency and degree. Most people are led to think only about frequency—the 'odds of success' part of the equation. In so doing, they might not give due consideration to the equally relevant 'cost of failure' issue—the degree to which they will be penalized for having tried to outperform. Both are legitimate considerations, but telling only one side of the story is not really offering advice—it is manipulating decision-making by using selective information. Regarding the choices above, no doubt many people would stick with their original choice. My point is that it would be reasonable to expect a number of them to switch, too. That switch would likely never occur if the additional information wasn't disclosed.

Position 5:   "Even if the odd active fund fails to beat its benchmark, the costs associated with active management are well worth it. A diversified portfolio containing a number of actively managed funds would surely allow the winners to overpower the losers if compared with a similar basket of passive products."

Evidence: The empirical results show the exact opposite effect. In 2009, University of Denver professor Alan Roth published his book *How a Second Grader Beats Wall Street*. Using thousands of 'Monte Carlo' portfolio simulations over differing time periods, he examined the odds of an all active portfolio beating an all passive one. In all instances, the odds were reduced as both the number of funds and the time horizon increased. In fact, in comparing competing portfolios of five active funds and five passive funds, the likelihood of the active grouping outperforming was 32% over one year; 18% over five years; 11% over ten years and 3% over twenty-five years.

Position 6: "My clients prefer that we work together using a commission structure. They would rather not see (or be reminded of) how much they are paying me."

Evidence: There is no definitive evidence on either side of this debate. While it is undeniably true that there are some clients who take a 'bury your head in the sand' approach to disclosures of various sorts, it is equally true that a large percentage of FSPs do not even offer an unbundled and transparent business arrangement to their clients. Where this is the case, one must surely agree that it is disingenuous to suggest that a commission-based arrangement is the client's 'preference' or 'choice.' Any FSP who works exclusively using a commission-based structure is not offering clients a choice. Rather, those clients are left with an ultimatum: work with me using commissions or work with someone else. It strikes me as being a bit of a stretch to say clients 'prefer' one option when they were never even offered the other.

By way of example, I acknowledge that I personally prefer a fee-based (unbundled) arrangement. I say this to my clients and the majority are happy to work on that basis. That said, a small minority (less than 10%) prefer to work using commissions and I accommodate those clients with the same level of service.

Back to Fact or Opinion

What we have here is a clear disconnect beween what evidence suggests and what practitioners (themselves the 'experts in the field') generally recommend. This disconnect has a number of potential explanations. We've already touched on how FSPs are taught and what their corresponding beliefs tend to be. There's the little matter of FSPs wanting to be paid while being generally afraid to provide their clients with a bill. There's the concept of doing what you know—many FSPs use active products and embedded compensation structures because 'that's just how it's done' in their eyes.

It may be that the greatest impediment to moving toward unbundled business models where passive products and strategies are offered a fair shake is the 'value proposition' that FSPs bring to the table in the first place. Many FSPs have spent their entire careers telling their clients that they add value by picking stocks, picking funds, the purposeful execution of fundamental and technical analysis and the shrewd ability to get people into makets as they're about to rise and to get people out as they're set to plummet. Can they support these claims with reliable data? In fairness, part of the problem here is that the theses cannot be reliably tested. How exactly does one test how one would have performed as a result of one not taking advice from an FSP? Furthermore, if proponents of this position cannot unambigouisly prove their viewpoints, it should be obvious that the other half of the problem is that their critics cannot unambiguously disprove them.

In my opinion, FSPs do not and cannot reliably add value

by doing those things that they generally insist add value. How does one tell valued clients that one's fundamental raison d'etre is a fraud? And so the façade of utilitarian purpose is maintained—even in spite of a truly massive body of evidence to the contrary.

Of course, causation and absolute certainty are different things. The causal link between smoking cigarettes and cancer is beyond dispute, yet there are many examples of people who smoke heavily and don't get cancer and others who don't smoke at all who do.

What is truly ironic is that there are a number of financial dealings that many fair-minded commentators feel can be significantly enhanced by working with a qualified FSP. Stock picking, fund picking and market timing are not among those things, mind you, but there are many people out there who feel the advantages are real nonetheless. We'll get into those things in Part 3 of the book. For now, we'll have to grapple with how to get FSPs to look into those mirrors they have been avoiding for pretty much their entire careers.

How does one respectfully demonstrate that the majority of one's peers are fundamentally wrong? Wrong—in spite of being intelligent, diligent, responsible and client-centred. In previous editions, I told the story of physicians in the 1950s doing their rounds and giving away cartons of cigarettes to patients who were stuck in the hospital over the holidays. How do you suppose they felt when the day came where 'cigarettes cause cancer' switched over from being a mere possibility—an 'unproven thesis'—to being a certifiable fact? Those doctors cared about their patients! They (mostly) kept up with journal articles to stay abreast of the latest research findings. They worked diligently and responsibly to gain their positions in society. Then, one day, the Surgeon General pronounces that cigarettes are indeed a leading cause of cancer. From that day forward, they were forced to come to terms with their own limitations and professional hubris. Something very similar is happening in the financial services industry right now.

I believe that, through inferrence and presumption, the financial services industry has effectively convinced most investors that markets are inefficient enough to be reliably exploited. Investors, in turn, have come to believe that by paying the industry substantial fees for research, insight and any of a number of forms of 'expertise,' they can reasonably expect to 'beat the market.' To date, however, this has been a mostly futile exercise. Acting as if something is so doesn't actually make it so.

The issue here is not whether people are allowed to have an opinion. Of course they are. The issue is whether they are manipulating a process in order to effectively impose their opinions on others who are coming to them for independent advice. Compare this with what many FSPs do today: they offer to work with people provided that those people accept their opinions about what kind of management is best.

I've been given a number of potential explanations about why an FSP might reasonably recommend active options nearly exclusively. Obviously, no one can discern collective motivations for certain—and motivations are likely to vary between FSPs at any rate.

The first possible explanation stems from simple habit. Many people (FSPs included) start out doing things a certain way and then simply continue doing things that way. Having always recommended actively managed products and strategies, there is a view that FSPs are merely 'doing what they have always done' and guilty of nothing other than perhaps failing to 'change with the times'—much like the doctors referenced above.

The second possibility is that FSPs sincerely believe that,

in spite of the overwhelming but non-unanimous evidence to the contrary, they can reliably pick those securities or products that will 'outperform' their benchmarks and/or peer groups. The view here is that these FSPs are conscientious, diligent, serious and earnest about their work and legitimately believe that they are doing what is best for their clients. Since there are always examples of products that beat their benchmarks over all time frames, it needs to be acknowledged that this is a plausible explanation.

Perhaps the most contentious explanation is that some FSPs are threatened by the democratizing impact of low-cost, non-embedded products. These are the sorts of people (and I have met a few) who say things like, "If I recommend passive products, then clients won't need me." The irony of this is that people are now caught in the net of recommending products that are likely to be inferior on the balance of probabilities simply to be able to justify their own inclusion in the decision-making process.

I've been holding mirrors up to my fellow FSPs for nearly a decade now. Some appreciate the forced introspection; others not so much. What was once heresy is increasingly being viewed as self-evident. I've referenced a large number of resources at back of the book for those people who want to examine evidence further. Have a look if you're interested. The industry's regulators insist that practicing FSPs cannot portray the things I've referenced above as facts. As such, I will simply end the chapter by saying that it is my opinion, and the opinion of a growing number of FSPs around the world, that stock picking, fund picking and market timing are simply not part of the job description of a truly professional FSP.

Investment Pornography

Sex sells. —Anonymous

There are many people who feel that the media, far from being the guardians of consumer interests, are really just unwitting lackeys for corporate interests. After all, who pays for newspaper and television advertising? And what would the media write about day after day if they clearly acknowledged that outperformance isn't persistent? The challenge for all FSPs is to cut through the clutter and get consumers to focus on the things that are both important and within individual investors' personal control.

Even if the urgency and immediacy of headlines were as important as implied, it would likely be too late for virtually anyone to act on the contents of those stories. By the time consumers read about a new earnings report in the paper or see the feature on the hot new product on television, it'll be too late anyway. If markets are indeed highly efficient, then by the time the information has been made available, the implication will have already been felt. If there's news that interest rates have gone up unexpectedly, the bond market will reflect that new reality in mere minutes, if not seconds. Calling your FSP the next morning to act on the 'news' is like locking the barn door after the horse has bolted. The industry has a term to describe those economic and political events that get people interested, even excited, but have virtually no real value: 'investment pornography.'

Background Noise

One thing that people need to sort out for themselves is whether something really is news or just investment porn. Ironically, unimportant but interesting tidbits of information grab financial headlines on most days. The information is usually nothing more than background noise in the busy hubbub of life for a person seeking financial independence. Part of the job of a good FSP is to act as a filter and to ensure that clients are not unduly swayed by these seemingly important sound bites that rarely add up to anything. Investment pornography can include, but is not limited to, the following items:

- changes in interest rates, employment rates and inflation
- fluctuations in currencies
- the price of oil, gold and other commodities
- where stock markets closed
- yield curves
- housing starts
- consumer confidence indicators

Anyone focusing on a time frame of twenty years or longer isn't going to care much about the day-to-day, week-to-week or month-to-month gyrations of any of these items. But people read about them nonetheless and people watch the business news daily. As the saying goes, "In the short run, returns are virtually unknowable; but in the long run, they are virtually inevitable." Truly professional FSPs won't make predictions about what any of the gyrations mean or will lead to because these fluctuations don't genuinely matter. Professional FSPs focus not only on things that matter but also on those that are within their control. At any rate, the market moves swiftly to incorporate new information, making it nearly impossible for ordinary investors to capitalize on that new information.

Not surprisingly, virtually every bit of financial news is nonetheless portrayed at least implicitly as something that could lead to disproportionate profit. Since that's where the media and the world outside would have consumers look if left to their own devices, STANDUP FSPs have a daunting task ahead of them, yet not for reasons that you might think. The media goes on and on about all the things we just itemized. As a result, who can blame consumers for thinking they're important?

At the time of publication, I'll have been a regular guest on BNN's program *Market Call* for about three years. I enjoy the experience immensely. I cannot help but marvel at how many callers say that the STANDUP approach is rare among FSPs. Since this approach is based on empiricism and transparency, it's odd that so few Canadians perceive their FSPs as having those qualities.

The other thing that I absolutely can't get over is how many callers press me for a forecast of one kind or another. I must admit that when you're live on national television, it is sometimes difficult to find a polite way to tell well-intended questioners that it would be irresponsible to provide a forecast about things that are, by definition, unknowable.

Of course, whenever someone offers a forecast, it is covered by the show's blanket disclaimer that the opinions of the show's guests are those of the guest alone and are not necessarily shared by the network or the guest's firm. Once again, I have no quarrel with other people having opinions—including those that diverge from my own. It's just that it seems to me that if there's so much broad, macro-level factual information that one can draw on, why would anyone want to spend time asking about one person's opinion? Opinions are like noses—everyone has one. Real value usually lies in factual information.

Unfortunately, as soon as someone is seduced by the hoopla of forecasts, trends and the like (opinions), they become far more likely to do something stupid with their money. Focusing on the wrong things can lead to making the wrong decisions. If FSPs can just get their clients to keep their eyes on the things that matter (facts), they will have likely earned their fees.

Here's an example of an opinion offered by someone who is less than indifferent to how someone in the audience might behave. Over the years, I've heard more than a few money managers say things like: "This is a good time to use active management." Now, they have their opinion and I have mine. How much of an impact does the 'current market environment' have on the fact (I use the word deliberately and advisedly) that all aggregate investing is zero sum before costs? In other words, it would seem to me that all markets are equally good or bad for active management and that the "this is a good time..." is little more than a sales pitch.

What is more, however, is when someone says "this is a good market for something," it would seem to me that a logical corollary would be along the lines of: "Will you also tell me when it's not a good time for that thing?" and "When was the last time when it wasn't so good?" and "If you really are looking out for my best interests, wouldn't you be equally eager to point out when to avoid something as when to embrace it?" In all my years, I've never ever heard a stock picker say: "This is a really bad time for active management."

The existence of investment pornography as exemplified by self-interested industry stakeholders merely complicates the questions surrounding good advice. If good financial advice isn't about understanding trends and making forecasts, then what is it about?

Behavioural Finance

I can calculate the motion of heavenly bodies, but not the madness of people.

—Sir Isaac Newton

The phrase 'you're only human' is used almost daily in describing the foibles of life.

One of the most interesting aspects of being human is that we sometimes focus on things that are fun while ignoring other things that are more purposeful. For consumers and FSPs alike, this can manifest itself in some perverse ways.

Professional STANDUP FSPs don't engage in anything other than abstract discussions about the direction or timing of the market or market performance. Everyone who has even implied an ability to make reliable predictions should move immediately to rectify the misconceptions that they themselves have perpetrated as a result. Consumers and FSPs alike should spend most of their time reviewing and adhering to a suitable asset mix and looking for planning opportunities. Beyond that, most of what FSPs do might be referred to as 'constructive behaviour modification.'

Instead of focusing on things that are controllable (cost, asset allocation, tax efficiency), the majority of FSPs focus on the most random and uncontrollable element of portfolio design: 'performance' as gained or lost through security selection and market-timing decisions.

Perhaps it's just more fun to focus on security selection and market-timing decisions. There's not much profit margin available in promoting a steady, suitable, 'buy, hold and re-balance' strategy, even though those things are highly important. On the other hand, there's a whole lot of money to be made in the monolithic industry focusing on security selection and market timing.

Any professional who is serious about putting the interests of the client first should acknowledge that the employment of active management is usually, to some extent at least, an exercise in corporate profit enhancement. The industry has shot itself in the foot. Having convinced all of society that security selection is actually worth something, it can't kick the habit and come clean with the whole truth because profitability would plummet. In Section 4, we'll look at some recent developments regarding what the financial services industry is doing to disclose and manage these conflicts. Until the spring of 2012, these conflict of interest disclosures were few and far between. Regulators have now made the professional, written disclosure of real and perceived conflicts a necessary pre-condition of doing business.

I know one successful FSP who has said, "We (FSPs) get paid for our opinion," and who has gone on to observe that, as a result, "We had better be right." I disagree. My view is that FSPs get paid for conveying causal relationships and assisting clients in making responsible decisions that take those relationships into account.

The Big Mistake

Perhaps the main duty of the FSP is to ensure that clients avoid 'The Big Mistake.' Of all the advances in the field of personal finance, there may be none more important than the fairly recent discoveries in behavioural finance. Behavioural finance is the study of how emotional decisions caused by human factors often lead to poor investment choices and re-duced investment returns. A growing body of research demonstrates how this 'human side' of investment decision-making has a major impact on actual performance outcomes. In spite of this, there's no reference in any textbook for FSPs to teach them how to stay the course and deal with the road-blocks associated with their clients' emotions.

Daniel Kahneman and Amos Tversky are likely two of the most influential social scientists of our time, but relatively few people have heard of them. Their ground-breaking research in the field of decision-making has precipitated a sea change in finance.[1] These men are psychologists, and they convincingly showed that humans are frequently less than ra-tional in making decisions within the context of uncertain outcomes. They also showed that people have difficulty in processing probabilities and maintaining a consistent stance depending on how propositions are framed. In 2002, Kahneman was awarded the Nobel Prize in Economics. Kahneman and Tversky offered copious evidence showing that the most basic assumptions of modern economics do not actually hold when tested with real people.

The Kahneman and Tversky research is particularly inter-esting when combined with the Nobel Prize-winning economics research from the previous year. In 2001, the Nobel went to George A. Akerlof, A. Michael Spence and Joseph Stiglitz for their work on markets with asymmetric information (where people on one side of a transaction have more and/or better information than people on the other side).

The research done by these thought leaders is about as empirically robust as any out there. They have shown that, as a matter of fact, large proportions of society are susceptible of decision-making quirks that are often self-destructive. In spite of this, FSPs are not taught about decision theory before they can offer advice.

Many FSPs would be well advised to consider the three possible ways of processing information: you could know something and know that you know it; you could not know something and know that you don't know it; and finally, you could not know something and be totally unaware of your own ignorance. This last situation is arguably the most dangerous. I suspect many FSPs don't recommend that consumers consider certain products and strategies because they are simply unaware of the evidence in support of them. In turn, the reason they are ignorant of the evidence is likely because they simply assumed they 'already had it all figured out,' and so moved on to other things.

While some experts believe there are investors out there who can exploit human foibles for personal gain, Kahneman doesn't think it can be done. Based on his own findings, he is of the view that markets are efficient. He says:

> People see skill in performance where there is no skill... People are overly impressed by the performance of money managers, who sell what they've been doing for the past few years. It is difficult to realize that you would get very similar patterns if there were no skill at all in picking stocks or running funds."[1] He goes on to say that: "...the idea that any single individual without extra information or extra market power can beat the market is extraordinarily unlikely. Yet the market is full of people who think they can do it and full of people who believe them. This is one of the great mysteries of finance: Why do people believe they can do the impossible? And why do others believe them?[1]

Qualified FSPs can be useful in offering reasonable counsel that comes from a perspective that should mitigate potentially self-destructive tendencies. STANDUP FSPs understand this intuitively. In spite of this, FSPs receive no formal training in the field of behavioural finance before they start in the business.

There are thousands of FSPs working today who had to demonstrate the ability to calculate intrinsic values of special warrants and the price of a security trading ex-dividend and cum-dividend. In reality, most never use these sorts of skills after writing their licensing exam. That same course material did nothing to explain behavioural concepts like anchoring or loss aversion, even though these and other emotional and intellectual blind spots go a long way to explaining investment experience.

Any FSP should understand that advice needs to be offered from the client's perspective and that the client is going to feel overwhelmed by some of the complexity and uncertainty of capital markets. University courses leading to an advanced degree in financial planning, therefore, also need to add an entire body of work to their course material dealing with tangible case study approaches on how to assist consumers in staying the course and avoiding 'The Big Mistake.' Imagine the good that qualified FSPs could do if educators actually taught them how to apply solutions to these problems.

Ironically, Kahneman and Tversky are also two of the biggest allies that stock and fund pickers have. People engaged in the business of security selection argue that if people make repeated mistakes regarding risk and reward, then clearly capital markets must not be altogether efficient. The behavioural finance research deals with individual decisions made by particular investors, whereas 'the market' is actually the sum total of all investors (private and institutional, large and small) that reacts to information as it becomes available. Therefore, even though individual investors might make inappropriate investment decisions, the market as a whole might not.

This is the essence of the problem. On the surface, many consumers have sufficient knowledge of capital markets to make adequate financial decisions. In spite of this, there is evidence that shows massive net redemptions when mutual fund values are dropping and massive net sales when markets are on fire. If the phrase "buy low, sell high" is such a trite little truism that any fool can understand, why do so many people ignore it and do just the opposite? Similarly, if the principle of diversification is so basic that it is seen as a motherhood issue that everyone understands and agrees with, why were so many portfolios wildly overweight in technology when the bubble burst at the turn of the millennium? Furthermore, why do citizens of every nation on earth invest disproportionately in their home stock markets? If they're all seeking the best possible risk-adjusted return, it should be obvious that they can't all be right. It seems as though the quest for performance can easily take a back seat to convenience and familiarity.

If left to their own devices, consumers will frequently make emotional decisions during market swings and manias, even if they later acknowledge (usually with the benefit of 20/20 hindsight) that they were not making logical decisions at the time. But people can make irrational decisions even when markets are behaving 'normally,' if such a description can be applied to markets at all. Professional FSPs should be able to save well-intentioned consumers from themselves in these times of weakness.

We all make cognitive errors because the brain is designed to deal with the important problems in life, but the perspective the brain uses to deal with more complex problems isn't always accurate. As such, an FSP might be able to apply the teachings of behavioural finance to help clients maintain a better sense of perspective. That, in turn, should lead to better decision-making. There's an old saying in poker: if you look around the table and can't figure out who the 'patsy' is, then chances are that you're the patsy.

Gambles

In the week between Christmas and New Year's in 2011, I was relaxing at home while reading Daniel Kahneman's *Thinking, Fast and Slow*. There, beginning on page 269 for those of you who want to look it up, was one of the greatest and most influential living economic thinkers on earth using gambling as a reference point for financial decision-making.

It's ironic that I had just given up writing a monthly column that I had been doing for nearly a decade for *Advisor's Edge Report*, and later, www.advisor.ca. That step away from regular contact with FSPs was due largely to my ongoing frustration in trying to get compliance people to allow me to write articles about investment decision-making that compared it to gambling.

The Kahneman book makes reference to two basic, over-simplified models of decision-making, called System 1 and System 2. Professor Kahneman explains that System 1 is nearly spontaneous and often wrong, while System 2 is more methodical but chronically lazy. He is interested in how people actually make decisions in stark contrast to the prevailing orthodoxy of all economic modelling. He challenges the most basic assumptions of economics—where the very premise of all models is one of people being sensible, consistent, rational, self-interested and utility-maximizing. That's the difference between theory and practice. You know the difference, right? In theory, there is no difference—but in practice, there is. Kahneman showed that people often make decisions that are less than intuitive and certainly inconsistent with the traditional premises of economics...and decisions are everywhere in life.

In terms of explaining why most FSPs prefer active management, it occurred to me that the decision of many FSPs to favour the active camp may be nothing more and nothing less than a simple decision to be persuaded by a narrative that, on the surface, seems plausible and to leave it at that without investigating further. In other words, perhaps most FSPs don't really honestly think about what they recommend in a critical manner. Rather, they might just do what they have always done—simply because that's the way they've always done it. As with the physicians and the cigarettes I mentioned earlier, this might be a simple case of intellectual laziness. I suspect that peer pressure has a bit to do with it, too.

One example is the so-called 'fourfold pattern'—one of the truly remarkable discoveries gleaned from the pioneering work done by Kahneman and Tversky. In it, they showed how people are risk averse when in a circumstance where there's a high probability of a gain and when there's a small probability of a large loss, but they're risk-seeking when there's a small chance of a large gain and large chance of a substantial loss.

Decisions involve trade-offs. Kahneman and Tversky showed that most people are inconsistent in their decision-making and that so-called 'cognitive biases' abound. What is more, the outcomes associated with competing choices are often not certain. People are allowed a reasonable degree of latitude to interpret things (data, trends, research reports, etc.) in whatever manner they see fit and to make recommendations accordingly. The problem is that we all have biases. Biases are interesting in themselves if they are confined to simple matters of opinion where reasonable people might differ. To the extent that people can change their behaviour for the better, shouldn't we at least look for opportunities to help them to help themselves?

What about facts? Should mere opinions be allowed to supersede facts? What about more subtle questions involving probabilities? If there are two competing courses of action and neither is certain to lead to a better outcome, but one is 90% more likely than the other to lead to a better outcome, can someone reputably advocate for the 10% option without even mentioning the option that is more likely to lead to a superior outcome?

This goes straight to the heart of decision-making because it goes straight to the heart of advice-giving. How does one provide responsible counsel in a world where some outcomes may be more probable than others but, at any rate, no course of action is unambiguously superior in all instances?

As one might expect, IIROC has a comprehensive rule book. (Don't all self-respecting self-regulated professions?) In it, there's a section regarding appropriate marketing material. The passage can be found in section 29.7(1) of the IIROC rules governing marketing material and FSP conduct. In my view, the interpretation of what can and cannot be said has engendered a form of de facto censorship. Unlike academics, FSPs are precluded from offering specific constructive recommendations for substantive change if/when those recommendations are deemed to be portraying the industry in an unfavourable light. How exactly can any situation improve if no one is allowed to respectfully point out any deficiencies in the first place? Then, when someone from outside the industry (i.e. who is not subject to IIROC rule 29.7(1)) says or does the exact same thing, that person is shunted aside as a 'mere' journalist or academic who 'has no idea what it's like in the real world because she/he doesn't have to deal with retail clients every day.'

The industry effectively self-censors internal critics and dismisses external critics—leaving the (presumptive) impression that everything is fine and well and under control. In my opinion, the IIROC rulebook contravenes Section 2 of the Constitution Act of 1982 regarding Freedom of Expression.

Some people may say, "Well, that's (advocating one approach exclusively) just the way financial advice has always been given." That may be. Of course, the same sort of reasoning was once offered to deny blacks and women the right to vote. Other people might say that these ideas are 'too new' and therefore not particularly reputable. I find that amusing. The idea of risk-averse decision-makers preferring options that maximize utility (as opposed to economic value) was first put forward by Swiss scientist Daniel Bernoulli in the 1770s, so the concepts are hardly new. Meanwhile, the nearly universal acceptance of Kahneman and Tversky's work speaks to how reputable the work is.

In a related matter, why do nearly all people in the financial services industry bristle at the comparison between gambling and investing? Gambling, as financial decision-making and advice-giving, often involves trade-offs between improbable positive outcomes.

My sense is that the former is portrayed as being random (which is accurate), while the latter is portrayed as being based on disciplined, serious research (all true) and is decidedly not random (unfortunately, not true). A little more than a decade ago, Nicholas Nassim Taleb wrote a book called *Fooled by Randomness*, in which he demonstrated the chimera of financial markets and financial decision-making beyond all reasonable doubt. No matter. It seems the industry cannot bear to hear the truth, no matter how clearly, empirically and respectfully it is put forward. As in *The Wizard of Oz*, inquisitive truth seekers are told to "stop pulling back the curtain."

While this is especially true for people who work in the industry, it is really only enforceable for that subset of society that works in the business. Academics who don't work directly in the financial services industry such as Daniel Kahneman, Nicholas Taleb and Michael Edesess have all demonstrated the inherent applicability of the gambling metaphor that the industry is so desperate to suppress.

The New Keynesians

The emerging role of the professional FSP is both an interesting and unique one. On one hand, we're talking about people who know minute details about financial things that most people never think of. On the other hand, FSPs have to stay tuned into their clients' deepest emotions if they ever hope to gain the necessary trust to get people to act in ways that may be contrary to their potentially dangerous natural instincts.

In short, a good FSP can be a valuable resource in understanding a number of concepts. In the future, being a trusted FSP will likely go well beyond simply managing money. Although FSPs know all about money, they have a particularly important role to play in educating their clients about themselves. Interestingly, the word 'educate' comes from the latin *educo*, which literally means to 'draw out.' Good FSPs will ultimately draw out the best in their clients.

It is becoming increasingly clear in the context of financial advice that most FSPs are left-brained people offering left-brained (i.e. logical and empirical) explanations for why things might happen and what to do in response. The trouble is, most people make financial decisions with the right side of their brain, the one that deals with the emotional aspects of decision-making.

Let's use the ideas of another well-known economist to illustrate the coming together of both conventional economics and behavioural economics when explaining the role of a new-age professional FSP. John Maynard Keynes was an extremely influential economist who felt that the primary role of governments was to mitigate the vagaries of the business cycle—to have highs that were less high and lows that were less low, while still growing the economy. He believed governments should spend more money (perhaps incurring a deficit) in order to stimulate the economy when things were slow and then spend less (or tax more) when times were good to make up for any previously incurred shortfalls.

Still, Keynesian economics is likely more universal than you might think. Instead of looking at the financial stability of a nation, why not draw an analogy with an individual household? The most basic truism of investing is 'buy low, sell high.' Conceptually, FSPs have a role with their clients much like governments had in implementing Keynes' ideas: They have to get their clients to do things they might not otherwise be inclined to do. Human nature being what it is, clients are inclined to buy when things are going up and to sell in a panic when the markets are heading south.

The role of a good Keynesian public policy administrator is to constructively temper the amplitude of the business cycle for the benefit of the greater public good. One might say that the parallel role of a good FSP is to temper the amplitude of client emotions. There's a distinct need to help people resist the temptation to buy just because the investment has been going up or to sell just because it has been going down. It is a behaviour that is self-evidently useful and intellectually simple. The problem is that that same behaviour can be emotionally difficult, leading to considerable losses.

DALBAR showed that quite clearly. Pioneers in behavioural finance such as Richard Thaler at the University of Chicago have done further academic research demonstrating that when people are confused and anxious, they do irrational things such as selling low and buying high, even as they profess to be sensible long-term investors.

Despite this situation, good FSPs can be useful in helping their clients to deal with some of the teachable moments of behavioural finance. Irrational trading tendencies can have another negative consequence: tax liabilities. A recent study showed that taxes eat up as much as one-sixth of the average mutual fund return, which is only 9% to begin with. Since approximately 54% of all mutual funds in Canada are held outside registered plans, this is a significant concern. Amin Mawani, Moshe Milevsky and Kamphol Panyagometh of the Schulich School of Business at York University in Toronto have researched the effects of taxation on mutual fund port-folios. In a recent study published in the *Canadian Tax Journal*, they conclude that "taxes exceed management fees and bro-kerage commissions in their ability to erode long-term in-vestment returns."[2] It is widely believed that a responsible FSP can help consumers to resist making questionable trades. Mind you, not every FSP is necessarily responsible—and those who are transactional generally make more money the more their clients transact, so how much help do you think they will be in their drive to imbue their clients' investing with some constructive behaviour modification?

In the United States, legislation now compels mutual funds to disclose after-tax returns. The York research turned up some interesting results, including the fact that when funds are ranked for their after-tax returns, the order generally differs from pure fund performance rankings. On average, funds moved up or down twenty-eight spots in the rankings compared to their peers as a result of their tax efficiency (or lack thereof).

Remember that only the most recent generations of MBA graduates have been taking mandatory courses in ethics. Similarly, new university graduates with a degree conferring the right to practice as professional and holistic financial advisors will need to address the very real gap in the education system as it presently stands. Our number-cruncher FSPs are going to have to write some essays, role-play with their classmates and do some interactive learning in diagnosing both the financial and the emotional distresses facing prospective clients.

FSPs have never been taught the importance of behaviour in investing, so they have come to the conclusion that behaviour must not be very important since it isn't being taught. We need to set the record straight right away and to teach our FSPs that investor psychology is a very, very big deal.

A Bias toward Inaction

Biases don't only exist in terms of what one buys. They also exist in questions like when one might sell. You've probably read a number of promotional pieces about people or organizations that have a 'bias toward action.' These are the people and companies that don't just stand around and watch the world turn, these are the doers of the world. Many people are comforted and perhaps even inspired by this kind of attitude, but personal finance is one field where they shouldn't be.

Extremes are dangerous in many endeavours, but when it comes to managing your finances, dormancy almost always beats hyperactivity. Nearly every major study on the subject has shown that portfolio turnover correlates negatively to performance. In layperson's terms: the more you trade, the worse you do—on average. Every trade involves costs, including trading costs, bid/ask spreads and possible tax liabilities. The more you trade, the more these costs eat into your returns. If left to their own devices, most people would likely trade too often. This often happens because people believe they can discern trends when random events cause prices to display trend-like attributes. Experts consider this to be clear evidence of overconfidence.

It's one of the great ironies about wealth management. Many people assume that in order to stay on top of your finances, you need to monitor them unflinchingly and to make swift, sure and informed decisions when circumstances change. Nothing could be further from the truth. As it turns out, the most successful investors are usually strategic thinkers who are prepared to wait years for things to pan out.

This is another area where FSPs can add value. They can act to encourage their clients to trade less by insisting that perceived trends are actually nothing more than coincidental and random outcomes and not the sorts of things that one should consider 'useful information' when trading securities. Unfortunately, a large portion of the industry does nothing to clarify this misconception and even goes so far as to imply causation where none exists. Newspapers that run contests where thousands of contestants pick a basket of stocks to see which will outperform over a short time frame merely legitimize security selection as a socially acceptable form of gambling that masquerades as an intellectual undertaking.

Until perhaps twenty years ago, investment management was almost entirely transactional, meaning FSPs only got paid when clients completed trades. In the recent past, as the paradigm of FSPs as value-adding, advice-giving professionals has become more prevalent, the financial services industry has moved from giving away advice and charging for transactions to giving away the transactions and charging for advice. Discount brokers and technology have played a major role in this shift. Today, do-it-yourself (DIY) investors can trade online for virtually no transaction costs, yet the market share of discount brokerages has not changed appreciably while their transaction charges have dropped. Of course, just because transactions charges are modest, that doesn't mean the trades are 'cheap,' since the other factors mentioned above should also be considered. People seem pretty competent in determining whether they need advice or not.

Research done at the University of Michigan and published in 2003 showed that purchase decisions made by mutual fund investors are influenced by salient, attention-grabbing information and that investors are typically more sensitive to in-your-face fees such as front-end loads and commissions than they are to operating expenses. As a result, they are more likely to buy funds based on performance, marketing or advertising. The research showed a consistent negative relationship between flows and front-end load fees. In contrast, they found no relation between operating expenses and fund flows. Their research showed that marketing and advertising (things that are generally embedded in fund operating expenses) accounted for this. The findings lend credence to the notion that mutual funds are sold, not bought, and that behavioural factors normally associated with poor consumer decision-making (such as being fairly oblivious to price) caused people to make some perverse decisions.

The financial services industry grew out of a sales culture that made money when engaging in trading activity. Therefore, people giving financial advice less than a generation ago had a clear personal financial incentive to get clients to trade more even though increased trading activity was repeatedly shown to do more for the FSP than for the client. Unfortunately, there was no way for consumers to determine whether advice to transact a trade was genuinely in their best interests or simply dreamt up by the FSP to increase revenue. Over time, individual securities were replaced by mutual funds as the investment vehicles of choice for most consumers.

Irrespective of the products used, it should be noted that SPANDEX FSPs think and act like salespeople, while STANDUP FSPs think and act like value-adding professionals. Unfortunately, when the system was set up, it was done in such a way that every transaction carried the potential for FSP bias. Since everyone has some degree of bias in their thinking, what sorts of steps do you suppose could be taken to confront the problem?

Part Three
Necessary Disclosure

Necessary Disclosure

One can resist the invasion of armies, but not the invasion of ideas whose time has come.

—Victor Hugo

Why are so many FSPs afraid to have a discussion about how and how much they are paid? It's ironic, given that their clients have already gone first in this personal disclosure about all the major financial things in their lives. Even though most FSPs have a pretty good sense of how much all their clients make, many continue to balk at reciprocating—and then go on about how the financial advice business is all about openness and trust.

The simple reason for this is that there's a fear of the unknown. Even though most people want to work with others in an upfront manner, there's a feeling among a significant number of FSPs that consumers will recoil in horror once they find out how much financial advice costs.

Who Wants Transparency?

Many observers are both amused and confused by some FSPs' inconsistencies. For instance, some FSPs lament about the costs of running a practice to their peers but go on to dismiss the high cost of the products they recommend to their clients. As with so many things in life, one's priorities are revealed through the choices one makes. If FSPs really want to reconcile rhetoric and reality, they should seize the opportunity to be consistent in their thinking. Doing so would allow them to demonstrate that they 'get it' when it comes to ethics, transparency, the alignment of interests and the importance of cost.

Having a strong entrepreneurial streak in them, many clearly understand that costs matter when running their own practices. Whether it's rent, computer software and hardware, photocopying costs, online access, you name it, FSPs are certainly minding their Ps and Qs.

A traditional brokerage arrangement would see an FSP accept a lower payout rate and with their firms covering a number of variable costs on their behalf. Today, many FSPs are asking their firms to offer the most competitive payout rate possible so they can outsource the variable costs of running their practices. Essentially, FSPs want their firms to give them the latitude to get their own product suppliers in order to control costs. They also want their firms to provide statements showing exactly how much each line item expense actually costs so that they can better monitor things. These FSPs are acting the way any other responsible small business owner would.

However, this is not what some FSPs do when making investment recommendations. There are FSPs out there who simply don't want to have a conversation with their clients about how they're getting paid, how much they're getting paid and how much their advice is worth. It is noteworthy that some FSPs may be using higher-cost products because they honestly believe it'll be 'worth it' in the long run. One way or another, FSP revenue depends on client performance and some FSPs would likely justify their use of pricier products because they expect that ultimate returns will justify the higher costs. One could argue, therefore, that these FSPs far more focused on maximizing returns (growing the top line) than controlling costs (growing the bottom line). The logic is that if the top line grows, then so does the bottom—all else being equal.

Many FSPs say they resist unbundling because they would make the same amount of money and the client would pay the same amount of money either way. This is not necessarily true. With unbundling, clients could easily substitute expensive products with cheaper ones and pocket the difference. If this were to happen, the FSP's compensation wouldn't change, but client costs certainly would! In fact, there's likely to be an arbitrage opportunity, where a saving (let's call it 1%) could be honourably split between an FSP and a client. Perhaps an FSP ought to be paid 20 basis points more? (A basis point is 1/100 of 1%.) Even if this were to happen, a typical client could still save 80 basis points and be substantially better off as a result.

Furthermore, how many FSPs have a letter of engagement (LOE) that sets out the obligations of both parties once they begin to work together? We've already looked at the cost of parts and labour. Although FSPs need and deserve to be paid, consumers deserve to know what they're paying and what services they should reasonably expect in return. In this regard, it's like anything else: an informed consumer is a good consumer. Just as with cars, cribs and carbohydrate-reduced diets, the more consumers know about products, the better their decisions.

Most observers would agree that there are three primary ways that an FSP might be paid:

1. An 'advisory' arrangement with transparent, asset-based fees
2. A 'professional' arrangement where there are hourly fees for deliverables

3. A 'customer' arrangement where the FSP merely facilitates product placement and receives an embedded commission as a result

It should also be noted that all Certified Financial Planners (CFPs) have been required to use LOEs for over a decade already. On one hand, this might not be too surprising since the industry doesn't want to come down too hard on those FSPs who at least have their hearts in the right place. Attempts are being made to assist FSPs (most of whom genuinely want to do the right thing) to actually go out and do the right thing. There are both STANDUP FSPs and SPANDEX FSPs out there. Without being too judgmental, the industry is trying to use carrots as opposed to sticks to get SPANDEX FSPs to make the leap that they have resisted until now and become legitimate professionals.

Good disclosure leads to better consumer decision-making. As such, the people who should want this kind of disclosure more than any other are the consumers who continue to insist that finance is too complex and full of jargon. Having a series of simple one- or two-page disclosures and engagements that have been stripped of legal wording is a great way to improve consumer understanding, which in turn should lead to better FSP-client relationships.

What's an Appropriate Level of Disclosure?

Disclosure is vital because it can form the basis of a strong working relationship. The more clients understand what is being done—and why—the more likely it is that they will 'buy in' to the advice being given. Furthermore, informed consent is widely seen as being a hallmark of any professional relationship where the person giving the advice is likely to have technical expertise that goes beyond the purview of what an ordinary person on the street might reasonably be expected to know.

Using the example of physicians and the link between cigarette smoking and cancer, when the evidence linking cigarette smoke to cancer began to show up in research papers, there were significant members of the medical community whose first reactions were denial. Suppose you were a physician in the 1950s who did not discourage cigarette smoking. In fact, suppose you actively encouraged it (as some did) as a benign means of relaxation. As time goes on, evidence mounts that your position is incorrect. Would you continue to cling to your position?

The dilemma that professional physicians faced was one of grave consequence. As the primary advisors regarding their patients' health and welfare, there was an obligation to alert patients to the risks associated with consumption of cigarettes. On the other hand, the evidence (in the early days at least) was not definitive and there were professional reputations to protect. What should a professional, patient-centred physician do? What would a patient whose health is on the line want the physician to do? Should concerns be raised when the evidence starts to come out or only once a sufficient body of evidence has been developed?

The concepts in this book are by no means unique. What about the recent rash of concussions in the National Hockey League? Is this due to a change in equipment or diagnosis or merely an unfortunate 'rough patch' where an unusually high percentage of players are afflicted? How should the league govern itself while the jury is out?

What about differing views about climate change? Most scientists are compelled by the evidence; some are not. Irrespective of which side is ultimately proven to be right, surely there must be some need to offer heightened awareness of decisions being made. Even if the concern turns out to be a false alarm, alarm bells can be justifiably rung. In broad, macro-level decisions, many people would rather endure an unfortunate false positive or two if it means the surfeit of caution can also prevent or at least better manage the consequences of inaction.

The idea of being a STANDUP FSP hinges on the twin pillars of research, which should be dispassionate and rigorous, and disclosure, which many feel should be compulsory. One pillar is never enough. Physicians learned this firsthand a generation or two ago. Those who tried to deny the evidence were ultimately seen, with the benefit of hindsight, as being less than professional.

There are always exceptions, but just because it is possible to smoke ceaselessly and not get cancer doesn't mean smoking is advisable or good for you. Harkening back to the previous section and accepting that individual outcomes are not absolutely certain, is the statement "cigarettes cause cancer" a matter of fact or a matter of opinion? After all, clear correlation is still not the same as certainty.

Once again, accepting that the social sciences always allow for at least a modest amount of uncertainty, most reasonable people would be comfortable saying that the carcinogenic impact of cigarettes is now a generally accepted fact. Looking back on the past half-century, it should be obvious that the medical profession could have been and should have been more forthcoming about the harmful effects of cigarettes. Have we learned as a society?

Given that most people agree that more should have been done to alert the general population sooner, what has society decided regarding the proper role of professional intermediaries such as physicians? Is mere disclosure even enough, or were physicians, governed by the Hippocratic

Oath, expected to actively engage in the constructive modification of their patients' habits? It might come down to what one considers to be material.

How exactly might a person define the word 'material'— as in 'FSPs must always disclose all material facts'—when making recommendations? Dictionaries suggest synonyms including "relevant," "substantial" and "pertinent." To my mind, any information that causes a person to change their opinion or behaviour is material. For example, if you were a smoker and I was the first to inform you that cigarettes cause cancer, I would say that this information would be material if it caused you to change your habits. One could quite properly add that this information could be relevant, substantial and pertinent whether one gives up smoking or not. But to me, changing one's behaviour is a pretty reliable sign of genuine materiality.

For a number of years now, I've been disclosing to my clients in writing that most actively managed mutual funds lag their benchmarks and that the few that seem to outperform cannot be reliably identified in advance. Not surprisingly, most of my clients resist using actively managed funds once they've been presented with this information, and yet there is nothing in the industry that requires that this disclosure be made.

It has become clear to me that disclosure is a significant contributor to consumer decision-making and can be used to manipulate choices.

FSPs and the companies they work for simply cannot have it both ways. Markets are either efficient or not. A 'third option'—one that suggests that both approaches may have merit—might also be useful. Regardless of where an FSP might come down personally on a matter of opinion, the most current and reliable evidence for both positions ought to be disclosed at the outset.

If market efficiency is merely a question of opinion, then surely everyone is entitled to their own beliefs. All correspondence should carry a disclaimer that states that other FSPs in the organization do not necessarily share the same opinions. Surely we have come far enough as a society to know that saying something is so doesn't make it so and that questions of empiricism should never be reduced to something as juvenile as a popularity contest.

According to many experts in finance, there is now sufficient evidence to allow fair-minded observers to conclude that markets are sufficiently efficient that it is improbable that one could reliably beat them through security selection or market timing. As such, one could argue that the failure of an FSP to disclose this evidence is about as inappropriate as a physician failing to disclose that inhaling cigarette smoke is linked to cancer.

It bears repeating that 'probable' does not mean 'certain.' As such, one could pursue a course of action that is more probable to yield superior results and do worse as a result of this attempt. Similarly, one can choose a course of action where an improbable outcome nonetheless bears fruit. The larger issue revolves around the concept of informed consent.

Losing about 1% in returns, while significant, pales in comparison to losing one's life. But this is the problem with disclosure: just how definitive does the evidence have to be and how dire do the consequences have to be before disclosure is required?

If there is a level of disclosure regarding the pros and cons of one approach or product without a similar degree of disclosure about something that is in direct competition, then how is a consumer supposed to make an informed decision about which way to go?

A critical aspect of real professionalism is that practitioners do not impose their personal views on others, but rather work collaboratively in a manner that the client believes is in her best interests. Obviously, if the FSP were to disagree, she ought to say so. Different people may look at the same information and come to totally different conclusions, but any professional offering advice based on information that is either not fully understood or not fully agreeable should disclose those details in a manner that allows the consumer to make an informed choice.

It would be disingenuous of any professional FSP not to at least portray all possible interpretations and alternatives fairly. Advisors are allowed to and indeed expected to advocate for one position over another but should do so only after giving all viewpoints a fair hearing.

The media is full of stories about how certain products or strategies are somehow better than others, when the outcomes are actually nothing more than random occurrences. Even when evidence comes forward that shows a way of doing things as flawed or a dangerous threat to society, it's extremely difficult to get entrenched corporate interests to change. There are powerful elements of industry that are making huge sums of money by doing things the old way. These interests will deny evidence and confuse the issue as much as possible and for as long as is possible in a desperate attempt to protect corporate profitability. This is nothing new. Throughout history, we have seen examples of corporate interests denying high-level empirical evidence out of brazen self-interest while simultaneously purporting to be working on behalf of the valued clients.

The Cigarettes of Our Generation

With the challenges within the financial services industry,

the heart of the issue is giving responsible advice. What role should a qualified FSP play? Do regulators have an obligation to force FSPs to tell their clients about the evidence involving market efficiency?

When the class action suits started in the tobacco industry, it was the tobacco companies (i.e. the product manufacturers) that were targeted for making harmful products without disclosing the material risks associated with their consumption. The physicians (i.e. the professional, advice-giving intermediaries) were typically spared lawsuits because they were seen as mere conduits and not the root of the problem. That, plus the product manufacturers had deeper pockets. If this precedent holds regarding market efficiency and associated disclosure, then mutual fund companies had better start putting bold disclaimers on the fronts of their prospectuses lest they share the fate of Big Tobacco. Legislators ultimately came to conclude that the welfare of the citizenry trumped the right of corporations to make profits and forced the disclosure on them.

Of course, unwittingly eroding your life's savings is less harmful than unwittingly shortening your lifespan. Still, while many people would suggest that their physical health is paramount, financial health would likely run a close second. In April 2006, Ontario's Minister of Health Promotion Jim Watson was quoted as saying, "If I had my druthers, I would not want to see tobacco anywhere in Canada."[1] Those are strong and uncompromising words. No doubt many people would be offended by them—perhaps they could claim that their rights were being trampled. Remember, however, that rights in Canada are subject to a 'reasonable limits' test and that one could argue that Watson's comments are reasonable under the circumstances.

No matter what you feel about their activities, politicians

have a responsibility to protect the welfare of their citizenry. Sometimes that kind of protection might require what to some might seem like draconian measures. If governmental protection is indeed what is required, then one could just as easily expect that bolder mutual fund disclosures are right around the corner.

Whether done at the micro level by a conventional broker or at the macro level by a mutual fund manager, security selection generally costs about 1% per year. Holding FSP compensation and other factors constant, this is an opportunity to increase client returns by 1% a year. Similarly, there's an opportunity to find a price point where both the FSP and the client are better off—at the expense of the people doing the stock picking.

Let's say a client is fully invested in a mutual fund portfolio with an average MER (annual cost) of 2.5%. The pre-tax cost could be broken down like this:

Product Overhead:	0.5%
Stock Picking:	1.0%
FSP Compensation:	1.0%
Total:	2.5%

Again, one must stress that there will always be examples of funds out there that ultimately justify their higher fees. It is and will likely always be possible to beat the market. The point here is simply that it is both improbable and not something that can be done reliably or with persistence.

Now let's have a look at a couple of possible alternatives, using the idea of parts and labour sold separately, where the overhead is the product 'cost' and FSP compensation is the financial services equivalent of 'labour':

Option 1: Pass Savings on to Client
Overhead: 0.5%
FSP Compensation: 1.0%
Total: 1.5%

Option 2: Divide the Savings
Overhead: 0.5%
FSP Compensation: 1.25%
Total: 1.75%

Option 3: Who Needs an FSP?
Total Cost (Overhead): 0.5%

When making comparisons to the status quo base case, it becomes clear that Option 1 passes on a 1% saving (alternatively depicted as a 1% increase in return) to the client. In Option 2, since many FSPs insist they are underpaid, they could increase their compensation by 25% annually (a 0.25% annual fee increase to the client) and still leave the client better off by 0.75% every year. And for those people who don't believe an FSP adds value, or those who don't believe they need the services of an FSP, they can save a truly massive amount of money by simply buying market-based products.

If you asked an FSP to rate where their loyalty lies—with the employer/suppliers, clients or their own families—very few would place the employer/supplier relationship anywhere other than in third place. If the client comes first, and any FSP loves their own family more than the company president, then either Option 1 or Option 2 would be preferred over the status quo. That's because the FSP and their clients are always as well off or better off under Options 1 and 2. Only the employer/suppliers are worse off. Let's say the portfolio in question would earn 9.5% annually before costs. What would that mean for an investor with $100,000 invested for the next thirty years? Here's what those portfolios would be worth once the thirty years were over:

Option A: $1,006,265.70
Option B: $938,681.73
Option C: $1,326,767.90

By the way, what would the client's portfolio be worth if the status quo format were used? Would you believe $761,225.50? In other words, Option 2 would not only increase advisor income by 25% annually forever, it would leave the client with almost $200,000 more to retire on. That's a clear win/win scenario! The only loser is the product manufacturer, but since the manufacturer consistently finishes third out of three in the great quest for loyalty anyway, neither FSPs nor their clients should be concerned.

Calibrating Disclosure

The financial services industry is still looking for the 'Goldilocks' level of disclosure: not too much; not too little. How much disclosure is required before making an advice-based decision anyway?

There are a couple of things that are now coming to the forefront. They are the 'value proposition' of certain financial products and the price of the associated financial advice. Let's look at the products first. Throughout history, there have been stock pickers who have beaten their benchmarks. However, the number of these outperformers has never been appreciably different from the number one might expect through random chance. Perhaps chance was the only thing driving these 'superior results,' not causal, value-adding research, insight and shrewdness.

For about fifty years, the debate has raged. Throughout that time, social scientists have been able to run more and better tests, with betters controls for survivorship bias, mandate consistency, start- and end-date bias and other material factors such as costs, bid/ask spreads and taxes. Both sides of this debate have scored some points over the years, but neither has scored a decisive victory.

Most consumers cannot do a reputable job of explaining what investment products cost or how much of that cost goes to the FSP. Meanwhile, many FSPs seem content to do nothing to correct any misconceptions that may have taken hold.

The Consequence of No Change

The system needs to be reformed. The cost of doing nothing is very high indeed, since the integrity of the entire financial services industry could be called into question. Figuring out an honourable way to leave the world of embedded compensation is job one, and everything else regarding the establishment of a true profession flows from it. The current situation cannot continue indefinitely because there are simply far too many dysfunctional investment decisions being made as a result of the bias of compensation considerations.

Eliminate the Bias

It is a truth very certain that when it is not in our power to determine what is true we ought to follow what is most probable.
—René Descartes

There are two primary types of bias in financial services: a bias for active products in favour of passive ones, and a bias in favour of embedded compensation products over unbundled products. In many instances, this is the same problem, since many active products are available primarily with embedded compensation and virtually all passive products are available without embedded compensation. This is why many FSPs profess to favour active management but still refuse to recommend some of the most highly respected funds available such as those from PH&N, Mawer, Chou, Steadyhand and Beutel Goodman. Active or not, no embedded compensation usually means no shelf space with most FSPs.

Our challenge in converting a mere industry into a bona fide profession is to eliminate all forms of bias so that FSPs' motives are not called into question. The obvious solution is to create a level playing field, and there is an equally obvious way of doing that: simply have all products pay FSPs the same.

There are two possible ways of meeting this objective: 1) increase the compensation on passive products by bringing it up to the level paid by active ones, or 2) reduce the compensation paid by active products, bringing it down to the level paid by passive ones. From an 'elimination of bias' perspective, either would work, but from a 'do what's right for the consumer' perspective, the second option is clearly more appropriate. In the final section, we'll take a look at professionalism's trends from around the world. One of those options is beginning to carry a little more heft these days.

Anyone who wishes to work without the input of an FSP should be allowed to do so without having to pay for that decision. Many observers believe that most people would be better off working with an FSP. That being said, though, what might be right for most people may not be right for all people, and it would be arrogant to suggest that someone's services are so vital that people should be forced to pay for them whether they use them or not.

The Final Frontier

Over the past several years, I've spoken to representatives at a number of advisory firms about their philosophies in order to get a sense of their values and corporate culture. My sense is that compensation models can go a long way in explaining (or at least predicting) belief systems. Companies will say their FSPs can work using either transactional or buy-and-hold philosophies. Either way, there's room. They say you can be a comprehensive planner or a simple investment specialist. Either way, there's room for that too. The FSPs can be commission based or fee based. Either way, they would be welcomed. In short, companies talk a good game about giving FSPs a suitable platform and then leaving them alone to run their practice as they see fit, provided that the FSP remains compliant.

In a society where intelligent and reasonable people might differ, those differences should be explored and discussed rationally. Is it anyone's place to tell others whether they should agree with or be opposed to same-sex marriage? What about capital punishment, abortion, euthanasia or other moral questions? The gay rights issue has been described as the human rights issue of our generation. I would go so far as to venture that the debate regarding the practical degree of market efficiency is the financial services industry's practice management issue of our generation. As with all other questions that cannot be answered definitively, surely there is no place for discrimination just because someone happens to disagree with another's opinion.

Even more reprehensible is the way many advisory firms have previously portrayed STANDUP FSPs who believe in market efficiency as bad apples, as if independent thought were a vice of some sort. Corporate representatives have been known to suggest that a belief in market efficiency is contrary to corporate values, even if those values include explicit references to the firm's not interfering with the FSP-client relationship! Perhaps it is time the politicians stepped in to put an end to this shameful and often self-serving conduct.

Do FSPs Recommend Going to Casinos?

Consistency is an important part of any undertaking and people constantly look to professionals to offer consistent, impartial advice tailored to their circumstances. Someone with certain symptoms could visit three or four physicians and presumably get the same diagnosis with each. Qualified physicians take a dispassionate approach to medical advice.

Increasingly, FSPs are talking as though they are professionals—but are they? More to the point, are the recommendations of FSPs consistent, impartial and rational? Surgeons are required to explain the pros and cons of various procedures to patients in terms that patients can understand, but the final decision rests with the patient, who will decide based on personal values, preferences and the facts involved.

There is considerable evidence that the majority of actively managed mutual funds lag their benchmark and that the handful that outperform cannot be reliably identified before the fact. So, would a professional FSP recommend to a client that they should take a trip to a casino and gamble with their life savings as a retirement strategy? Both feature the possibility of improbable but outsized returns. Accepting that there are risks associated with both activities, do the rewards offer fair compensation for the risks involved?

We all know that FSPs will tell their clients it's unwise to be so cavalier with their money as to risk blowing it at a casino, but that's the point. If the analogy holds, then FSPs would have to acknowledge that it's similarly unwise to pursue active management—and for exactly the same reason. Both offer the possibility of winning in exchange for the probability of losing. People can't have it both ways. A major concern here is disclosure. When someone deliberately fails to tell the whole story in an attempt to manipulate an outcome, motive can certainly be called into question.

In the future, FSPs will need to stop hiding behind exceptions as an excuse for making blanket recommendations. Everyone knows that there are people who have smoked two packs a day for seventy years and never had cancer. Everyone also knows that there are people who died of cancer before age forty even though they never took a single drag. While there are exceptions in both cases, there is clearly an established and clinically proven link between cigarette smoking and cancer, just as there is a clear link between actively managed products lagging passive ones. The costs of portfolios are the carcinogens of the investment world and active strategies cost more than passive ones.

Doctors don't actively recommend that patients take up smoking, do they? They might acquiesce, but that's about as far as it goes. I'm okay with acquiescence. Far be it from me to deny someone of their right to be wrong. That's why we need better disclosure on product packaging. I'm not suggesting people shouldn't be allowed to 'try their luck' if that's their choice. Casinos, cigarettes and actively managed mutual funds are all legal in Canada, but only two of the three are widely seen as socially questionable.

Reconciliation Time

All this raises the question of why, after all this time, has the industry still not formulated a consistent, logical and rational perspective on the value of qualified financial advice? There are those who believe the financial services industry is inconsistent 'because it can be' and that remaining so maximizes profitability. The status quo drives STANDUP FSPs crazy because they want to do sensible things, but the industry has become so focused in its quest for profit that it doesn't even bother pretending to be sensible.

To make matters much worse, consumers are still being made to pay trailing commissions to discount brokerage firms where advice is neither requested nor received. This suits sales-oriented FSPs very well of course, because they can tell their clients that it 'costs no more' to buy (A Class) mutual fund products from them than from a discount broker.

This sort of positioning really drives STANDUP FSPs batty. By paying firms that offer no advice (discount brokerages) the same as those who offer advice (advisory firms), product manufacturers send an implicit message that the advice being offered is worthless. The STANDUP FSPs in the advice channel are of the opinion that with friends like that, who needs enemies? That fee is supposed to be for the FSP's advice, wisdom, specialized knowledge and guidance. At a discount brokerage, there is no FSP to offer any of this, but the embedded compensation to the firm persists.

The 'value proposition' of qualified advice would be appreciated far more if it were put out in the open where people could see what they are paying and have discussions around the value of what they are getting in return. Unbundling—the removal of all embedded compensation from all product offerings—would accomplish this quite nicely.

Parts and Labour Sold Separately

The essence of a genuine professional man is that he cannot be bought.

—H.L. Mencken

One of the great conundrums of the business of offering financial advice for a living is that some products offer more embedded compensation than others, while some offer none at all. This can cause a huge bias in the product recommendations made by FSPs and casts doubt on whether they can be considered true professionals under current circumstances.

Many believe that the only way to be sure about the appropriateness of advice and suitability of recommended products is if the link between products and compensation is broken once and for all. Otherwise, the motive of the FSP can and will always be called into question. The principle of the primacy of consumer interests is so entrenched that it applies to all walks of life. Let's look at auto mechanics.

Pretend that we have a simple matrix regarding parts and labour. You can use quality replacement parts or cheap knock-offs as one decision and you can install them yourself or hire a mechanic as another. Now let's pretend these variables are linked. What if your actual options were only twofold? What if you need to choose between quality parts installed at home by yourself or knock-off parts installed by the mechanic at the garage? Which would you choose? The choice invites some implicit trade-offs between cost, quality and convenience. Both options have benefits, both have drawbacks.

Think about this from a consumer's perspective, especially if that consumer is like me around a garage. I don't know a carburetor from a caliper. I need help. Imagine if a mechanic told customers that if they want the work done at his garage, they would have to agree to using inferior, knock-off parts. You can use quality parts if you do the work yourself, but you have to use knock-offs if you get someone else to do it for you. How would you feel if your mechanic gave you this option? Wouldn't the first question be: "Why can't I get the good parts and still pay you your hourly wage to install them, Mr. Mechanic?" Indeed.

As a consumer, how would you feel about a system in which embedded compensation encourages the people offering advice to offer a potentially inferior product? Shouldn't consumers be encouraged to choose products based on merit alone?

Auto mechanics are onto something. When the expectations are set out clearly and in writing before the fact, it is difficult to challenge what they've done if it accords with those expectations.

The cardinal rule of the financial services industry is that the client comes first, and FSPs are expected to subordinate their own interests to those of their clients. Part of this rule involves a 'no surprises' commitment to professionalism. This is a noble objective, but one that is open to wide interpretation. If a prospective client sees two different FSPs on a matter and receives different advice—either about planning concepts or products to be used—does this mean one or the other is being negligent? Provided they are reasonable, each set of recommendations should be considered. But there is a problem with most investment recommendations: embedded compensation.

F Class Mutual Funds

The introduction of F Class mutual funds over a decade ago was a huge step in the right direction. These are mutual funds with the commissions and trailing commissions stripped out. The difference in cost is equal to the difference in FSP compnesation—plus applicable taxes. Many years later, the industry still panders to the lowest common denominator since mutual fund research websites typically only publish numbers for A Class funds. Essentially, Corporate Canada will happily throw STANDUP FSPs a bone by manufacturing unbundled products, only to pretend that those products don't exist after having done so.

Since the products' costs are reduced by the exact amount of embedded compensation, the unbundled format allows consumers to make a clear distinction between mutual fund management expenses and FSP compensation. Now it is time to take a closer look at what consumers are really getting. Most embedded compensation equity mutual funds in Canada have a management expense ratio (MER) of about 2.45%, made up of trading and administrative costs of about 0.45%, a 1% fee for the mutual fund company and a 1% embedded advisory fee and tax. There are often additional trading costs that don't even show up in a fund's MER.

The aforementioned advisory fee is called a 'trailing commission' if you are an FSP running an ad in a local newspaper and a 'trailer fee' if you are a fund company executive doing an interview with the same newspaper. Every FSP advertisement I have ever seen requires the FSP to refer to trailers as "commissions." Meanwhile, every interview I've ever read of an executive from a manufacturing or distribution firm refers to trailers as "fees." Clearly, they cannot be both simultaneously.

It never ceases to amaze me how corporate interests can

conveniently fudge their own rules of conduct when it suits them. Whether trailers are in fact commissions or fees clearly cannot depend on who is doing the talking. Furthermore, since the two concepts mean very different things, the more accurate depiction ought to be the standard.

Most people wouldn't care much how trailers are described, but we should clearly have one set of rules for everyone. In a desire to offer certitude, it should be noted that the CRA views trailers as commissions and that IIROC requires that all marketing material refer to trailers as commissions. That said, surely everyone would agree that precision should not be compromised by using very different terms interchangeably. My sense is that moving back and forth between two very different terms simply as a matter of convenience only confuses people. Perhaps that's what the sales element of the financial services industry wants. Whichever you believe trailers to be fees or commissions, surely we can all agree that they cannot be one thing for one audience and another thing for another—especially if the terminology is primarily dependent on who is doing the talking.

The embedded compensation side of the mutual fund industry is so convinced people need FSPs that they set up the system so that consumers have to pay for FSPs whether they use them or not. These same companies then tell FSPs with a completely straight face that they are firmly committed to the advisory channel. If this were true, they would either prohibit discount brokers from selling their products or, at the very least, insist that if discount brokers want their products on the shelf, they should use the F Class versions.

Embedded compensation mutual fund companies won't do either because they are interested in distributing their products as widely as possible. Profitability and maintaining market share supersede any loyalty to their primary distribution channel. It would be refreshing if just one embedded compensation company stood up and walked the talk by removing its products from the shelves of discount brokerages as a gesture of solidarity with and commitment to qualified advice.

Most discount brokers are getting a great deal in this arrangement: the same compensation as qualified FSPs with none of the work or liability! Truly professional FSPs don't back down from the notion that qualified professional advice costs money. Most FSPs don't stand up for this concept. Some observers feel this illustrates that the FSPs who condone this practice might secretly doubt whether or not they really add value.

But what would happen if discount brokers couldn't sell embedded compensation funds? For starters, discount brokers would be a lot less profitable than they are now. They would likely have to raise transaction charges or new account fees just to remain marginally profitable. The pricing gap between the advice and DIY channels would close, but it would never go away. Qualified financial advice costs money.

Other Professions

Direct fees are charged for tax preparation. You can do your own taxes and save yourself some accounting fees or you can delegate the task to a qualified professional. This professional will simplify your life, do a responsible job and charge you a predictable fee for services rendered. In the future, consumers are simply going to have to decide whether they are going to act as their own advisor or pay for advice, and, if paying for advice, what a fair price might be.

Some professionals cost more than others in the same field, so the notion of identical pay for identical product placement regardless of FSP seniority and sophistication will also change. In a transparent fee-based environment, everyone knows instinctively that it costs more to get a partner at a specialized Bay Street law firm to do legal work than it costs to get a small-town generalist lawyer with a storefront office at the corner of Main and Elm. It stands to reason that FSPs with more experience, credentials, profile and aptitude will command a higher fee than raw rookies out of the chute once fees become the prevailing compensation model for FSPs.

Some consumers who are currently on the fence and use an FSP only grudgingly might move to discount brokers; the advice channel obviously doesn't want this, but the market segments itself pretty clearly. In general, people either want to work with an FSP or they don't, just as people choose whether to do their own tax preparation. There should be an opportunity for consumers to engage in a meaningful self-selection process without any implicit penalties associated with personal choices that minimize the revenues of financial services firms.

If qualified advice costs money, it logically follows that it will cost more to work with an FSP than to do the work yourself. Under present circumstances, there is no real reason why people disposed to investing in traditional embedded compensation mutual funds wouldn't want to use an FSP. Any value added is worth the inescapable fee that is being paid anyway. This is not the case if portfolios are constructed with individual securities and ETFs.

The system obviously needs to change. There are billions of dollars invested in mutual funds at discount brokerages that are paying these firms embedded fees while no value-added services are being rendered. That's tens of millions of dollars that discount brokers are earning annually that rightfully belongs in consumers' pockets. As it stands today, you can file your own tax return, hope you don't miss anything and save yourself a few bucks in the process. You can defend yourself in court, take your chances with the judge and save yourself some legal fees. What you cannot do is invest by yourself using embedded compensation funds without paying full advisory fees. The same holds for insurance (more on that later). These pricing biases simply have to end.

I do not believe the system should continue to condone pricing structures where consumers have to pay for professional advisory services even if those services are neither requested nor rendered. The most obvious solution is to abolish embedded compensation products altogether. The myth perpetuated by some FSPs that advice is 'free' would be exploded. Those who want advice would pay advisory fees and those who do not want advice would be able to forgo them.

What Do Most FSPs Recommend and Why?

The incontrovertible fact no one seems to grasp is that it is always the client who ultimately pays the FSP for services rendered. So many FSPs say they recommend embedded compensation funds because only embedded compensation funds pay them. Let's be clear here: no funds pay FSPs. Only consumers pay FSPs. The difference is that embedded compensation funds have devised a seemingly benign way of collecting FSP compensation from the client and distributing it to the FSP. Make no mistake: In one way or another, FSPs are paid exclusively by their clients.

Many SPANDEX FSPs fear the elimination of embedded compensation because the status quo protects their personal financial well-being. Making a voluntary transition from commissions to fees involves a painful restructuring of their business model—certain short-term pain for presumed long-term gain. It might also mean that the FSP has to acknowledge that a good deal of his presumptive value proposition cannot be reliably substantiated. In spite of how most FSPs talk about taking a long-term view, they are human and there is still the matter of short-term pain of reduced income that has to be endured during the transition. If the transition is to occur with even a modicum of integrity, there will be a significant drop in income.

Pain or no pain, the need for reform is clear. Consumers rely heavily on advice from intermediaries, although many consumers have almost no understanding of the costs of obtaining this and are similarly unable to properly gauge its quality. The advice itself is often compromised by the incentive effects of embedded commissions paid by product providers. The commission-driven sale of these products remains the norm, leading to persistent concerns about consumer detriment. Research has shown statistically significant evidence of FSPs recommending one provider's offering over another because it paid a higher commission.

The good news is that transparent and unbundled business models have been gaining market share over the past few years. When the second edition of this book came out, the proposition was still seen by many as being "too new" and "unproven" regarding wide-scale acceptance. Today, there's a large and growing plurality of FSPs who work this way and the value proposition has been so thoroughly proven as to be considered mainstream. It seems there's a growing recognition that the key elements of an unbundled product shelf represents a win/win proposition for consumers and FSPs alike.

There remain many FSPs who earn commissions and who genuinely want to become true professionals. The trouble is, given their past history, they don't know how to make the leap. How do you tell a client who has been with you for twenty years and never paid you a direct fee in his life that you now believe he will be better served by paying a direct fee?

The other impediment to meaningful change is that it is difficult for many FSPs to do the right thing and become STANDUP FSPs when competitors are making easy money by picking the low-hanging fruit of consumers who are oblivious to their options. By preying on consumers who are insufficiently sophisticated to know there are other business models out there, SPANDEX FSPs continue to co-exist with STANDUP FSPs, and many people are unable to distinguish between the two. As is often the case, change comes more quickly to those places where competition is fiercest and stakes are highest. Most of our major cities feature a wide range of STANDUP FSPs offering their services to the public. Many mid-sized (100,000 people or so) cities will likely have a few STANDUP FSPs by now, too. Many of the 'old school' FSPs continue to do brisk business in rural areas—simply because competition is less stiff and consumers are often less demanding.

Where Does FSP Loyalty Lie?

The choice comes down to the FSP making a decision about whose interests will come first: the client's, the FSP's, or the product supplier's. Anyone looking at this rationally would agree that corporate interests ought to finish third in this little contest, but that's not the way it usually goes. The client is always supposed to come first and, with a few caveats (e.g. fees to clients cannot be so low that FSPs go out of business), most FSPs would suggest that the preferred order of priority should be:

1. Clients
2. FSPs
3. Corporations

Nonetheless, in many instances, the order is actually reversed. Consumers could confront FSPs with the question of 'who's your daddy?' Unbundling allows for the truth to be spoken and for appropriate actions to follow. Putting the client first is part of every FSP's fundamental fiduciary responsibility. Sadly, the industry is set up to make that exceedingly difficult and the people being hurt the most (consumers) remain indifferent.

Proponents of the embedded compensation model argue that consumers are not demanding a fee-based arrangement from their FSPs and often don't understand important differences if and when they are presented to them. If a vast majority of consumers are essentially indifferent, why should anyone, including regulators and legislators, care? This indifference is largely due to consumers being blissfully unaware of how embedded compensation can cloud the judgment of FSPs. You can't be outraged by something you don't understand.

Embedded vs. Unbundled

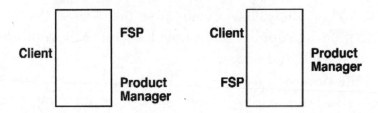

Whose side are you on? By moving to an unbundled format, FSPs can demonstrate that they are aligning their practice with their clients' best interests. Without bundling, FSPs are perceived as sales agents for product manufacturers.

Since the industry allows FSPs to select their own business model, there is considerable resistance toward the complete unbundling of parts (investment products) and labour (FSP fees) because the short-term pain is certain, while the long-term gain is anything but. Not only do FSPs have an emotional bridge to cross, there's also the matter of having to pay mortgages along the way. Remember that there are also some FSPs, notably at banks, who receive a salary for their work. Part of the problem is that many advisory firms have been slow to put platforms in place that would allow FSPs to serve their clients in an unbundled manner. There are a number of FSPs who want to move to a more professional business model but are being thwarted by their employers.

On the client side, the most compelling reason to move to a fee-based arrangement is that it closely aligns client interests with FSP interests. Since clients are paying fees based on the size of their portfolio, FSPs have a clear incentive to make portfolios grow and to mitigate portfolio declines. The more the account grows, the more the FSP makes; the more the account declines, the less the FSP makes. The fee-based model might also allow for fee deductibility for non-registered accounts that would not otherwise be possible. Unfortunately, no model is perfect. As with other arrangements, there is no incentive for an FSP to counsel a client to pay down non-deductible debt.

It should be stressed that even if FSPs firmly believe it is in their clients' best interests to switch, they cannot force any client to share that view. Both FSPs and consumers naturally resist change. If you're a consumer who is working with an FSP you trust, ask yourself one question: "Would I be prepared to take a considerable voluntary risk in my own career, knowing that it could take perhaps six full years for me and my family to be as well off as a result?" Since people tend to avoid pain if possible, I suspect most would honestly answer no, even though six years is a reasonable time frame for FSPs to expect when running the gauntlet.

A car is a depreciating asset and will one day be worthless due to normal wear and tear. Better made cars cost more but generally depreciate at a slower rate, so spending relatively more may be a sensible consumer decision. Investment assets, on the other hand, generally appreciate over time, so the best value is often secured by using products that cost the least, allowing for maximum appreciation of value over time. This is an important distinction. Virtually all other consumer products add value by minimizing depreciation, while investment products add value by maximizing appreciation.

Compensation Logic

Have you ever met an accountant who sends himself an invoice after preparing his own tax return? It would be a bit silly, wouldn't it? In fact, the concept is entrenched in law. For instance, you can hire a maid or a gardener to do work around the house, but you can't legally pay yourself (or your spouse) for doing the same work.

Accountants bill their clients for services rendered, but there are millions of Canadians who file their own returns and forgo paying professional fees in the process. Whether it is wise to use a tax professional depends on the complexity of one's situation and one's ability to implement appropriate tax strategies. It is a personal decision that is made on a household-by-household basis. People generally do what they believe is in their own best interests.

No one in their right mind would bill themselves and then add the bill payment to their personal income. If an accountant was making $100,000 a year, would she bill herself an additional $1,000 to prepare her own return? She would have to pay about $450 in tax that would otherwise not be due if she did.

In spite of the ridiculousness of sending yourself a bill for services rendered, this is what virtually every FSP does today. This is because most FSPs buy mutual funds with embedded compensation for their own accounts, even though the fund companies would allow them to buy funds without embedded compensation instead. Even those FSPs who work at a conventional brokerage firm bill themselves for their own accounts. Does this sound like FSPs might be compromised in some way? Would you entrust your life savings to someone who acts in such a dysfunctional manner? What credibility do FSPs have when they seem more interested in boosting their gross income through increased sales volume than in making sensible financial decisions with their own money?

The culture and predisposition toward sales, to the point where damage might be done to the financial well-being of FSPs themselves, need to change. This is a culture that has been deliberately fostered by product manufacturers and distributors. Would you expect your accountant, doctor or lawyer to act in such an illogical manner? Would you have faith in their professional services if they did?

Embedded compensation mutual fund companies have had F Class mutual funds available to Canadians for over half a decade now, and they insist that brokerage and planning firms have agreements and systems in place with all clients where F Class funds are being purchased. The rationale is that they wouldn't want clients getting advice without paying for it. Of course, paying for advice and then not getting it (as with A Class funds offered through discount brokerages, for example) is perfectly fine.

No FSP in their right mind would offer F Class funds to their clients without charging a separate fee because personal bankruptcy would surely follow. One can only do so much de facto pro bono work.

The industry recognizes that it is unfair for FSPs to have to bill themselves for doing their own financial planning (even though most FSPs continue to do so) but does not recognize that an embedded fee for 'advice' where no advice is given is a rip-off for consumers. If you're getting professional advice, you should expect to pay for it. It follows that if you're not getting advice, you shouldn't have to pay for it.

What Do Parts Cost?

The simple continuum we looked at earlier gives you a sense of what parts might cost. Most ETFs generally cost anywhere from 0.08% to 0.55%, asset class F Class mutual funds generally cost between 0.25% and 0.65% and actively managed F Class mutual funds generally cost anywhere from 0.73% to 1.90%, so there's considerable room for variability depending on the products you use. In order to make a more meaningful disclosure to consumers, FSPs could offer a listing of actual costs associated with each unbundled product. This way, consumers could see for themselves what the products cost and could simply add the FSP's fee on top. The total cost of the portfolio is simply the weighted average of the sum of the parts.

It should be noted that many FSPs will be justifiably worried that if they cannot earn commissions, they will have to make this type of disclosure. These transactional FSPs understand that they may well be forced out of business by more professional FSPs who are able to work in an unbundled environment. They will also likely resist the implementation of professional standards for the same reason. It's time the industry smoked out the salespeople—these FSPs will fight financial services reform as though their lives depended on it. Many advisory firms make the matter even worse, while some SPANDEX FSPs add considerably to the corporate bottom line.

In a very real sense, the lives of sales-oriented SPANDEX FSPs depend on commissions. They will speak of the nobility and honour of earning commissions and of the many decent people who have done so for generations. They will say that they themselves are beyond reproach in their personal business practices and will resent any inference to the contrary. These people miss the one inescapable fact that virtually all consumers understand intuitively that the term 'professional salesperson' is an oxymoron.

What Does Labour Cost?

There are plenty of FSPs who make recommendations that are motivated at least somewhat by compensation issues. The first rule in the financial advice industry is that the interests of the client come first. But how is this monitored? At present, as long as the FSP can rationalize an investment as being consistent with client objectives, the investment choice goes unchallenged. Many believe that the petroleum industry has done a good job of educating consumers about the constituent parts of the costs of their products. Big Oil has chosen to put pie charts on many of their pumps in order to demonstrate how they arrive at their price for gas. Of course, many believe this is because they want to point the finger at government taxes as a means of deflecting anger. Nonetheless, while the motives would be radically different, financial product manufacturing companies could easily follow suit if they were genuinely committed to more and better disclosure. Similarly, STANDUP FSPs could do a better job of offering meaningful disclosure, too. Here's an example:

Explanation of Compensation

Remuneration is always tied to one of three factors: invested assets, fee-based deliverables and unavoidable commissions.

Option 1: Direct Fees (based on the household assets invested)

- Investment products have no embedded compensation. Fees are paid directly and transparently by the client.
- Superior flexibility due to lack of restriction on future trading activity.

Fees are in accordance with the amount of assets in portfolio(s) of the client(s). Fees are 1.4% on the first $250,000, 0.6% on all additional assets, with a flat $20 transaction charge.

Option 2: Fee for Services (not related to products at all)

- Written recommendations regarding planning objectives.
- Written financial independence calculations (perhaps including a sensitivity analysis).
- Any ad hoc projects involving reviewing, analyzing, and recommending planning objectives.

Where this option is chosen, the total fee depends entirely on the time involved. The FSP's time is charged at $300 per hour and his assistant at $50 per hour.

Option 3: Payment via Commissions

Some products such as life insurance and oil and gas flow through limited partnerships pay a commission to both the FSP and the advisory firm. These products are not available as a component of the standardized fee-based format. These products are recommended only when applicable to the circumstances of the client(s), and investments in these products are not used in the calculation of fees in Option 1. For example, if a client invests $500,000 initially and an additional $100,000 into a limited partnership, the fee calculation would be made using only the $500,000 invested (i.e. there is no offset provision). Please ask about specific compensation amounts if purchasing one of these products, since actual formats and amounts can vary significantly.

By signing below, you acknowledge that you have read and understood these three compensation formats.

Signature _____   _____
                 Client   Date

Signature _____   _____
                 Client   Joe Brilliant, FSP

Once accounts are over $250,000, the annual fee becomes a blend of the differing marginal rates. This blended fee drops as accounts get bigger. Think of it as a volume discount. The 1% benchmark that many media people seem to think is reasonable is reached at $500,000. Accounts below this amount would cost more than 1% per year, and accounts above this amount would cost less. A $1,000,000 account, for instance, would attract an annual fee of $8,000 (0.8%).

A fee-based format recognizes three concepts: the alignment of FSP and client interests, the economies of scale implicit in the rendering of qualified advice, and the need to weed out inefficiencies at various thresholds (price points). Since FSP compensation is now linked to the size of the portfolio and not the placement of any product in particular, there is a clear consistency of purpose. If the account goes up, the FSP makes relatively more. If the account drops, the FSP makes relatively less.

Many FSPs make the point that they need more than 1% as compensation for taking on smaller clients since these clients involve nearly as much work as larger ones. The logic cuts both ways. If small accounts should command a premium, then large accounts should be accepted at a discount. The marginal fee rate format takes economies of scale into account.

Under this scenario, the marginal fee model could involve charging a small processing fee (e.g. $20 per trade) on securities trades where the FSP receives no compensation. This wrinkle can more closely align the interests of the client, the FSP, and the advisory firm. Better still, clients could be given a certain number of free trades annually. Trading costs money and should only be used to improve the portfolio. Increased activity beyond a prescribed limit can be charged to the client.

Beyond purposeful rebalancing, trading activities should be kept to a minimum. The FSP of the future will work in concert with clients to ensure all aspects of their financial affairs are attended to. This partnership with the client should be aimed at attaining financial independence in a suitable time frame and then maintaining a consistent quality of life beyond that point.

Beyond that, the most important elements of the relationship should be put in writing so that there can be no doubt about who is doing what.

The Ramifications of Unbundling

The test of a first-rate intelligence is the ability to hold two opposed ideas in the mind at the same time, and still retain the ability to function. One should, for example, be able to see that things are hopeless and yet be determined to make them otherwise.

—F. Scott Fitzgerald

The majority of FSPs are decent people. This is true whether they are fee based or commission based. It is widely accepted that there is no meaningful correlation between FSP competence and the compensation model used by that FSP. Both models (fees and commissions) are generally thought to have equally thorough and creative practitioners. As with any line of work, there are some who are better than others, irrespective of compensation model.

That being said, it is vital to distinguish between competence and professionalism, which are very different things. Competence seems to be evenly distributed, as far as anyone can tell. Professionalism, on the other hand, is at least somewhat determined by the manner in which one works with consumers.

Management Expense Ratios (MERs) and Loads: What's the Difference?

No matter how much the industry likes to think progress has been made in explaining how mutual funds work, most consumers still don't get it. This struck me while speaking with a client. I wanted to make a clean break: clients were going to work on either an unbundled-fee basis or not at all, and the time had come to choose.

The client then surprised me. She said a friend had told her that it was cheaper to buy no-load funds. This is only true with a limited number of fund families. In most instances, clients who work with FSPs use traditional third-party funds. In this case, the MER is usually identical whether the fund is purchased on a 0% front-end basis (with no load for early redemption) or a back-end load basis.

The cost of a mutual fund is its MER. This is generally the sum of FSP compensation, fund company compensation, trading and regulatory costs and GST/HST. Newspapers report returns net of MERs, so if a fund shows a 7.5% rate of return with a 2.5% MER, it earned 10% on the year, deducted 2.5% through the MER and passed the difference on to unitholders. Many consumers still don't understand that.

From a client's perspective, deferred sales charge (DSC) funds retain the identical MER as no-load funds but have a charge associated with them if they are redeemed early, generally within the first seven years after they are purchased. If the fund is held until the DSC expires, there is absolutely no difference between a DSC fund and a no-load fund, not in cost, content, tax treatment or anything else. It should also be noted that while investors may always switch from one fund to another fund within the same family at no cost, there may be tax consequences in non-registered accounts.

However, if it turns out that for any reason the client wishes to sell the DSC fund early, there will be a charge. This drops over time. The friend of my client could potentially be right if DSC funds were used improperly. In this instance, the client would have paid the MER along the way but would have also incurred a DSC upon disposition.

It should be clear that the real difference here is how the FSP chooses to be paid. This decision should always be made in consultation with the client. The A Class mutual fund options are either more money up front and less in future years (commission based) or some flat amount based on assets annually (embedded-fee based). Neither is right nor wrong, it is simply a matter of personal preference. Client cost is identical.

The difference in the two structures is how the FSP's compensation is amortized. If an FSP is paid 5% up front and the fund only costs 2.5% a year, it should be obvious that the mutual fund company is out of pocket in the short term. As a result, the company would want to recoup its payment to the FSP should the fund be redeemed prior to the DSC schedule running its course. Since the FSP has already been paid and the client has presumably been told that this is a long-term proposition and that there are virtually always options within the fund family that would forgo these charges, the client is asked to foot the bill.

If the client chooses to liquidate less than 10% of that fund prior to the amortization period (DSC schedule) running its full course, these charges do not apply since this is con-sidered a modest redemption made for liquidity / cash flow purposes and not a large-scale sell-off. The 10% option can be exercised annually but is non-cumulative. In other words, a client cannot redeem 20% for free in year two if there was no redemption the previous year.

The GST of Financial Advice

The thing that keeps most people from working with a fee-based FSP is the fee itself. If consumers have worked with an FSP who didn't charge fees directly, the quantum of the bill was probably never openly discussed before...an 'ask me no questions and I'll tell you no lies' kind of approach. Putting FSP compensation out in the open changes that.

Perhaps the easiest way to understand the visceral hatred many people feel about paying fees (especially in years when markets are going down) is to consider how we reacted as a nation to the Goods and Services Tax (GST) when it was first introduced. Note that many provinces have since moved to a Harmonized Sales tax (HST). I was working on Parliament Hill in the summer of 1990, doing a work term for my graduate studies program in public administration. A special committee was set up to look into the effects of the GST on consumer prices. All manner of people and organizations came forward to express fear and loathing about the proposed changes to Canada's fiscal policy. People instinctively resist change.

Members of the government of the day went to great lengths to explain that the tax would now be 'transparent'; it would now be out in the open, whereas previously it had been embedded in the price of the final product. Government members insisted that the GST would be replacing an outdated tax system that charged large amounts for some things (manufactured goods) and nothing at all for others (services). Again, many consumers today believe they are paying a load to buy a product (a 'good' called a mutual fund), while they feel they are entitled to free advice (a service) along the way.

The position of the government was that all things, both goods and services, should be taxed equally and that the tax should be out in the open, making it politically difficult to raise taxes in the future. Consumers weren't buying it. Putting a tax on sales receipts where none existed before created the distinct impression that taxes were going up, even though the GST proved to be revenue neutral.

More recently, it is widely accepted that the campaign promise of GST cuts was both bad public policy and excellent retail politics. Perhaps now readers can get a better sense of why so little progress has been made in unbundling products and advice to date. The players in the financial services industry are collectively scared of the backlash that they believe is likely to follow.

By putting their fees right out in the open, FSPs will be made to do business much like other professionals. There will be a constant assessment on the part of clients as to whether they are receiving true value for the services provided and advice rendered. The changeover must occur without undue damage to either the FSPs' welfare or clients' portfolio values. Both parties need to have their interests honourably represented if this transition is to move forward.

Independence and Advice

There are many tricky situations tied to embedded compensation for people who offer financial advice. From a FSP's perspective, the primary issue has always been the need to earn a fair and reasonable living. Ironically, the question of real independence is often secondary.

For instance, many FSPs in the same firm, or even the same office, may use entirely different products when making recommendations to the public. Traditional third-party (embedded compensation) mutual funds, while diverse, are still quite similar in that the FSP gets paid simply and consistently, irrespective of which product or security they recommend.

From a client's perspective, when working with an FSP, the issue is about getting high-quality, unbiased advice. For them, it all comes down to: "Can I trust this person to recommend what is truly appropriate for my circumstances?" No matter how ethical, empathetic, competent and professional the FSP seems to be, clients instinctively wonder if the products and strategies being recommended are what's best—and for good reason. What's needed, therefore, is a clear and wholesale adaptation of the more widely accepted elements of professionalism.

Part Four

Professionalism

What Adds Value?

All great truths begin as blasphemies.

—George Bernard Shaw

One of the great assumptions of active management is that it 'makes sense.' In other words, people assume it is sensible and practical to pay an expert a fee to try to do better than a market average. This is often the case even though the experts, taken together, constitute the very market that they're trying to beat. The aggregate return cannot be reliably exceeded by the majority of participants (unless the results are severely skewed). One definition of insanity suggests that doing the same thing you've always done, yet expecting different results, is a form of madness. In a zero-sum world of macro-level investing, the net benefit is nil, while the cost drag remains real.

It makes no sense to pay someone else a fee to gamble with your money unless you are highly confident they can add value along the way. As such, one should be fairly certain that the person one hires to add value is in fact doing just that. Many FSPs have come to the conclusion that the world is too complex and that they would rather hire 'expert professionals' (i.e. money managers) to run specific mandates within their clients' portfolios. Whether the FSP is trading securities herself or subcontracting that decision to a specialist, the situation holds true. Here's what Chet Currier, a columnist at *Bloomberg News*, had to say:

What mutual funds have always had to sell is diversification, convenience, liquidity and something called 'professional management.' Well, the customers can get all the diversification, convenience, and liquidity they want from index funds that avoid the costs of security selection...active managers deserve to be paid only for the amount by which they outperform the index, known by the shorthand term 'Alpha.' Because active managers as a group stand little chance of beating the market (they are the market and they cannot hope to beat themselves), those active managers as a group deserve no pay at all.[1]

But if active managers do such a collectively poor job on the performance side as to not be deserving of any pay at all, why on earth would any professional, independent, client-centred FSP ever recommend using their services, much less making that kind of recommendation on virtually all occasions? It appears that there has been an undemonstrated presumption of accretive conduct at play. Of course, there are empirically confirmed examples of individual active managers who have outperformed both benchmarks and passive alternatives. The thesis being explored here revolves around the concept of informed consent. Even though there is evidence that this can be and has been done, there is no reliable evidence that it can be done predictably, reliably or persistently.

Credit Where Credit Is Due

People pay mutual fund managers a fee to manage a portfolio with a mandate to outperform a certain benchmark. If the manager is outperforming the benchmark after fees, consumers should say, "Thank you very much," and not begrudge the fee. If, on the other hand, the manager lags the benchmark, either a new manager should be hired or the consumer should cut the losses by simply buying the benchmark or its nearest facsimile.

As long as the manager posts a return (net of fees) that exceeds the benchmark, they're adding value. 'The better the manager, the higher the fee that can be charged' is the logic. Presumably, that manager could charge the same as competitors and still be handsomely rewarded, since investors would be pleased to give them a disproportionate percentage of total assets to manage. In other words, savvy consumers should not be opposed to high fees in and of themselves. However, they should be opposed to any fees that are worth less than what they cost.

Think of it in these terms: the more a product costs, the more it lags, all else being equal. Lowering the cost merely increases the likelihood of better performance—it guarantees nothing. It should also be stressed that there are exceptions in both directions: cheap managers who lag their benchmarks and expensive managers who beat their benchmarks.

Since most actively managed mutual funds feature embedded compensation and most index-type investments don't, there is often a second performance burden for most actively managed mandates to overcome. Active management proponents properly argue that it is unfair to compare one strategy that generally pays FSPs to another strategy that generally doesn't. Ironically, this is another reason to get on with the elimination of embedded compensation. Without it, a true apples-to-apples comparison is impossible for all funds with similar mandates but different compensation models.

Why Work With an FSP?
What if the 'value added' comes from something other than security selection? It is widely accepted that most con-

sumers want to work with qualified FSPs. For them, it is important to talk to someone face to face, and regular contact is important—even if purposeful security selection is a mug's game.

One of the great ironies of the financial services industry is that many observers believe that FSPs generally do add value. They do so, for the most part, while using actively managed mutual funds that generally subtract value relative to passive products and strategies. Mutual fund companies know this and continually tell FSPs how great they are. In fact, it is far more likely that any value that is added will come from changing peoples' trading behaviour and not from picking investments or timing markets.

Index providers talk about cost only because without an embedded payment mechanism for FSPs, that's all they have to go on. It might be said that an often inferior product line has co-opted the complicit loyalty of those FSPs who recommend these products. One could argue that this is a low form of bribery. The *Oxford* dictionary says a bribe is: "a sum of money or another reward offered or demanded in order to procure an action or decision in favour of the giver."[2] Given the strong tendency for FPSs to recommend products with embedded compensation, one could easily make the case that something else is indeed entering into their decision-making and influencing their conduct in this manner.

Do FSPs Really Add Value?

This is a difficult thesis to test in a meaningful way, because you'd need to control for the alternatives that were not chosen in order to make meaningful comparisons. How does one quantify decisions that were not taken, especially with certain types of clients, when calculating FSP value?

Although the question is a contentious one, there seems to be a prevailing opinion that FSPs do add value, just not the way most people think. People sometimes think about ditching their FSPs and pocketing the difference in cost savings. Essentially all FSPs would consider that to be penny-wise and pound foolish—albeit with a bias. Do FSPs really add enough value to justify their fees?

If your FSP's only value proposition is stock or fund picking, then it is more likely that a case can be made for firing them. But before you decide to do things on your own, make sure that that really is all that your FSP does. Many elements of financial advice never show up on a quarterly portfolio report.

Behavioural finance research shows that people feel the pain of a loss more than twice as strongly as they feel the joy of a gain, so loss minimization is a big potential 'win' for FSPs. The mathematics of capital markets means that a 50% market decline from a previous peak like the one that ended in March of 2009 requires a 100% rise just to get back to the previous level. Furthermore, virtually everyone suffers from some quirks of human nature that cause them to do irrational things for some seemingly sensible reason. The problem is that people who rationalize often end up telling themselves rational lies. Good FSPs can help people who suffer from these quirks. Well over half the population thinks they are above-average drivers. Maybe the same holds regarding stock and fund picking. Overconfidence can be a devastating character trait that needs to be properly tempered.

When discussing financial matters, it is generally accepted that fear and greed motivate people. Let's face it: people are far more emotional than rational when it comes to their money. Most FSPs promote their services as offering return maximization (greed), while the value of working with a professional FSP is more likely to be gained through the peace of mind that comes with loss minimization (fear). This is especially true as accounts grow larger.

Investors Behaving Badly

A landmark study conducted by CEG Worldwide examined investor behaviour for the period from January 1990 to March 2000. Aptly entitled "Investors Behaving Badly," it showed quite compellingly that FSPs have a positive impact on their clients' financial lives. It also showed that the traditional foundations of financial planning, such as setting financial goals, were often not in place for DIY investors, who were more inclined to be moved by short-term influences as a result. How many DIY investors do you suppose have an investment policy statement?

Specifically, DIY investors were more likely to trade too frequently, which more often than not led to poor market timing. It is well documented that portfolio turnover correlates negatively to returns. These DIY investors often chase a hot stock, hot fund or hot asset class, effectively buying near the top of the market when they execute the trade. In 42 of the 48 Morningstar mutual fund categories studied, higher net inflows occurred when performance was best. In doing this, DIY investors often focused unduly on immediate past performance and ignored the principle of diversification, something any qualified FSP would pay primary attention to when designing a portfolio. As a result, the study found that many DIY investors missed out on potentially better results due to their failed attempts at market timing. Investors are supposed to buy low and sell high, while it seems that most people are naturally inclined to buy high.

What about DIY investors' sell discipline? Not only are DIY investors unduly confident in their own investment selections when values are dropping, they frequently delay in returning to the market after getting out. They reason that they need to be confident that the market is indeed moving upward again. Investors need to be right more than half the time when engaging in this kind of market timing (both when to get out and when to get in) in order to do as well as simply buying and holding. Most truly professional FSPs are sufficiently humble to know that predicting the future is a daunting task that should not be undertaken casually.

John Bogle has noted that in the early 1950s, portfolio turnover stood at about 25% and that it has steadily increased to the point where rose to over 100% at the turn of the millennium.[2] How's that for discipline and a long-term perspective? In fairness, this is data for all fund investors, both those working with FSPs and those doing their own investing. I've spoken with dozens of FSPs over the years and they don't encourage their clients to trade nearly that often. Still, society seems to be moving away from true investing and toward some form of what might be called institutionalized speculation. I met a fellow in the spring of 2012 who had been trading securities successfully in his own account for over a decade (with meticulous notes to prove it), so there are exceptions.

Furthermore, the CEG study showed that since DIY investors had consistently higher redemption rates and shorter holding periods, higher tax bills naturally followed. By not staying invested, they often missed those days when markets moved ahead strongly, something FSPs could have helped prevent. The average DIY mutual fund investor realized a return of 8.7% versus a market average of 10.9% over similar time frames. The lesson should be clear. Most DIY investors unwittingly take on more risk than those who work with an FSP, setting themselves up for self-destructive behaviour when things go sour.

The primary role of an FSP is to help clients achieve their financial objectives, whatever they may be and however they are defined. Beating a market index, or some composite of multiple indexes, is seldom how truly professional FSPs position their services. Rather, they should tell their clients that it is their role to get them retired and keep them retired with the least trouble by making smart financial decisions along the way.

Looking back at the CEG study, it seems there were three reasons why investors generally behaved as badly as they did in the 1990s: the market, the marketers and the media. The market at the turn of the twenty-first century was seductive. Everyone seemed to be making money and people who took a rear-view-mirror approach (expecting the near future to be much like the recent past) jumped in as the fear of loss was replaced by the fear of being left behind. Marketers capitalized on both disintermediation, the notion that information that was once only available from a controlled source (e.g. stock quotes in the 1970s) is now readily available to the general public, and the seemingly endless stream of good news. Investors took comfort in all the positive spin they were bombarded with. Finally, the media created a mania. People extrapolated the 'good news' and believed the music might never stop.

What have we learned in the past twenty-plus years? What if individual investors are mostly irrational? In other words, what if you believed the price of a security was incorrect, but you bought it on the expectation that someone else (a 'greater fool,' perhaps?) would come along and offer you even more money for it, thereby transforming an otherwise bad investment into a good one? If you bought a stock simply because you were pretty sure the price was going to go up (due to human nature and in spite of your opinion that there was no rational reason for this to happen), that could be considered prudent, perhaps even shrewd. Is this investing or speculating? The case could be made either way.

Irrespective of your own viewpoint, it may be comforting to know that the 'efficient market' and 'behavioural finance' camps see the primary role of FSPs as maintaining discipline and setting and managing expectations. As a result, the two camps offer the same advice, which might double as an admonition of what a good FSP should be doing:

- Diversify within and throughout asset classes
- Re-balance when your asset allocation deviates materially from the target
- Put your money in low-cost investment products
- Pay attention to what you can control (trading behaviour)

Two experts in the field of behavioural economics—Richard Thaler and Sass Sunstein—recently released a book entitled *Nudge*, which talks about people's behavioural problems and proposes some potentially constructive solutions. Their primary thesis is that certain people—dubbed 'choice architects'—can play an important role in gently guiding decision-making. Their main rule is the application of 'libertarian paternalism,' whereby choice architects can nudge people toward what are likely to be superior alternatives without (and this is crucial) in any way compromising their right to choose other options.

My view is that FSPs are perhaps the most influential choice architects that ordinary people interact with on a regular basis. That means FSPs have both a great opportunity to direct informed decision-making and a huge responsibility to do so conscientiously.

The Four Quadrants of Financial Services

There are four combinations of active/passive and FSP/DIY. Although nothing is absolute, it seems that most of the time, (lower cost) passive trumps (higher cost) active and people with FSPs trump DIY investors, although exceptions exist. Let's explore the underlying assumptions and characteristics associated with each:

	Advice	**DIY**
Active	1 Active Advice	3 Active DIY
Passive	2 Passive Advice	4 Passive DIY

Quadrant 1: Active with an FSP

This is likely where most people are today. They work with an FSP who they hope will add value through insight, discipline and planning opportunities and use actively managed investment products to do so. The thinking is likely that both active portfolio management and the input of a trusted FSP are expenses worth incurring in the pursuit of one's financial objectives.

Quadrant 2: Passive with an FSP

This quadrant has likely the fewest people in it, although it is likely growing faster than the others—and for good reason. It is the quadrant that I favour and it acknowledges that working with a qualified, trusted FSP is likely to be worth the additional cost, but also that using active managers to implement the strategy is often a waste of time, energy and money.

Quadrant 3: Active but DIY

This is a somewhat curious quadrant, especially for those people using A Class mutual funds. The assumption here is that the consumer doesn't need an FSP for investment advice or advice regarding taxes, estate planning or other financial issues but nonetheless believes that active management adds value and that superior active managers can be reliably identified in advance.

Quadrant 4: Passive but DIY

This is a respectable quadrant if you are reasonably astute, have a simple situation and are disciplined in your investment approach. Anyone with the time, temperament and training to manage their own financial affairs could quite properly be in this quadrant and pocket the savings in the process.

My view is that the passive with advice combination (quadrant 2) is likely the best, even though it is likely the least used format. This is changing, of course, and the value proposition is beginning to gain market share—mostly at the expense of the more traditional (quadrant 1) approach.

The point that needs to be underlined is that the active/passive debate is only one consideration that needs to be resolved for many consumers and that the advice/no advice decision is a separate question. In an unbundled world where cost-effective, tax-effective, broadly diversified products are widely available without any constraints from embedded compensation, there is absolutely no reason why one decision should have any impact on the other. Both can be contemplated independently and strictly on the basis of merit. Of course, as long as embedded compensation exists, there is always a strong likelihood that the independent consideration of these two decisions will be compromised.

The above chart assumes an investor is using either entirely active or entirely passive investment products. There remains a legitimate case to be made for using both approaches concurrently. Similarly, there are a number of consumers who use FSPs for the bulk of their net worth but carve out a small amount of 'play money' where they dabble on their own.

As a result, the four quadrants are somewhat oversimplified. There's no easy way to accurately reflect these nuances and uncertainties, but this should help to determine both where you are currently and where you ought to be once you've thought everything through.

Get Advice If You Need It

Everyone has an opinion on the need for and value of advice. Not surprisingly, nearly all FSPs think advice is important. There are some people who are able enough or whose circumstances are simple enough that they can do things adequately on their own.

Reasonable people might differ on what percentage of the population needs advice, but since a lot of advising involves discipline, process, perspective and similar things that are not easily quantified, there's nothing close to a consensus profile of a person who should use an FSP as opposed to one who might be successful going it alone.

As a general rule, most commentators would likely say that most consumers would be well served by working with an FSP, although it is probably fair to allow that there is a subset of the population which would be entirely justified in forgoing these services, too. Whether the percentage of the population that should work with an FSP is 50%, 70%, 90% or some other number isn't really the point. The point is that the decision is largely circumstantial and difficult to quantify reliably.

The Tyranny of Overconfidence

Many of the reasons for seemingly dysfunctional behaviour are rooted in behavioural economics—the study of how human emotions, biases, tendencies and perceptions shape investment decisions, and seldom for the better. To the extent that we know these quirky tendencies can colour our thinking, we need to take action to effectively curb them. Anyone can tell people not to panic when markets are down, but that is often easier said than done.

As such, anyone who is still uncertain about whether they should be working on their own or with an FSP might re-examine the chapter on behavioural finance. Think of market gyrations as the equivalent of a cheesecake buffet to a person on a diet. If you can resist its temptations on your own, then perhaps you don't need additional assistance. If, on the other hand, you think you'll need the financial equivalent of a personal trainer to keep you honest with your resolutions of disciplined good health, then hire one.

Accordingly, many of the best FSPs help in ways that the wider public wouldn't normally consider or expect. Research shows that virtually everyone is subject to certain behavioural quirks that can often be detrimental to one's long-term goals. The emerging field of behavioural economics is demonstrating that these 'predictably irrational' (to borrow a phrase from Dan Ariely) behaviours can lead people to unexpected (and often undetected) activities of self-sabotage. Perhaps the most dangerous of these is overconfidence.

Overconfidence is a common condition that we would all do well to consider when investing our money. Men have been shown to be 'hard-wired' to be more overconfident than women, by the way. Still, virtually everyone would be well advised to be a little more humble when it comes to stock picking, but stock pickers are typically anything but humble.

I have yet to meet a money manager who will admit to being below average. I've only met a handful of FSPs who are willing to acknowledge that their results have been no more than middling when trying to identify superior managers, even though we've already seen that the industry has a collective track record that is embarrassing. Every stock picker on the planet, it seems, thinks they're smarter than their average peer. Statistically, it is a self-evident truism that approximately half of all money managers will end up with a performance that lags the peer group and that, after fees, the average peer group will lag the benchmark.

The preceding paragraph is something that is demonstrated annually by researchers at Standard and Poor's. Every year in the spring, they release their SPIVA (Standard and Poor's Index Versus Active) report for data going to the previous year-end. Every year since it was first produced, that report has shown that the majority of active managers lag their benchmark...and that the proportion that outperforms drops as the time frame lengthens. Rather than including data that will be dated, it would likely be better to encourage readers to simply do an Internet search of the acronym SPIVA, where you will find details about the research itself, as well as the methodology behind it. Of particular note is the controlling for survivorship bias, something that many fund companies fail to talk about when promoting their products.

Certain FSPs and commentators may point out that, in

buying passive products, an investor is virtually guaranteed to lag benchmarks, since passive products cost money, too— and they make no attempt to add Alpha along the way. This is undeniably true. It is also true that people who utilize passive approaches are highly unlikely to underperform by much more than their costs. It should also be noted that if an investors is working with an FSP, that would constitute an additional drag on performance in the form of additional costs.

Around the same time as the CEG study, in 2000, another study was released entitled "How Well Have Taxable Investors Been Served in the 1980s and 1990s?" Published in the *Journal of Portfolio Management*, it looked at the index versus active debate in three important ways. It used after-tax performance to measure success and failure, it compared active managers to passive ones (as opposed to an index, which has no associated costs) and it used a time horizon of nearly twenty years (the annual SPIVA studies span only the previous five years).

About six out of every seven funds trailed the passive option (the Vanguard 500 index fund) net of taxes. What is more, those that outperformed did so by only 1.28% a year, on average, while the approximately 86% of laggard funds posted a performance that was 3.19% lower than the passive alternative—on average. You might want to refer back to this paragraph when reviewing the bell charts near the end of the book.

My sense, though, is that real client-centric FSPs are inquisitive about robust research and try their level best to bring the best products and strategies to their clients. And the best are at least aware of these reports' findings (you can read the SPIVA reports at www.spiva.standardandpoors.com). If you're really bold, go to www.stanford.edu/~wfsharpe/art/active/active.htm to download an article by William F. Sharpe, where he shows the incontrovertible logic that demonstrates how the average actively managed product must underperform the average passively managed product.

The bad news for many consumers is that reliable out-performance is a doubtful proposition no matter who is doing the talking. The good news is that it doesn't really matter much. If there is only one concept that you take from this book, I believe it ought to be that good financial advice is not about security selection or market timing.

FSPs could be doing a huge service to their clients by saying, "Look, there are three parties to this arrangement here: me, you and the product manufacturers. I'm interested in working for your best interests. What if we fired the active fund companies and passed the 1% saving (the typical cost differential between active and passive products) on to you?" This should be a no-brainer. Every FSP is expected to put their client's interests first, so shouldn't that decision rest with the client?

Fair-minded people can differ, but it boggles the mind that so many FSPs fail to give their clients a choice—and yet insist that they're putting their clients' interests first. When presented to clients this way, I'm sure that a large portion of them would prefer passive products. The STANDUP FSPs of the world are doing precisely that. They're going to their clients and open-endedly asking them what they would prefer. Not surprisingly, these FSPs have been gaining market share.

Note that it is FSPs who are in the position of control, i.e. they are the 'choice architects.' They essentially decide whether actively managed products get an extra 1% (adding 1% to client cost) or if they should be replaced by more cost-effective products with similar mandates (thereby saving the client about 1% in annual, ongoing costs).

This is especially true when one considers the emotional

baggage that often accompanies failed attempts (no matter how well-intended) to outperform. Moshe Milevsky is a professor of finance at the Schulich School at York University. Here's what he had to say about regret:

> .... As your investment time horizon increases, the probability of regret decreases exponentially. In other words, financial risk has an embedded dimension of time. It is meaningless to talk about whether or not something is risky or safe without addressing the relevant time horizon and the financial alternatives. So, is the stock market risky? Well, that depends. Using only a short-term horizon, it's absolutely risky. Using a long-term horizon, I would argue that most equity markets probably are not. Are GICs, treasury bills, Canada Savings Bonds and term deposits safe? Well, once again, that depends on time. In the short term, they're the safest things available. After all, federal and provincial authorities implicitly guarantee them. Their returns are reliable and predictable. But, in the same manner, I would argue that over the long term, they are the riskiest places for your money. In sum, risk is in the time of the beholder....[3]

It cannot be stressed enough that this kind of explicit disclosure, featuring the informed and active consent of the client, should be viewed as a clear win/win for FSPs and clients alike. Ironically, when this business model was first put forward, it was seen as being radical and even heretical. Indeed, when *The Professional Financial Advisor* was first published in 2003, it created a significant amount of controversy within the FSP community. The notion of unbundled, professional, client-centred advice should not be controversial in the least. It is—truth be told—a decidedly mainstream and highly democratized way of looking at things.

There's also some room for maneuvering here, because the business of giving professional financial advice is 'scalable.' It is simply not four times as much work to deal with a $1,000,000 account as it is to deal with a $250,000 account. Accordingly, once a family of accounts passes through a reasonable threshold (again, let's assume $250,000), there's an opportunity to offer a 'volume discount' that would not be possible in a world of bundled and embedded FSP compensation. In this new world, some FSPs could quite properly say, "Since I'm adding value here and saving you some money, how about if I keep a portion of those savings for myself?" This is especially true with smaller, higher maintenance accounts (perhaps less than $250,000). The FSP could say, "What if I charged you 1.4% on assets instead of 1%? True, I'd be getting more money, but you'd be getting someone who is more aligned and client-centred, and you'd still be saving 0.6% annually." On a quarter million dollar account, that still amounts to $1,500 a year.

Let's run down a quick list of overall benefits:

- greater overall professionalism
- transparency of product and service pricing
- elimination of bias in product recommendations
- clear delineation of services to be provided—with reciprocal client obligations
- possible tax deductibility
- possible increased FSP compensation
- possible reduced consumer cost
- focus on what is important
- clear alignment of FSP and client interests (no incentives to churn accounts)

Know Yourself: For Both Consumers and FSPs

Consumers need to be able to make a meaningful comparison between what they're paying and what they're getting in return for their advice dollar. My experience is that most do a good job of self-assessing whether or not they should be working with an FSP. The cost differential between using an FSP and going it alone as a DIY consumer is often not as great as the media would have you believe, even if you consider only investment management and set all other planning concerns aside. While it will certainly cost more to work with an FSP than to do it yourself, it may well be worth the added cost. Professional FSPs can help to identify those areas that require attention and ensure those other areas are suitably addressed.

There are other benefits that clients need to understand about using a STANDUP arrangement, too. The most important of these is transparency. There is no direct economic benefit to working with someone who charges a direct fee to a client as opposed to being paid by a product supplier, but there is usually an added level of comfort in having all the cards on the table. When the only way an FSP is paid is directly by the client, you get a clear sense that reasonable efforts are being made to do the best job. The mind tends to focus when the chequebook is pulled out.

This, of course, is how most other professionals get paid, so consumer understanding and acceptance should be high once the transition is complete. Until now, STANDUP FSPs had effectively been penalized for being early adopters of a professional paradigm. Now, they are reaping outsized benefits for moving to a more client-centred model that clients likely wanted all along but never really knew existed. The model is becoming almost mainstream and the 'early mover advantage' has likely already evaporated.

Given that many FSPs genuinely want to do the right thing and that there's now a clear opportunity for FSPs to finally do it, what needs to happen next? The short answer is that a large plurality have already voted with their feet and transitioned their practices to become STANDUP FSPs.

Based on the 'Law of Diffusion of Innovation,' the innovators and early adopters have likely already altered their business models in keeping with the new paradigm. We're now reaching the 'tipping point' where the early majority of FSPs seem poised to make the transition to transparent fees using products that offer no embedded compensation. When that happens, the late majority and the rest will have little alternative but to be dragged into the more professional paradigm. It seems almost inevitable.

A decade ago, these FSP were seen as early adopters, but 'leading edge' was also 'bleeding edge' in terms of acceptance. Today, these same FSPs are the early majority, as billions of dollars' worth of retail account assets are being converted from the traditional model to the new one every year.

The FSPs who have not yet made this transition may soon have to resolve once and for all whether or not they will function using a model of professionalism and put the best interests of their clients first. If they elect not to, they may well end up being left behind.

We've already talked about behaviour economics in general and overconfidence in particular. Having completed the transition to a more client-centred business model, FSPs can use the following tangible tool in assisting their clients to have the focus and discipline necessary to avoid the self-defeating investment decisions of the old paradigm.

Get an Investment Policy Statement

To think is easy; to act is difficult; but to act as one thinks is the most difficult of all.

—Johan Wolfgang von Goethe

Of all the things a STANDUP FSP can do to assist a client in reaching their goals with focus and clarity, writing a suitable Investment Policy Statement (IPS) is perhaps the most critical. The simple act of putting an IPS in place is one basic value-added activity that, by itself, deserves an entire chapter. That one thing would be to put a suitable Investment Policy Statement in place after getting a consumer to complete a comprehensive questionnaire (at least twenty questions) that is purposeful and forces the investor to consider the trade-offs involved in reconciling risk and return.

An Investment Policy Statement (IPS) sets out the most important aspects of a portfolio: risk tolerance, strategic asset allocation, expected real rate of return, investor experience, time horizon, liquidity and so forth. It is a 'portfolio blueprint' that ensures decisions are made in a consistent and purposeful manner—and it goes a long way to getting retail investors to focus on what's important.

We often hear of medical professionals referring to the need to eat a balanced diet. That generally means eating appropriate quantities from the four major food groups: grains, fruit and vegetables, dairy products and meat. The same could be said for building a balanced portfolio. People need to invest in judicious amounts of stocks, bonds and cash. Similarly, there are clear elements of good health that apply pretty much across the board: exercise regularly, get plenty of rest, drink plenty of fluids—those sorts of things. For financial planning, analogous sayings include: 'pay down non-deductible debt,' 'save a portion of everything you make' and the ever popular 'buy low; sell high.'

It would probably be a bit silly to extend the metaphor too far, but the general principles of 'everything in moderation' and 'diversify for safety' are clearly appropriate for both lifestyle and personal finance. One can surmise from the many people today hiring personal trainers, going on any number of diets, popping any number of supplements, and practicing yoga that there's clearly a movement afoot to do better. The decision to get outside help if necessary is a logical extension of that desire for self-improvement and wellness. So it is with personal finances. Most good advisors are like coaches: they won't tell us what to eat or what exercises to do because, for the most part, we know all that already. Coaches and trainers motivate us to do better and hold us accountable for our behaviour. That's what good FSPs do too.

STANDUP FSPs make sure you invest in a balanced portfolio the way a personal trainer would make sure you eat a balanced diet. They don't care whether you eat apples or oranges, so long as you eat reasonable portions of fruit. They don't care about whether you have toast, Corn Flakes or Cheerios for breakfast, so long as you eat reasonable portions of grains. So it is with good FSPs. To them, the identity of individual stocks or funds is secondary to the concept of balance—they just want to make sure you're not loading up on one thing to the virtual exclusion of everything else. That's not healthy, yet that's what many people would do if left to their own devices, not held accountable by someone who can offer guidance and perspective.

Beyond that, the management of finances is much like managing anything else: you need to focus on what you can control. This should be obvious because if you can't control something, you can't really manage it. No one can control where stock markets are headed, but people shouldn't worry unduly about that, anyway. Pretending to have control of things when you don't is just a way of fooling yourself with a false sense of security. People desperately want to have control over their finances and are sometimes willing to put undue faith in those who claim to offer it. When it comes to capital markets and their behaviour, there is no control— only focus and direction.

As with physical health, there are some people who are disciplined and savvy enough to do what needs to be done so they can remain in excellent health without any coaching at all—with others, not so much. In terms of your physical health, there's likely room for improvement no matter who you are. The same goes for financial health. The question that only you can answer is: "Just how much do I need a financial coach?" If you are honest with yourself, it will likely come down to a simple (albeit speculative) cost/benefit analysis. If the value added meets or exceeds the cost expended, you should probably hire someone to help keep you accountable to yourself for your goals. Instead of doing one more rep or one more lap, you've got someone urging you to set aside an extra $100 a month or to set up that college fund immediately.

Does Anyone Understand Gary Brinson?

Back in 1986, some ground-breaking work was done on the subject of the determinants of portfolio performance. Updated in the early 1990s, research done by the highly respected Gary

Brinson and his team delivered the following finding: "Data from ninety-one large U.S. pension plans indicate that investment policy dominates investment strategy, explaining on average 93.6% of the variation in total plan return."[1] This research dealt with how much a diversified portfolio might deviate from its investment policy and what explained that deviation. It did not look into questions of performance and was more descriptive than prescriptive in its nature.

Between the technical language used in the study and the lack of training of most people who read it, it may well go down as one of the most misquoted pieces of scholarship in modern history. Virtually everyone in the financial services industry wanted to quote the research, but few people really understood it. Unsuspecting FSPs (we have already delved into how they are 'educated') were quick to jump onboard to promote the benefits of strategic asset allocation in general and portfolio optimization techniques in particular.

Corporate marketing departments, many of which were equally eager to legitimize the profit-maximizing wrap accounts coming out around the same time, talked glowingly about the importance of asset allocation. Looking back, it seems corporate interests twisted the research to get it to say whatever their marketing departments wanted it to say. This usually had little to do with the actual findings. Virtually everyone involved in implementing the findings got it wrong, and it is hard to believe the industry-wide error wasn't at least somewhat willful. Brinson's research broke down the investment management process into three sequential decisions:

1. Choose the asset classes to be used.
2. Choose the normal weightings of those classes.
3. Select the securities to populate the portfolio.

When it comes to investment decision-making, Brinson showed that the tail is wagging the dog and has been for as long as people have been investing. He defined the first two decisions as the investment policy and the third as the investment strategy.

Brinson demonstrated that the third and final decision explains very little in terms of the average variability of returns. Almost all the average variability in returns was explained by the first two decisions. Which of these three decisions do the media focus on almost exclusively? The third. Which of these three decisions do most of us (FSPs included) generally focus on? The third. The companies that manufacture these sorts of products do little to set the record straight about causation. Here's what Brinson himself had to say about asset allocation services that use active management:

> Most individual investors probably should not be paying an active management fee. They would be better off to use some passive or low-fee instrument for their asset allocation. Furthermore, investors should be skeptical of anyone who cannot prove a long record of success when they imply they can enhance your returns by giving asset allocation advice.[2]

Many years ago, I had an epiphany. A wrap program I was recommending to many of my clients had just undergone a fairly significant product enhancement. New RRSP-eligible investment pools were being introduced to allow clients the opportunity to legally skirt the foreign content restrictions in RRSPs, which had just been increased to 30% of the book value of the amount invested. The higher foreign content limit for registered plans combined with new RRSP-eligible funds meant a lot of clients went from just under 20% foreign content to over 50% foreign content in their registered port-folios. By adding these new funds, clients were able to enhance their expected returns without changing their risk tolerance.

Over the months that followed the introduction of these new investment options, clients were sent revisions to their investment policy statements that showed how their expected return (the 'managed account premium') would increase, while the expected standard deviation (i.e. variance) of their portfolios would remain unchanged. In effect, these funds had extended the so-called 'efficient frontier' of how well investors could do on a risk-adjusted basis. They allowed the program to develop an entirely new frontier that was superior to the old one at all levels of risk tolerance. Expected returns increased, while expected risk remained unchanged.

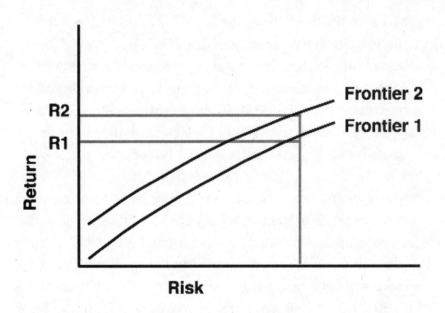

Best of all, the changes were entirely consistent with the responses given to the questionnaire used to design the original IPS. My epiphany, therefore, was a direct result of the validity and importance of decision number two. The same asset classes that had always been used were now being used in different proportions than had previously been the case and had improved the universe of possible client portfolios as a result. This all came about through the intrepid skirting of Canada Revenue Agency's foreign content limits for RRSPs, which have since been scrapped altogether.

Anyone who believes that asset allocation dominates portfolio return considerations should refrain from timing the market or engaging in either stock picking or fund picking. That's almost never what happens in practice. As a result, there are many observers who believe that instead of being the knowledgeable experts that the marketing machine portrays them to be, thousands of 'professionals' don't properly understand the products the industry is selling. Commentators have long lamented that a marketing culture seems to have overtaken the culture of stewardship within the financial services industry.

The dogma expounding the primacy of strategic asset allocation persists even though most people adhering to the dogma have likely never even read the Brinson research, much less understood it. The Brinson research shows that security selection accounts for less than 5% of any given portfolio's variance in performance on average—and the effect was often negative. People in general, and FSPs and the media in particular, have simply been focusing on all the wrong things in their reading, writing and investing.

Decision One: Choose the Asset Classes

The choice of asset classes matters greatly. The concept of how much one investment moves in relation to another is called correlation, which is vital when contemplating which asset classes will be used in constructing a portfolio. Just as combinations of risky stocks exhibit less risk than individual securities themselves, combinations of asset classes can have less risk than individual asset classes. Two investments that move in lockstep have a correlation coefficient of 1.0. Those that move in exactly opposite directions have a correlation coefficient of –1.0. Those that move randomly, where movement in one asset class has no bearing on the movement of another, have a correlation coefficient of 0. These are said to be non-correlated. Asset classes that move similarly are said to be highly correlated, while those that move somewhat similarly are said to be weakly correlated and those that move in opposite directions (even if only modestly) are said to be negatively correlated. Most asset classes are at least somewhat positively correlated.

In general, the less asset classes are correlated, the more portfolio risk is lowered. It is also important that these asset classes not be particularly volatile of and by themselves. As a general rule, risk decreases as the number of randomly selected asset classes increases. Diversification improves the risk/return trade-off and the best form of diversification is to add more asset classes.

In most instances, any twelve-month period would see some asset classes go up and others go down. It is rare indeed to have all asset classes move in the same direction over even a relatively short time frame. Risk can be thought of as the range of possible outcomes for any given asset class over any given period of time.

Decision Two: Choose the Normal Weightings

The second decision that Brinson says investors need to make relates to the proportions of the asset classes used by investors. As we saw earlier, changing the mix can go a long way to enhancing return, and risk needn't necessarily increase as a result. The discipline of decision number two should be enforced through an effective IPS.

Any strategic asset allocation needs to be formally written down so that it can be purposefully adhered to. Whatever number is chosen, there should be a written discipline to re-balance back to that target. It might be done automatically or manually. It might be done when there's a significant market movement or at a prescribed point in time. How and when it is done is secondary. The important point is that once an asset allocation is set, there should be a system in place to keep it within those parameters and to evaluate whether those parameters continue to be appropriate.

Decision Three: Select the Securities

The third decision is where virtually the entire industry lives: picking stocks and funds and timing the market. This is next to useless. To begin, active management is not a pre-condition of strategic asset allocation; in fact, it can be a sig-nificant hindrance. Actively managed pools of capital are less pure than asset class indices. In other words, the tendency to pursue decision three using mutual funds almost certainly compromises control over decision two to some extent. Since the second decision is more important, why would a rational person skip over it just to get to the third?

As soon as an FSP recommends one manager over another, it automatically raises the question: "Why did you recommend this manager?" If security selection is so minor an explanatory variable as to be nearly insignificant, one wonders why so much thought should be given to manager selection in the first place. How professional is it to make a very big deal out of something that is of little consequence?

Obviously, FSPs have to recommend something. Since they could be philosophically indifferent to—or at least willing to contemplate—both active and passive management, why not let the consumer decide? Is there any better and more compelling way to communicate the relative unimportance of security selection? If it was a big deal, surely the FSP would have a strong opinion. If it's not, why should an FSP care either way?

Anyone who is truly committed to the primacy of strategic asset allocation should be comfortable with investment options that seek to replicate the asset class they are benchmarked against in the purest, simplest, cheapest and most tax-efficient product format available. Professional FSPs could simply spell out the risks and limitations of each and then let clients decide based on their own comfort levels, perceptions of risk and personal preferences.

Virtually every firm in the industry today goes out of its way to downplay the fact that the fees they are charging for portfolio management through security selection within an asset class usually do more to benefit themselves than their clients. They are deliberately telling less than the whole story. Although these firms and the FSPs who work there also do a number of very good things and are quite concerned about the welfare of their clients, when all the cards are not on the table, there is still work to do. We need to put an end to the misdirected attention (and the presumptive importance) that has been allowed to take root by many financial industry participants and most of the media. The surest ways to improve a portfolio's risk-adjusted returns are to either alter the mix of investment options or to strategically add new asset classes that have favourable risk/return characteristics.

The 90% Solution

Few things in life are certain. However, most reasonable people would likely agree that if something holds true 90% of the time, then that's about as good as one could expect in light of inherent uncertainty. As fate would have it, the number 90% comes up frequently as a threshold that explains a number of important but disparate things in the field of capital market research.

First, research done in the 1980s by a team led by Gary Brinson showed that strategic asset allocation explains more than 90% of a portfolio's variance over time in a diversified portfolio. Although there were other factors, it was clear to Brinson that most of any given portfolio's volatility could be explained by the extent to which it deviated from the prescribed mix of stocks, bonds and cash.

Second, research done by Eugene Fama and Ken French shows that more than 90% of a portfolio's return can be explained by looking at three factors. The so-called 'three factor model' shows that market (stocks vs. bonds), size (small vs. large) and valuation (value vs. growth) are the primary drivers of returns. Tilting a portfolio toward stocks in general and small, cheap companies in particular can enhance long-term performance, albeit with slightly more volatility.

Taken together, these bits of information paint a clear picture of what a rational and prudent investor should do given the uncertainty of capital markets. That investor should buy a wide variety of cheap investments that track broad asset classes and tilt them toward value stocks and small company stocks to maximize long-term, client-specific, risk-adjusted returns in proportions that are consistent with their own circumstances. That's also exactly what professional FSPs should recommend.

It bears repeating that nothing is certain and that there

are 10% exceptions to the research noted above. Still, it is rather disingenuous to point to exceptions in an attempt to disprove something that is generally true. If FSPs are going to be viewed as professionals, then surely they should be required to make full and clear disclosure of the most likely outcomes given the balance of probabilities associated with any recommended course of action. Although the ultimate outcome of any decision can never be totally certain, investors deserve to know their odds of success before an FSP counsels them to act in a manner that is contrary to research.

Getting a formal IPS in place allows FSPs to construct purposeful portfolios that consider the clients' unique perceptions of risk and reward by setting allocation limits on pre-agreed asset classes by focusing on those factors that have been shown to be of most importance. With that said, there are a number of other things that FSPs can do to assist clients in their decision-making.

What Do STANDUP FSPs Do?

Never doubt that a small group of people can change the world. Indeed, it is the only thing that ever has.

—Margaret Mead

Above all else, today's FSPs need to demonstrate in clear terms that they are working for their clients, not their product suppliers or employers. Consumers are becoming increasingly aware of the conflicts that FSPs face. Once the hierarchy of loyalty has been established, other elements of good advice are sure to follow. Some of the items that follow are activities that are generally accepted as having some degree of value in the marketplace. Others are simply attributes and/or by-products of a STANDUP value proposition. The list is not exhaustive. Rather, the intent here is to show readers what sorts of things they might reasonably expect from a STANDUP FSP. On top of the need for FSPs to explain these elements of professionalism compellingly to their clients, there is the additional need to focus on the truly important aspects of a solid advisory relationship.

Information about asset classes, risk, return, co-variance and standard deviation is nice, but it doesn't matter one bit to typical investors largely because the nuances are beyond them. Many would rather buy into the investment pornography of forecasts, predictions and guru worship. Sadly, these same people often leave the logic and portfolio design to FSPs, who are usually just as likely to buy into the prevailing paradigm.

More than anything else, this may be why many investor advocates believe regulators and legislators need to step in to protect investors. After all, there are only so many STANDUP FSPs out there and they can only do so much.

We have already seen a significant organic and voluntary shift in value propositions within the FSP community. Still, since most major brokerage and financial services firms aren't actually in the business of truly educating the public, they might try to gain control over how people think by stressing their access to information and superior research, among other things. Unfortunately, in a world that reacts in milliseconds to new information, that 'advantage' has essentially been arbitraged out of existence. Prices change almost instantaneously when new information is released. By the time anyone can put together a research report, its contents will be dated. At any rate, it is illogical to expect to be able to exploit a mispricing and to then expect that the mispricing will persist after the exploitation. People simply can't have it both ways.

Look at it this way: a physician who stubbornly refuses to use new procedures or medicines is considered unprofessional. Blatant refusal to stay current can lead to malpractice suits. Physicians are mandated to protect the health and welfare of their patients and full professional disclosure is simply a part of how true professionals conduct their affairs. Similarly, it would be difficult for an FSP to be considered a true professional if the advice they offered did not incorporate the fullest breadth of products and services currently available.

Scientific Testing And Necessary Disclosure Underpin Professionalism—STANDUP. That's the answer. What we need now is for the remaining FSPs to stand up to the financial services establishment and to stand up for their clients. This is exactly what has been happening. The intellectual and moral emancipation is exhilarating!

In addition to looking at what STANDUP FSPs do, it might also be helpful to examine why many people think their way of doing things is superior to the way most other FSPs work. The following items are not all necessarily attributes that are exclusive to STANDUP FSPs, but it has been my experience that the best FSPs often feature these attributes.

Deductibility of Investment Counselling Fees

This is a misunderstood and often improperly quantified benefit. The Income Tax Act allows for the deductibility of investment counselling fees under section 20 (1) (bb). Although the matter is contentious and ill-defined, the prevailing and conservative view is that financial planning fees (e.g. those associated with a financial independence calculation and illustration) are not deductible. As a result, many FSPs have taken to doing their financial planning work for free, provided the investment counselling fees are sufficiently large.

The problem is that professional counselling fees are only deductible if they do not apply to registered accounts. Counselling fees for registered plans (RRSPs, RRIFs, LIRAs, RESPs and the like) are not tax deductible. Only the fees associated with non-registered accounts (also known as cash accounts or investment accounts) are tax deductible. If a consumer has both an investment account and a registered account with an FSP, the deductibility is prorated and allowed on a proportional basis. There are many people who feel the Income Tax Act needs to be rewritten in order to clarify the issue of deductibility of financial planning fees and whether deductions should be allowed when F Class mutual funds are used.

Since fees for advice regarding securities trading (whether discretionary or non-discretionary) are potentially deductible, while commissions are certainly not deductible, there is also a minor debate going on regarding 'free' transactions in a fee-based account. Some firms allow households a certain number of trades based on overall asset levels, while others insist on modest cost recovery charges (e.g. $20/trade) in order to separate transaction charges from advisory fees. Some accounting firms take the position that, in order to be entirely and unambiguously compliant with CRA's intent, the inclusion of 'free trades' have real costs that, while modest, could compromise the deductibility of the totality of any fee. The honourable thing, they say, is to reduce fees modestly and to charge separately for transactions to remove any doubt about possible de facto transactional subsidies offered in the form of free trades.

Both opponents and proponents of direct fees have likely misrepresented deductibility at one time or another. Opponents say that since there is a de facto deduction through the reduction of gains in an MER, there is no benefit whatsoever. This is true only if talking about instruments that earn interest income. Conversely, proponents imply that the benefit of the deduction is absolute and applies in all circumstances. This, too, is erroneous. As is often the case when two sides try to persuade relatively unsophisticated consumers about the merits of their way of doing business, the first casualty is truth.

It is true that products with embedded compensation already offer a de facto deduction through the reduced income or capital gains realized through MER deductions. This reality is ignored by some FSPs who overstate the benefits of deductibility in the furtherance of making a sale. A $100,000 investment in a bond fund that earns 3% (2.5% after backing out an embedded, 50-basis-point trailing commission) leads to $2,500 in taxable income at the client's top marginal rate in a cash account. If the same fund is used in an F Class format and an identical fee is charged, there is no benefit to the consumer from a tax perspective because the deduction occurs at the same marginal tax and inclusion rates.

What about vehicles that earn capital gains? The capital gains inclusion rate of 50% is a major benefit to many people working with fee-based FSPs because a larger deduction derived from claiming investment counselling fees against all sources of income leads directly to higher after-tax client returns. There is a very real and substantial benefit to charging client fees directly, however

- the fee needs to pertain to a non-registered account or deductibility is lost
- the fee needs to pertain to capital gains or dividends, which are taxed at a preferential rate, allowing the investor to capitalize on the 'inclusion rate spread'
- the actual amount of the benefit depends on the client's marginal tax rate

If either of the first two circumstances exists, there is no benefit either way. If the third exists, the benefit of direct fees may be reduced if the client in question is not in the highest marginal tax bracket since the spread between any given rate and 50% of that rate goes down as the rate goes down.

Directability

Another potential benefit of working with a professional STANDUP FSP is directability. Directing fees to be paid from outside one's account provides a major benefit to consumers that most people simply never think of tapping into. It is the flip side of deductibility and allows the consumer to decide who will pay the fee and from which account. If all fees are associated with a registered account, there is no benefit from a cost perspective. Transparency is nice, but it does not add to the bottom line since fees aren't deductible for registered accounts. While fees for a registered account cannot be deducted, they can be paid from an investment account or bank account. This can maximize tax-deferred compounding in a registered plan.

Let's say you're fifty-nine years old and have $600,000 in family RRSPs growing at 7% a year before fees. If you can pay a 1% fee from outside the plan, it will compound tax free until age sixty-nine at 7%, rendering a total portfolio size of $936,250. However, if the fees come from the investments while inside the plan, the de facto growth rate is reduced to 6%, rendering a portfolio worth $879,644. The amount paid by the consumer is essentially the same throughout (1% on the annual portfolio size), but there will be an additional amount in excess of $47,000 available when the RRSP is converted into an RRIF in a decade.

The benefits continue later in life. Even though the RRSP matures and is converted into an RRIF once clients are in their seventieth year, the benefits continue for as long as the client lives; there is merely a need to redeem a small portion of that portfolio on an annual basis. Still, if the client lives to be ninety years old, there will be an additional twenty years in which the RRIF earns a de facto return that is 1% higher than it would be using conventional billing methods.

A simple way of approximating the growth rate is to use the 'Rule of 72.' This states that the rate of return divided into 72 gives you the length of time in years it takes to double your money. A portfolio earning 6% doubles in about twelve years, while a portfolio earning only 4% doubles in about eighteen years. When the time period is forty years, that 2% difference in compounding is absolutely massive.

A young person could hypothetically add six digits to his retirement portfolio simply by paying his fees separately (outside of the account). If this hypothetical young financial independence seeker is also maximizing his annual RRSP contributions, the results can be truly staggering. Since the RRSP contribution limit is now indexed to inflation (how many financial plans have you seen that reflect this assumption?), this person could potentially make annual RRSP contributions in excess of $23,000, thereby adding to the benefit every year.

This even works for non-registered accounts. Not only can consumers reduce their tax bill by deducting fees, they can minimize portfolio shrinkage by paying fees from their bank account. There are also applications for income splitting. If one spouse is in the top marginal bracket while the other is a homemaker, the high-income spouse can pay fees for all family accounts (including children, trusts, etc.) and deduct the fees (where deductible) at her top marginal rate. This is really a combination of deductibility and directability, but you can see that there are potentially large benefits here too.

All this leaves more money in consumers' pockets. The best thing about fee directability is that it represents a win/win scenario for FSPs and consumers alike. In this case, the FSP is no worse off, having received an identical level of compensation, but the consumer is better off because there is more money left in the account at the end of the relationship.

Working with a STANDUP FSP

A whole raft of 'value-added services' from yesteryear is now being given away as financial information becomes a commodity. The FSP middlemen can be easily bypassed, and they therefore need to do other things in order to truly add value for those who want to use their services. If financial advice is not synonymous with stock picking (or its first cousin, fund picking), then what exactly is it that FSPs do to earn their compensation? Although security and fund selection don't generally add value, many other things that good FSPs do actually do add value. It's pretty much the exact opposite of what most people think.

Let's take a quick look at some of the things traditional FSPs used to do. These services include stock quotes, consolidated statements of holdings, asset allocation, proprietary securities research and trade execution. Do you notice anything about this list? All these services can now be accessed by anyone who has a computer with an Internet connection. All of them are absolutely free, save for trade execution, which is almost free.

In doing this, let's take a step back. FSPs need to be clear about their true role. Many people have useful ideas about what that role ought to be. Because of his vast experience in helping FSPs with this question, I asked Dan Wheeler, Director of Global Financial Advisor Services at Dimensional Fund Advisors, for his perspective on the role of qualified advice. Here's what he had to say:

> The role of the advisor is really a defensive role. The advisor is there to manage expectations, to make sure that all the bad things that can happen to people and their capital do not happen—things like market timing and tactical asset allocation. If you're moving money in and out based upon some type of economic forecast, you endanger the person getting the capital market rate of return and getting to the point where they want to be years down the road.[1]

If Wheeler is right (and I believe he is), then what kinds

of things can FSPs help with and what kinds of additional activities might a consumer want to consider?

An Ongoing, Iterative Process

It needs to be noted that good financial advice is not a one-time event. Instead, financial advice giving is an ongoing, iterative process. People graduate from school, find work, get married, start families, pay off debts, take on mortgages, get promotions, endure disabilities, buy second properties, suffer temporary setbacks and experience myriad other things. Life happens. Circumstances change and so should the plan.

Consumers need to be able to change with the times in managing the various developments in their lives, and FSPs should enable their clients to focus on all aspects of their financial lives, with the most important things being addressed first. A financial plan is usually done at the beginning of a relationship in order for an FSP to win an account, but it is often not reviewed. Therefore, there isn't a formal plan, just a brief written action plan focused on narrow investment matters and perhaps the provision of insurance. Some commentators are fond of saying that if financial planners were charged with financial planning as a crime, most would be exonerated because there wouldn't be enough evidence in their files to support the charges.

Planners, advisors, brokers and other FSPs who go by similar titles should all be engaging their clients in regular processes and procedures to make sure they are on track with their plans. This assumes there are written recommendations that have been put in place and that could pass as financial plans to begin with.

Clients can work together with their FSP to complete self-diagnostic checklists on a wide variety of financial matters including client awareness, investment planning, investment policy statement monitoring, debt management, tax planning, estate planning, disability and income protection and asset protection. A qualified, professional FSP has a pivotal role to play. Since financial advice is not free, consumers should quite properly consider what they're getting in return for their money.

This is often a challenge because consumers can have a perverse sense of perspective regarding what it is that FSPs do. Many resent paying their FSP if they have lost 10%, even if markets have lost 20%. Conversely, many don't mind paying if their portfolio has gone up by 10%, even if markets on the whole have risen by 20%. Neither is a particularly rational or healthy approach, and both are focused on strictly investment outcomes. Consumers tend to look at portfolio performance in isolation, with a tendency to focus on loss aversion. A more appropriate approach might be to look at portfolio performance relative to life goals, accepting that some years will be better and some worse than others. Some commentators have suggested that there are really only three attributes that are important for FSPs to have. They should be able to:

1. Spot problems and identify solutions
2. Motivate people to act/change their behaviour
3. Emotionally detach the client from investment markets

Although this is a clear and simple synopsis of what FSPs can and, in my own opinion, probably should do, it should also be stressed that they probably should not be doing any of the other things that many consumers and the media pundits seem to think they should be doing. The role of the STANDUP FSP is to help consumers navigate the emotional minefield of financial decision-making.

Simplification and Perspective

Perhaps the easiest way to describe the function of an FSP is to assist investors in overcoming their own irrationality. FSPs can also add value through simplification. To the extent that an FSP can simplify and enhance your life by doing spade work, filtering data, developing shortlists, calculating adjusted cost bases, securing T3s and T5s, interacting with other professionals or simply coaching you to top up that RRSP, there are benefits. Putting a price on it is virtually impossible, but it would be hard to deny that these activities are worth something to most people. A true STANDUP FSP works as an overall advisor for all financial matters. Proper orientation includes the following attributes:

- Diversify both within and through asset classes (asset allocation)
- Aim to capture asset class returns (i.e. not seeking 'Alpha')
- Are cost sensitive
- Understand and explain risk/return trade-offs
- Focused on clients, not markets

Meanwhile, and in stark contrast, most SPANDEX FSPs have the following attributes:

- Generally pick stocks and/or mutual funds
- Try to time the market
- Focus unduly (perhaps exclusively) on investment returns
- Chase performance
- Focus on investment products, not clients

Financial Planning

Depending on whom you talk to, there are a number of purported attributes to financial planning. In reality, the test is quite simple. According to the most reputable financial planning organizations worldwide, including the Financial Planners Standards Council in Canada, the six-step process to financial planning is:

1. Understand the client's situation
2. Clarify goals and objectives
3. Identify any particular barriers or unique circumstances
4. Make written recommendations with clear alternatives
5. Implement the chosen route
6. Review the plan regularly

Most people reading this book will not have the tools to purposefully implement all the required aspects of a comprehensive financial plan, many of which require specialized knowledge that qualified FSPs (i.e. CFPs) might not have. A comprehensive questionnaire should be required that goes into great depth on matters of tax and estate planning, business succession, proper use of insurance and advanced financial planning solutions. The point is that in order to make the most of qualified financial advice, the person offering the advice needs to be completely thorough in practicing her craft. These other planning-oriented skills are often more specialized and therefore more valuable, although many people might not need that level of advice if their situation is relatively straightforward.

All else being equal, there are three primary ways to increase investment returns:

1. Reduce fixed income exposure and increase equity exposure
2. Increase value investment equity exposure
3. Increase exposure to small and mid-sized companies

There are three primary tax-reduction strategies:

1. Deduct all allowable expenses
2. Defer taxes until a later date when you might be in a lower marginal bracket
3. Divide taxes so that family members in lower brackets can pay less tax

People may also wish to consider the appropriateness of universal life insurance policies to meet tax obligations upon death and to provide tax-free growth while clients are alive and tax-loss harvesting options if suitable alternatives are available.

Finally, consumers should remember that financial independence projections are made using assumptions only. If it turns out that someone falls short in their independence projections, there are only four possible assumptions that can be altered:

1. Savings rate: clients could save more on either a monthly or annual basis
2. Rate of return: returns are fairly predictable provided one takes a longer view
3. Retirement date: waiting longer increases savings and delays depletion
4. Reducing lifestyle in retirement: this should only be considered as a last resort

All things considered, the professional FSP can play many vital roles. As an educator, they can teach clients how to frame their expectations. As a coach, they can help them retain a proper focus. As a financial physician, they can work to find the best treatment available based on investment science. Along with these important roles come a number of important challenges, such as convincing clients that their own brain often misleads them and keeping investors calm when markets are choppy.

When I talk to friends who move up the corporate ladder and into management, many say their biggest challenge is managing people. I think to myself that they don't know how easy they have it. Professional FSPs have to manage people who are often irrational, emotional and unaware of their own biases in dealing with their life savings! They do this in a context of the popular media constantly acting as though unimportant things are actually extremely important.

Annual surveys by the consulting firm Dalbar have come to track the ongoing existence of the 'behaviour gap' that explains why typical mutual fund investors lag average mutual fund returns. Through these 'Quantitative Analysis of Investor Behaviour' studies, there is little room for doubt that investors suffer from significant behavioural biases.

While the magnitude of the performance leakage varies from year to year and over various reporting periods, the consistent finding is that investors underperform their funds—often by stunningly wide margins. The 2011 study, for instance, showed that the twenty-year annualized (time weighted) return for the S&P 500 was 9.14%, while the annualized return for the average investor using funds that are benchmarked against the (dollar weighted) S&P 500 was 3.83%. Essentially, the study shows that the average U.S. stock fund investor earns returns that are far lower than the returns of the market as a whole—a stunning testament to the importance of behaviour in investing.

The reason for this, it is widely held, is that many investors are prone to do the exact opposite of the age old adage 'buy low; sell high.' Instead of being focused and disciplined, investors seem to only invest by using the rear-view mirror and expecting that the recent past is a suitable guide for what one might expect in the near future. Instead, what is more likely is a reversion to the mean, where good periods follow bad ones and bad periods follow good ones.

Attempted market timing is a classic portfolio strategy error. Throughout history, market timers have come and gone with no meaningful evidence of any capacity to predict things in a manner that is statistically significant. The past is always clear when viewed from the perspective of the present.

Drawing on the earlier comments about behavioural finance, it should be noted that investors often behave badly due to any of a number of other behaviourally motivated biases: fear of regret, myopic loss aversion, anchoring, the endowment effect, representativeness and overconfidence being the most likely remaining culprits. Research shows that even those who do understand risk often act irrationally in spite of their comprehension of these concepts. If the primary role of FSPs is to help their clients earn adequate returns while employing additional related wealth-management services, then anything that assists in performing that role should be taught from the outset.

Perhaps the gravest error is the presumption of persistence. Tell me if you've ever come across this statement before: "Commissions, trailing commissions, management fees and expenses all may be associated with mutual fund investments. Please read the prospectus before investing. Mutual fund returns are not guaranteed, their values change frequently and past performance may not be repeated."

This is, I'm sure you'll agree, a standard disclaimer found on mutual fund prospectuses and advertisements across the country. Everyone knows it. Everyone has seen it.

My question is: why do so many people act as if it isn't true? If past performance cannot be relied upon for decision-making, why do so many people use that as their primary determinative consideration when choosing mutual funds? If the disclaimer said, "Reading tea leaves cannot be relied upon for making investment decisions," could an FSP credibly go to a client and say, "Here are the products I have chosen for you based on our proprietary reading of your tea leaves"?

Here's a simple exercise in logic. Let's not use past performance, tea leaves or chicken entrails to make forward-looking decisions. Let's just call the matter in question 'Process X.' The simple point is not what 'Process X' involves; it is about the reliability, repeatability and persistence of results. No matter what the actual process is, if it is unreliable, then stop relying on it!

At issue here is the notion of persistence. Ever since Mark Carhart's pioneering study on the subject more than a generation ago, it has been widely recognized that the performance of mutual funds does not persist in any kind of a reliable fashion—except that expensive, underperforming funds tend to continue to be so. Ironically, even as past performance is a lousy predictor of future performance, current costs are an excellent predictor of future costs (translation: costs persist). There's also a well-established negative correlation between cost and performance.

In offering advice to clients, I believe people should do what management thinker Rosemary Stewart suggests: focus on our sphere of influence rather than our sphere of concern.

We may be concerned about performance, but we can't reliably control it. Meanwhile, we can control product costs (or at least select products based on costs) and those are highly likely to persist.

Management of anything depends on how you work with the things you can control. If you can't control something, you can't manage it. No one can control mutual fund performance going forward. As such, I wonder why so many FSPs continue to make product recommendations that are based primarily on past performance.

In short, there are a number of things that a qualified FSP can do to assist people in arranging their financial affairs, but in most instances, those things are behavioural in nature. For some people, however, the prevailing opinion may be that an FSP is unable to add enough value to justify the associated costs. While this is likely true for only the minority of investors, the position is a legitimate one. If you forgo the services of an FSP altogether, you'll save yourself whatever you would have paid that person. Since the cost is easily quantifiable, the real question may well be one of how well you would do if you were managing your financial affairs on your own. I would be remiss if I didn't point out the alternative scenario for comparison and consideration.

Do-It-Yourself Advice

Nothing astonishes men so much as common sense and plain dealing.
—Ralph Waldo Emerson

It needs to be acknowledged that under the right conditions, some people would indeed be better off if they simply fired their FSP, pocketed the difference and did everything themselves. Is there some way of reliably determining whether you should use an FSP or do things yourself?

Unbundling for DIY Investors

One of the dirty little secrets of the financial services industry is that discount brokers aren't really offering discount products when it comes to most mutual funds. The term 'discount brokerage' might be one of the great marketing ploys of our time. Simply put, if you're buying an A Class mutual fund at a discount brokerage, there's no discount at all. So if you're going to be your own investment manager, for goodness' sake, whatever you do, don't use A Class mutual funds.

At the heart of this challenge is the fact that mutual fund companies consistently portray trailing commissions as a sort of fee for ongoing advice. That portrayal is inconsistent with that of both the Investment Funds Institute of Canada (IFIC) and CRA. Instead, IFIC and CRA view trailers as a form of deferred commissions, not a fee for ongoing service. The little game of positioning oneself through sneaky semantics is clearly at play here. It seems SPANDEX FSPs like to refer to trailers as 'fees' because it sounds better. After all, fees are what professionals charge, while commissions are paid to mere sales representatives. Alas, saying something is so doesn't make it so. The government, regulators and self-regulators have all spoken: trailers are commissions.

Nonetheless, when FSPs get letters from fund companies thanking them for their business, they often begin with phrases like: "Your service fees are detailed below...." The double standard in depiction is both self-serving and reprehensible. With discounters, there's no doubt about what you get: no advice with the same embedded compensation going to a non-existent FSP. How's that for a value proposition? Of course, if one were to use other investment vehicles such as individual stocks, traditional no-load funds, bonds, royalty trusts and ETFs, there would be a cost saving associated with forgoing advice.

With that none-too-subtle nuance cleared away, here's an obvious question: why would anyone pay a commission, deferred or otherwise, on a product that wasn't even sold by a representative? Given that most A Class funds at discount brokerages are bought on a no-load basis, there isn't even a deferral—the payment (typically 1% for equity funds) goes on in perpetuity. In the eyes of both investor advocates and STANDUP FSPs, the practice is nothing short of outrageous. In fact, the current industry structure is decidedly against DIY investors. The implication of this pricing structure is that advice is worthless. After all, if a product costs the same with advice as it does without advice, how much of the price can be attributed to the advice that came along for the ride?

A major regulatory reform that still needs to take place is that discount brokerages should be prohibited from operating this way. Clients pay FSPs a fee for advice. Quality advice is not free and should never be portrayed as being free. If there's no advice being offered, there shouldn't be an additional fee associated with buying or owning a product. My experience is that STANDUP FSPs are justifiably outraged by this. In stark contrast, SPANDEX FSPs don't mind at all. To them, it simply justifies their existence, as they tell their clients: "It costs no more to work with me."

One way the discounters could reconcile their stated position in the marketplace with what they actually do is to create yet another class of mutual funds with the help of some regulatory overseeing. These funds would only be available to clients of discount brokerages and not available to the wider public.

Since they would be manufactured exclusively for the use of DIY investors, these might be called DIY or discount units or D Class funds. If A Class funds feature embedded compensation, I Class funds offer a manufacturer's discount and reduced compensation and F Class funds offer totally unbundled compensation, one might think another means of slicing and dicing compensation isn't necessary. But what about compensating the discount distributor of the product? It would be unreasonable to charge clients for advice not rendered (A Class), but it would be equally unreasonable to expect discount brokerages to sell funds without getting any money for their services. What if there were a smaller embedded compensation going to discounters for their trouble? Perhaps 15 basis points (0.15%) would be suitable payment in this circumstance. Perhaps discount brokerages might be justified in charging for transactions on these types of funds.

The cost of buying a mutual fund as an administrative transaction is the same whether that fund is offered in an A Class, F Class or D Class format. Whatever system is ultimately adopted should be fair to everyone. Charging consumers for non-existent advice is contrary to most people's sense of decency. To date, Melanie Aitken and Canada's Competition Bureau have not stepped in to put an end to this abominable practice. It ought to end.

At a 15 basis points (bps) premium, the discount brokerages would at least be getting something for their trouble of providing DIY investors with a reasonable alternative. They would be offering consumers real choice in the marketplace without feathering their nests.

Unless D Class funds are made widely available, it is entirely possible that certain mutual fund investors will actually save money and gain a potential tax deduction by working a with a fee-based FSP as opposed to doing it themselves! In addition, if working with a fee-based FSP, the consumer would also be getting qualified advice that could save money, time and aggravation—not to mention coaching and behaviour modification.

The Three Ts

There are two primary consumer segments in the financial services marketplace: delegator/collaborators and do-it-yourselfers. Many people have an intuitive gut reaction about which camp they fall into and work in accordance with that gut feeling. There are a number of consumers who simply don't need an FSP. Nonetheless, the generally accepted principle is that people should, at a minimum, possess the 'Three Ts' necessary before they attempt to manage their own financial affairs: time, temperament and training. Here's a quick self-diagnostic exercise to help you determine which group you fall into:

Time

- Do you review your portfolio at least annually, even if you change nothing?
- Do you act without being reminded of major deadlines?
- Do you plan for your future in a meaningful way?
- Are you a 'doer' who is not inclined to procrastinate?

Temperament

- Do you maintain your asset allocation in turbulent markets?
- Do you maintain your savings rate over time?
- Do you sleep as well as usual in turbulent markets?

Training

- Do you have the capacity to handle your own circumstances?
- Are you even aware of how complex your situation is?
- Are you aware of planning concepts beyond basic strategies?

Of the three attributes, it should be obvious from the previous chapter that the one that I consider to be easily the most important is temperament. Self-sabotaging behaviour can be deadly—and without a second pair of eyes reviewing your behaviour, you might not even be aware of it. With that said, if you honestly answered yes to all ten questions, you probably don't need an FSP. If you answered no only once or twice, you might already need an FSP. If you answered no three or more times, you almost certainly should be working with an FSP. There are certainly people who can honestly answer yes to all ten questions. Most people, however, cannot.

Know Yourself

People simply need to decide. Do they want cost savings or value-added assistance in arranging their financial affairs? It comes down to whether you believe an FSP can add value through planning, discipline, insight, additional services or just peace of mind. It also comes down to whether the person you hire is worth what you pay. If you already have what it takes to plan your affairs and manage your portfolio, then off you go. Consumers need to be honest with themselves. They shouldn't either rush off to find an FSP or blindly stick with an FSP if they believe they can do just as well on their own.

It would be wonderful if there were a simple, reliable way to determine whether any given individual would be better off working with an FSP or going it alone. There isn't. It comes down to whether you have the confidence in your own abilities to do the necessary work for your unique circumstances.

At $250,000 of investable assets, a comprehensive approach is often required to make sure everything is addressed and coordinated. This might involve getting a team of related professional advisors working together to ensure they are all on the same page. Wealthy individuals are increasingly turning to qualified professionals precisely because of the complexity and interrelatedness of financial management.

Consumers need to know what matters to them and to know their own strengths, weaknesses and tendencies. Given that most consumers have already decided whether to work directly with an FSP, it is unlikely many will reach a different conclusion when the cost of doing so is brought into the open. There may be a handful of consumers who might switch their stance, but generally speaking, the expectation is that those who are currently with an FSP will stay with an FSP and those who are DIY consumers will be happy to remain DIY consumers. Even as the price of trading has dropped steadily, the percentage of discount brokerage accounts and assets under management has remained quite constant for over a generation now.

No matter how disciplined you are, there's no sense in doing things yourself if your situation requires a deeper level of preparedness. Consumers need to determine where they fit. There is absolutely nothing wrong with being a DIY investor as long as you know yourself and can be certain there will be no regrets if you work this way. Think carefully about your decision and be prepared to live with it.

One area where you might likely have no choice but to work with someone else is in regard to the appropriate amounts and types of insurance you have in place.

STANDUP Insurance Advice

It is the mark of an educated mind to be able to entertain a thought without accepting it.

—Aristotle

Until now, most of the discussion surrounding financial advice has revolved around investment options. Real integrated wealth management needs to cast a wider net. It should encompass financial planning, estate planning, tax planning, risk management and investment management. Accordingly, any client of an FSP who is genuinely trying to integrate advice on all aspects of their financial life will find the process conspicuously incomplete if it does not consider the proper use of various forms of insurance.

Insurance provides financial risk management. It comes in various forms but at its core is used to mitigate the financial risk associated with an unfortunate event such as a death, disability or critical illness. Insurance in its many forms is a product that offers fuzzy lifestyle benefits that are often difficult to quantify, largely because people have different impressions and values surrounding the notion of quality of life.

Those who make a living selling insurance are often thought of by the wider population as being less than true professionals. When going through a life insurance illustration, much of the discussion surrounds emotional hot buttons associated with something going horribly wrong. The image of people crossing the street in order to avoid coming into contact with an insurance representative holds true. In spite of this, there are many people working in the insurance industry in a highly responsible and professional manner, offering solutions more appropriate than anything else available. These solutions are often both complex and highly specialized.

The appropriate use of insurance is a vital part of integrated financial management. This is especially true for affluent people because the applications are almost endless. The wealthy might need to shelter money from taxes, protect their human capital (earning power), control the risks inherent in small businesses, make charitable gifts or pass a meaningful estate on to future generations. Insurance is often the most effective and tax efficient way of doing so.

Insurance Issues

Standardization and professionalism are big issues in the insurance industry, too. Almost everyone in the field agrees that we need identical and consistent wording concerning the definitions of ailments that can be easily understood in lay terms. If the terminology is easier to understand, it will be easier to explain and easier to help people get the coverage they need. Until now, every provider has had its own definition of the threshold needed to constitute a critical illness (CI). Imagine having a mild heart attack (or 'infarction') and having the claim denied because it was 'too mild.' Work has been done recently to standardize definitions, but much uncertainty remains.

Consumers need to understand that there is no such thing as a free lunch. If one CI provider is cheaper than another, it is likely not that the company is ultra-competitive or because the company actuaries have mispriced the product. The most likely explanation is that the company's definition of what constitutes a critical illness is narrow and therefore less likely to trigger a payment. As in life, with insurance you get what you pay for. Professional conduct requires consistent, plain and professional disclosure of the matter at hand. As a well-known commercial says, upfront companies shouldn't hide important details in the fine print...yet that's what many non-insurance customers would likely say is going on if you asked them.

The other contentious wrinkle in CI coverage is that there remains some uncertainty about whether or not the death benefit (paid out to a living person upon diagnosis of a critical illness) should be tax free. You'd think the tax people would be clear on this one way or another. In spite of this, CI coverage is rapidly becoming a major tool in the professional FSP's kit.

Even a passing consideration of disability, critical illness and long-term care coverage would go a long way toward meeting the test of providing life management to people who need it. People often make financial decisions without fully contemplating the consequences of things not going exactly as planned. Truly professional FSPs will insist that all bases are covered. On the whole, a good principle to apply when considering insurance is that there must be a genuine insurance need, otherwise it is almost certainly not right. The corollary of this principle is that insurance does have a valid place in many portfolios and might even offer the best possible solution to a person's financial problems. The appropriateness and type of insurance depends primarily on the situation.

Some companies have taken the opposite approach to solving the problem of coverage calibration. They have elected to bundle coverage for life, disability and critical illness into a single premium that covers all of the above.

The pricing seems to be competitive, so this would serve as yet another example of how insurance differs from traditional investment products in form and in structure.

Segregated Funds

The insurance industry features a mutual fund counterpart called segregated funds. They are similar to mutual funds because they offer investment options to clients, but different because they feature an insurance component offering a guarantee if held for ten years. At present, most insurance companies generally only protect 75% of the amount invested. Segregated funds also offer a 100% principal guarantee with the ability to lock in and reset a (presumably higher) value with a death benefit if the unitholder passes away. Segregated funds also offer creditor protection in case of professional liability or insolvency and generally cost about 50 basis points more than similarly mandated conventional mutual funds and bypass probate considerations in most cases. Consumers need to consider whether the benefits outweigh the costs.

Unlike conventional investment products, however, licensed representatives are allowed to sell segregated funds without ever completing a "Know Your Client" form to ensure suitability. In other words, there is no requirement to demonstrate that the funds being recommended correspond to the lifestyle or general objectives and needs of the person making the purchase.

This represents a massive gap in the overseeing and regulation of the financial services industry. There are simply no quality control assurances for the sale of segregated funds in the marketplace. Even more disconcerting is that there are no requirements for branch managers to oversee segregated fund recommendations and no requirements for audits to ensure suitability. There is also no such thing as an unbundled F Class segregated fund. Anyone who wants the product will have no choice but to purchase it in a bundled, embedded compensation format. Again, is this because FSPs don't want it or because insurance companies simply refuse to provide it?

Many life-licensed agents have little training in investment planning. The opposite is equally true: most investment specialists have little training in insurance. A little knowledge could be a potentially dangerous thing. Having a life licence allows people to sell segregated funds even though they are de facto mutual funds and require a rather different knowledge base. No matter where or how an FSP entered the industry, there are likely to be deficiencies in her skill set when dealing with products that are secondary to her original, sales-oriented value proposition.

Some FSPs with an insurance background have been known to recommend highly concentrated investment mixes in pursuit of maximum returns. This would almost certainly not be permitted in the more closely regulated investment industry. As with investment planning, there is no one to make sure that client illustrations are reasonable, so recommendations like this can be and have been made with virtual impunity. Brokerage firms and mutual fund dealers have branch managers to review trading, but insurance managing general agencies (MGAs), the counterpart to an investment firm, have no analogous person in the hierarchy.

On top of this, there is no mandate to complete segregated fund trades in anything other than a paper-based transaction system. This lack of mandatory electronic order execution means that trades can be completed many days after the original order is placed with potentially damaging consequences if investment options are moving up smartly. Unlike standard mutual funds, there are added problems when redeeming the annual 10% free units from segregated funds.

This is one more reason why the insurance side of the financial advice industry has found it difficult to move to an unbundled and transparent business model.

Guaranteed Minimum Withdrawal Benefits

In the past half-decade or so, one of the biggest success stories in terms of product innovation has been the introduction and quick market embrace of Guaranteed Minimum Withdrawal Benefits (GMWBs)—a particular type of segregated fund. Somewhat like annuities, and possibly due to the on-going demise of defined benefit pension plans in Canada, these are insurance-based products that offer a black-box sort of solution to investors by providing a guaranteed annual income based on a lump sum contribution or series of contributions at the outset. As of 2012, some of these were already being closed down, however, due to problems with both pricing and investment options in an ongoing low interest rate environment.

In some instances, the products are being re-jigged in order to cost more. In others, guaranteed payouts are being dropped from 5% to 4% in order to maintain viability over the long term. There has been precious little growth in capital markets around the world in the first decade and a bit of the new millennium. Innovations that seemed 'too good to be true' a few years ago are now running the risk of being precisely that.

As a general observation, it might be fair to say that anyone who thinks ordinary investment options are difficult for the average consumer to understand should look at life insurance products and concepts. If you want to see convoluted applications and marketing, then these products are for you, especially the complex and divergent bonus structures put in place by various companies as they compete for business on the life side. By trying to add value and flexibility, they often add cost and complexity. Perhaps most shockingly, many FSPs are at a loss to explain the terms and conditions associated with many bonus structures. If the person recommending a product doesn't truly understand how it works, what chance is there that the person buying it will ever understand?

Furthermore, FSPs often have a tough time moving their practices between insurance MGAs. In other words, customers had better get it right the first time because wrinkles can be awfully difficult to iron out if changing FSPs or if an FSP changes firms.

Almost any meaningful comparison between competing product illustrations and assumptions involves calling in experts to reverse engineer the options. Insurance companies actually like this because they can honestly say, "There's nothing else on the market like this product." Differentiation using complexity is good for insurance companies because there's no meaningful way for consumers to make apples-to-apples comparisons. Of course, these companies all say that the client comes first and none of them are pushing for a greater degree of structural uniformity and product transparency.

The Ultimate Bundled Product

People in marketing departments long ago realized that insurance wasn't the easiest product to sell. This is a result of the complexity of the products but also because people are resistant to dealing with their own mortality and have difficulty dealing with intangible products, especially if they won't be around to enjoy the payoff.

The intellectual gap has been bridged somewhat with the release of life policies that combine life insurance with investment benefits. Known as whole life, these are investment-enabled insurance products where all the money seems to go into one pot to cover both investments and insurance. This is the original financial services version of bundling. The problem with these products is that they are highly inflexible. Consumers are paying for insurance and investments simultaneously. Since people are paying for both and haven't figured out how to be dead and alive simultaneously, the products have fallen into disrepute. This is a little unfair, since policyholders can always access the paid amount through the cash surrender value once the whole life policy is in force, but the general limitations remain a very real concern.

Whole life policies can be useful for affluent people who are certain they will not need to access the money they are putting into the policy over the course of their lifetime. Some people bought whole life in the past when it might not have been the most appropriate solution for their circumstances. In these cases, sensible FSPs looking at the situation often advise policyholders to keep these policies but stop paying into them once there is sufficient cash reserve to meet future obligations.

This attribute has some roundabout benefits. The major benefit is that insurance is now self-funding and that no money will be required later, when insurance may be prohibitively expensive, if you can get it at all. The second reason is that there might be a modest amount of growth in the face amount, allowing for de facto protection against inflation. The third reason is that people can borrow against the cash surrender value of whole life policies, allowing them to leverage out a tax-free income.

Somewhat Unbundled Insurance

A new generation of insurance products, released in the 1980s, is called universal life (UL) insurance. It was promoted as being far more flexible because it allowed policyholders to manipulate their funding patterns to better meet their needs and to have more input on the investment options within the policy. In this respect, insurance representatives are light years ahead of their investment representative cousins. But just because the products' bells and whistles are unbundled, it doesn't mean the products are transparent in their compensation structure. The commissions for a 'buy term and invest the difference' and a UL policy should be identical because one is effectively a bundled version of the other. Unfortunately, they are not. Still, not wanting to be depicted as dinosaurs, actuaries and marketing people got together to revamp their insurance products to make them more responsive to consumer wishes. Flatter bonus structures are a good example of this. Universal life policies are usually minimum-funded with lower growth of cash (side account) values and a lower cost of insurance in comparison to whole life options.

Increased consumer payment flexibility can also mean reduced consumer discipline. The phrase "you can pay me now or pay me later" has truly frightening consequences when the choice to pay later means risking default if your income drops or other financial circumstances change for the worse.

It's usually best to pay as much as possible up front. Paying more early on mitigates the risk of vanishing premiums that don't actually vanish. A universal life insurance contract allows for premiums to be paid and growth to be credited to the policy in the form of the account value. That value can dwindle as monthly deductions and withdrawals are made. It should be obvious that a professional FSP is nearly certain to add value, given the myriad permutations involved. As with investment products, the challenge is to ensure that the advice given is genuinely consistent with the client's needs. There are a number of options to consider:

- death benefits can be level or increasing
- cost of insurance can be yearly renewable term (YRT) or level
- investment options are available both as active and passive strategies
- premiums are flexible regarding amounts and timing
- the availability of withdrawals
- the availability of leverage
- riders to enhance coverage
- the ability to change any of the above once the policy is in force

The insurance industry would have us all believe that flexibility is the same as unbundling. Although the compensation aspect of insurance products is not unbundled, the industry would argue that the considerable flexibility of a modern-day UL contract is effectively unbundled because it involves exact charges for fees and mortality and exact charges for premiums and growth with a wide array of combinations and choices between them. This complexity can lead to a number of problems that are unique to the insurance side of offering financial advice. These need to be considered fully and addressed in a way that dovetails with the red flags that have already been raised on the investment side.

Whole life and universal life policies give the insured person the ability to deliberately overpay premiums in order to establish a tax-sheltered investment account that will grow and ultimately pay the premiums at a later date, thereby offering 'permanent insurance' once the policy is fully funded. It is this unique feature that has caused many wealth management experts to sometimes refer to permanent insurance as the last great tax shelter or the best kept secret in personal finance due to the preferential tax treatment of death benefits.

Compensation Disclosure

Just as FSPs tend to recommend equity mutual funds over fixed income funds when equity commissions are higher, there's a perception that the insurance advice being offered may not always be the most balanced and in the best interests of the consumer. Not surprisingly, commissions tend to be much higher for more complex products. Think of term insurance as insurance that is rented and other forms as insurance that is permanently owned.

The inference of compromised independence is unfortunate because there are a number of circumstances in which a clear and compelling case can be made for a permanent insurance solution over a renewable term solution. For example, everyone acknowledges that term is cheaper, but premiums at the end are exceedingly high, and eventually, temporary coverage isn't even offered. In contrast, permanent insurance policies are guaranteed to pay out potentially huge sums to the insured's next of kin. When approached from this perspective, it appears entirely sensible that permanent insurance should cost more. It should also be noted that one might often be able to convert term coverage to permanent coverage down the road—under certain circumstances, of course.

Technically, FSPs do not have to accept a commission and cannot reduce the premium to the client by the amount of the commission being paid. If they could only reduce the client's premium as an offset against not receiving a commission, there might be a way to charge ongoing fees for insurance in a way that is similar to ongoing fees for investments.

For instance, the FSP might recommend a term to 100 (permanent insurance) option that seems to suit the client's needs very well. What might not be disclosed is that although the first-year commission might be 40% of the premium, there might also be an override from 100% to 200%. Overrides are like a hidden quota system. Companies pay them for increased business. As a result, an FSP might be given an incentive to put all business through one insurance provider in order to qualify for the largest override possible. That's fine if that company has competitive products in all fields of insurance, but what if there's another company that can provide superior coverage? In that instance, the FSP might recommend the company with the bigger override (what's best for him) rather than the company with the best coverage (what's best for the client).

The surest way to accurately disclose compensation for insurance at present is after the fact because there are a number of variables that affect compensation along the way. Consumers can be shown what the anticipated FSP compensation is for alternative proposed solutions and can ask for an explanation from the FSP if the most strongly recommended solution is also the most lucrative for the FSP. If the FSP can make a compelling case for why that solution is being recommended, then the client should give it serious consideration in spite of the fact that the FSP stands to earn more. The provincial financial services commissions (who regulate insurance) require that all FSPs disclose how they are paid— but not how much. It seems that insurance compensation disclosure in Canada remains governed by a mindset of 'don't ask; don't tell.'

In spite of the obvious benefits of compensation transparency, there is a very real concern in the industry that consumers might recoil in horror when they learn how much

FSPs stand to make if placing a large policy. It would be a shame if people resisted a solution simply because they fear it is somehow wrong that someone could make so much money in meeting that need. If an FSP can demonstrate that the market will bear a high level of compensation for meeting a client need, you'd think the client would find that reassuring (it must be hard and meaningful work if it pays that much).

As with investment products, disclosure and full client education are vital in making an informed decision on placement or rejection of insurance. The average consumer, however, has no clue about how to read and understand an insurance quote. In spite of this, consumers are asked to initial and sign these applications and illustrations, verifying both the formal explanation and personal comprehension of the contents. There is usually nothing about the compensation of FSPs in these illustrations, yet the actual dollar amount could easily be included in the illustration.

Until the mid-1990s, FSPs could be licensed to sell either insurance or securities, but not both. Earnest people trying to solve financial problems on behalf of their clients by using the widest possible array of tools were constrained by regulators who insisted they could only go to work with half a tool kit. This is just another example of the traditional sales paradigm holding sway and FSPs having to play the hand they're been dealt by corporate interests.

The brokerage and insurance industries grew up as silos, each disdainful of the other. Prior to the days of comprehensive wealth management, this adversarial approach was seen as being sensible. Until the 1990s, FSPs had to choose what kind of products they would offer and often had to force a product solution onto their clients based only on what they were legally permitted to recommend. Insurance people sold insurance products even if investments made more sense.

Investment people sold investment products even if insurance made more sense. Mutually exclusive licensing arrangements made for numerous inelegant planning solutions and needlessly forced consumers to work with multiple FSPs.

Clients were largely oblivious to the silliness of separate licensing arrangements and the planning solutions they spawned. They simply assumed that the person they were talking to would recommend whatever was appropriate as opposed to what was expedient and what they were permitted to recommend. Ethical FSPs referred clients to other professionals if they were not equipped to deal with the situation properly. Even today, regulators still expect FSPs to have separate files for insurance and investments for the same client, even though member firms promote one-stop shopping for financial services.

Active and Passive Insurance Options

If a consumer invests in a passive option through an FSP in an investment framework, it might cost 0.5%, but the FSP receives no compensation unless they charge for it separately. If the consumer buys an actively managed mutual fund, it will cost perhaps 2.5%, but the FSP receives a 1% trailing commission. There's a 1% saving to the client when holding FSP compensation constant. In other words, an apples-to-apples comparison of active and passive investment options might involve a choice between an index at 0.5% and an F Class mutual fund at 1.5% because neither pays the FSP anything.

In an insurance environment, the FSP gets paid the same whether the client buys an active or passive investment vehicle within the permanent life policy, but the client pays 2% more. Passive investments in an insurance contract might cost 2.85%. Active investments in an insurance contract might cost 4.85%. We've already established that insurance products cost about 2% more than identical pure investment products. We've also established that unbundled active products cost about 1% more than comparable passive ones. Doing the math, an unbundled active investment might cost 1.85%. Add on 2% for insurance costs and we get an expected MER of 3.85%. But active insurance products generally cost about 4.85%. Why the extra 1%?

In the world of DIY investing, consumers are forced to pay a 1% trailing commission to discount brokers who offer no advice. In the world of insurance, that 1% trailing commission equivalent is found in the form of higher consumer MERs. The FSP gets the same compensation regardless of the investment vehicle chosen. The net effect is that insurance companies are padding their pockets by comparing costs of active management with compensation to passive management without compensation. They keep the missing 1% as pure profit. Many FSPs recommend passive strategies within insurance policies even though they recommend active strategies in investment accounts. It is highly instructive that in an insurance environment, FSPs are happy to recommend the cheaper product and pass the savings on to their valued clients provided it does not involve taking a personal pay cut. Most UL products feature the use of indexes for the investment component. As a result, FSPs have some explaining to do. Why do they typically recommend actively managed products on the investment side but passive investments on the insurance side? If the FSP sincerely believes that one format is better than the other, shouldn't that format be recommended in both cases? If the FSP is indifferent, shouldn't we expect to see similar proportions of active and passive strategies in both investment and insurance products?

DIY Insurance

Dealing with the need for insurance is far more complex than many people realize. Consumers have no real alternative but to purchase these products from someone who stands to earn a commission for recommending them. Nonetheless, I still encounter a wide variety of SPANDEX FSPs who are adamant that consumers should never be given the option of buying insurance without an FSP as the intermediary. In my view, this is an arrogant position to take. No matter how useful one's advice or services might be, consumers should always be allowed, when taking into account their own self-interest, to forgo those services and do it themselves. Even when SPANDEX FSPs are right, the market shouldn't deprive consumers of their right to be wrong.

There are no discount brokers for insurance. Potential client savings would be enormous if there were because virtually the entire premium a client pays in the first couple of years goes to paying the FSP. Wouldn't it be nice if a consumer could go to a website, answer a suitability questionnaire, compare relevant quotes and ultimately get insurance coverage while saving the embedded commission?

Consensus remains that most Canadians are underinsured. A lot of room for human error remains and the consumer in question might buy the wrong kind or the wrong amount of insurance as a result. Of course, the same can be said for our collective attitude toward DIY investment options, yet no one bats an eye when people buy investments without corresponding advice. What's interesting is that medical advances might be making DIY insurance more of a reality than ever before. Research regarding DNA and the human genome may well radically change underwriting procedures in the near future. Assessments regarding health risks might be more accurate than ever—simply by providing a few drops of blood.

If the parts and labour are sold separately, then consumers should have the ability to opt out of advice for any and all products and save the corresponding compensation for non-existent advice in the process. Consumers will have to understand that although they might save a considerable amount in premiums, they might do an even greater amount of financial damage to their personal affairs if they take this approach. Liability is like that; once you take matters into your own hands, you have no one else to blame if things go awry. Advice costs money. Forgoing advice, therefore, should cost less.

A very real problem with disintermediation of specialized knowledge and services is one of information pilfering. For instance, a person could join the Automobile Protection Association and get access to 'no haggle, no hassle' providers that sell new vehicles for a modest markup over what they paid the manufacturer. It should come as no surprise that some cost-conscious consumers speak with their local dealership about the makes and models they are most interested in, take them for a test drive and then go through the APA to buy that vehicle at a lower price through a pre-screened distributor. That's how I bought my last car. For people who work in sales, it should be obvious that no matter how much value is added to the decision-making process, if there's no sale, there's no payment to the person with the specialized knowledge.

Given that current tax law already reflects a more enlightened view of FSP compensation for disclosure, one would think FSPs who recommend insurance would also favour a similar tax treatment for DIY insurance purchasers. If it is unreasonable to pay tax on services provided by yourself, it should be equally unreasonable to pay for services if they are never provided at all.

Regulatory Oversight

As with the securities and mutual funds industries, regulators are becoming more vigilant these days. In a draft of its 2012 Statement of Priorities and Strategic Directions, the insurance regulator known as the Financial Services Commission of Ontario (FSCO) is determined to become more aware of what FSPs actually tell their clients when making insurance recommendations. In fact, FSCO has gone so far as to say it aims to "determine how the life insurance industry is ensuring that consumers get appropriate information to make informed decisions when purchasing life insurance products" (*Investment Executive*, May 2012, pg. 1)

Clearly, the principle of informed consent is finding its way into the insurance business, too. This is the first time that financial literacy of some sort has made its way onto regulators' radar screens. For many years, the prevailing view was that insurance needs to focus more on the end user. Until now, the insurance aspect of advice was seen as a laggard within the wealth management industry.

The new FSCO initiative is aimed at ensuring suitability. If suitability is not properly considered in the process and cannot be supported by things such as correspondence and documentation, the primary liability will rest with the FSP— as the person who had the most direct contact with the client. Questions like "What did you say?" will demand clear responses, as well as demands for FSPs to show their notes regarding competing product options, evidence that the FSP knows both the client's needs and the product's attributes (pros and cons) and that all this be wrapped around a clear justification for the recommended course of action.

It seems life-licensed FSPs are more resistant to compensation disclosure than any other type of FSP. That's a shame because the consumer's interests should always be paramount.

I know of some prominent (and highly professional) FSPs who are afraid of the day when its quantification becomes mandatory. As good as they are, they don't believe the public will have much sympathy once they learn how much money can be made in the business.

The idea of a level-compensation alternative (as opposed to the lion's share being paid at the time of sale) has failed to take hold. Meanwhile, insurance is similar to the brokerage industry in that there is no requirement to get a related designation or do any more than the industry-mandated minimum regarding continuing education. For instance, there are only a few thousand Chartered Life Underwriters (CLUs) in Canada but approximately 70,000 insurance registrants. Perhaps 12,000 of these registrants are members of some professional membership organization.

There has been much speculation regarding how a true profession could be created in this environment. Some believe the way to professional status could best be achieved by having provincial regulators make it mandatory for insurance-licensed FSPs to join a professional membership body (there are a couple) and then have that body, in turn, set more rigorous (mandatory) standards for things such as designations, errors and omissions insurance, continuing education, letters of engagement and so forth. As it is, the life side of the wealth management business is, in the estimation of one active and esteemed member, 'virtually unregulated.'

When someone uses the services of a lawyer or accountant, that person knows how much the service costs because that person gets a bill for services rendered. There are still too many FSPs today who think and act like sales agents. The gauntlet is being thrown down here. A profession is evolving into existence from a sales-cultured industry before our eyes. What will FSPs do to answer the challenge?

The Inexorable Global March to a STANDUP Paradigm

Be who you are and say what you feel because those who mind don't matter and those who matter don't mind.

—Dr. Seuss

Progress almost never proceeds in a straight line. Instead, it tends to proceed in fits and starts where long periods of relatively static circumstances are punctuated by spasms of reform. When the first edition of this book was released in 2003, the idea of STANDUP advice gaining acceptance bordered on heresy. Times have changed and progress has been set in motion. Slow motion…but real progress.

Looking back, many will recall that more than a decade ago, the Ontario Securities Commission's Fair Dealing Model (FDM) got a good deal of flak from its detractors. There were those who thought the name implied that investors had been getting less than a fair deal all along. The FDM was a first attempt to modernize and professionalize the industry. Still, I remember doing a speaking tour in 2003 to audiences of advisors in major centres including Calgary, Vancouver and Toronto where the hundreds of FSPs present were (how do I say this euphemistically?)… 'less than pleased' with my aligned message of unbundling, transparency, evidence-based advice and greater professionalism. Since I was in the minority back then, the SPANDEX element of the industry tried to intimidate me and others like me into silence.

Of course, the intent of the proposed reforms was actually to imbue the regulatory system in Canada with a series of mandatory activities where mere unenforced best practices had previously been employed. People who don't like substantive reform have to find some excuse to oppose it, and many stakeholders got their backs up simply because of what the model was called—all the while remaining ambiguous about the actual intent of the model itself. Many even went so far as to agree with it in principle. Some groups offered constructive recommendations based on flaws in the FDM, too. Change takes time.

By 2006, when the second edition of this book came out, Ontario had already passed the work it had done on the FDM on to the Canadian Securities Administrators in the hope of taking enhanced regulatory oversight on matters such suitability, reporting and transparency to the national stage. Discussion about the proper role for FSPs and the relationships and conflicts that were still very much part of the system was found in every trade journal and at every office water cooler. Shortly thereafter, I began to notice a change in the way my message was being received. The SPANDEX FSPs who had been trying to intimidate me a few years earlier were becoming less vocal, and the STANDUP FSPs who had been hiding in the woodwork were beginning to step forward. The tide was turning!

The whole reason these changes have been enacted is because the status quo had lost so much credibility that drastic actions were required. In some parts of the world, such as the U.K. and Australia, desperate times have led to desperate measures.

In Canada, times have been equally desperate, but the measures taken have been decidedly muted in comparison.

While other parts of the world have been rocked by major scandals, Canada's scandals—astonishingly—seem modest in comparison. The market timing scandal of the mid-2000s is one example. There, a large number of mutual fund companies allowed hedge funds to trade units of their funds overnight to take advantage of timing discrepancies. Critics have compared it to betting on horse races after the race had been run. Not surprisingly, the companies who engaged in the activity pointed out that there was nothing in the industry rule book that expressly prohibited such practices. Of course, just because something isn't illegal doesn't make it ethical or acceptable in any way.

The actual list is much longer and the regulatory record of debacles speaks for itself. In addition to the mutual fund trading scandal, there was Portus, Norbourg, Bre-X, Nortel, Hollinger, Atlas Cold Storage, Royal Group, Livent, YBM Magnex and Biovail—all of these malfeasance incidents were in the news in the past fifteen years and most of them occurred far more recently than that. The string of regulatory embarrassments has caused Al Rosen, head of a firm called Accountability Research, to quip: "I personally rank securities regulators somewhere below politicians in terms of credibility."[1]

Back to the former FDM. The Canadian Securities Administrators (CSA), the provincial and territorial regulators from across the country, were the new custodians in charge of regulatory reform. Their intent was presumably to homogenize a number of the original OSC ideas to make them applicable to all provinces and territories—to the greatest extent possible, at least. Such is the sorry aftermath of leaving it to Westminster to interpret the clear intent of the *Constitution Act* of 1867 until the middle of the last century.

Politics and regulation being what they are, the price of wide-ranging interprovincial agreement seems to have been the perpetual relaxation of standards. The good news is that we have made progress. The bad news is that the progress has been relatively modest and painfully slow in coming. What has emerged from the exercise is the newly christened and newly enacted Client Relationship Model (CRM).

Unlike other jurisdictions (e.g. the U.K. and Australia), our regulators have elected not to require that the client and FSP have a discussion about what services will be provided and how they will be paid for. Instead, Canada has simply opted for disclosure to be materially heightened by both FSPs and their firms. Risk management is something that advisors and their firms are now required to avoid if at all possible, and to disclose and control at any rate.

The requirements regarding relationship disclosure and conflict management were added immediately upon the adoption of CRM on March 26, 2012. Avoiding and addressing conflicts, including the perception of conflicts, must now be spelled out in writing prior to new accounts being opened. Existing accounts also require that these same disclosures be made before trades are completed. More stringent requirements will be enforceable on the first and second anniversary of this date regarding relationship disclosure.

While most people would say it is self-evident that FSPs and their firms are in implicit conflict given that they want to make money off their clients and the more they charge, the less the client gets to keep. After all, this is the first time that even such basic conflicts have been acknowledged in writing by the entire industry with no exceptions.

Perhaps this might be a good time to review how the line has moved in determining client account suitability. Until the spring of 2012, the factors to be considered when assessing the suitability of a particular product or security for a client included: current financial situation, investment knowledge, investment objectives, risk tolerance and any other factors that might be deemed noteworthy. Going forward, four new considerations for suitability have been added. They include: relationship disclosure (IIROC rule 3500), conflict of interest management and disclosure (rule 42), suitability assessment (rule 1300) and performance reporting (rule 200.1).

In addition, FSPs are now expected to consider the client's time horizon and the portfolio's overall compositional risk level in doing suitability assessments. Speaking personally, I'm rather surprised to learn that those factors were not considered as part of the original suitability review process.

Six months after the original CRM adoption (September 26, 2012), the third rule regarding suitability assessment comes into force. That's when the new test of 'trigger events' will come to be enforceable regarding suitability standards. Until that date, account application forms were to be updated only when there was a material change (e.g. divorce, new job, birth of a child, new residence) to a client's circumstances or for any trade that was inconsistent with the client's profile. As of that date, accounts are to be managed while bearing in mind certain trigger events which might transpire. For instance, the market drop of about 20% from the spring of 2011 to the autumn of that year might cause a client's asset allocation to deviate materially from what was deemed to be suitable when the account was opened.

Alternatively, issuers could face trigger events, too. For instance, Research in Motion could be re-characterized as being rather less than a blue chip stock. Alternatively, a security (or number of securities) could be transferred 'in kind' from another institution. That transfer might cause the characteristics to deviate materially from how the suitability was initially assessed and a review would be in order. Yet another example would be if the client changed FSPs within the same firm.

Under CRM, all of these sorts of re-characterizations would trigger a phone call to see if the client wanted to either place a trade or two to move within the original guidelines or to reset the guidelines altogether. Can you imagine the looming flurry of activity, especially in volatile markets?

While the new regulatory framework allows for all manner of FSP compensation, it also requires that the methodology of calculation and quantum of compensation be spelled out clearly in advance of doing business. Among the intentions of compensation disclosure is an end to the days of advisors selling mutual funds on a deferred sales charge basis under the pretense that the advice is 'free.'

Performance reporting is the last of the four major reforms to be implemented as a result of CRM. At this time, it would be impractical to try to place a deadline on when that will become mandatory. For now, it might be best to acknowledge that the industry has agreed in principle to move toward standardized account reporting in the future and to leave it at that. The expectation is that someday clients will be able to receive their quarterly statements with annualized return data over varying time frames as part of their reporting. This could go a long way to determining whether or not advisors are truly delivering on the things they said they'd be delivering on. Accountability can be wonderful!

When considering all of these reforms, many have come to believe that the likely outcome of all of this will be 'revenue compression' for both FSPs and the firms they work for. The expected compensation going to FSPs and their firms may drop as a result of the increased transparency that will be part of the industry. While no one has a crystal ball, I personally doubt that the resulting revenue compression will be all that significant. In a business where the major players are protective of their profit margins, price competition has been shown to be relatively modest.

There are other changes, too, but those are the highlights. While Canadians can be justifiably proud about having made tangible progress, some get the impression that Canada has become a laggard in balancing the legitimate interests of advisors with the interests of investors who feel hard done by due to what some feel has until now been a general lack of transparency and deliberate minimization of significant conflicts. As the saying goes, however, better late than never.

The International Trends

Other jurisdictions have taken a different approach to the regulation of the securities industry and the advice that goes along with it. This might be a good time to double back to consider what's going on in other parts of the world. Canada is seen as going its own way on regulation—at least for now. Similarly, the global downturn of 2007-2009 cast a pall on ratings agencies and investment bankers the world over. Asset-backed commercial paper that was deemed to be of the highest credit quality turned out to be little more than a diversified basket of mortgages that were offered to people and institutions who had no real capacity to pay once rates rose and property values plummeted. It seems the extent of the regulatory steps taken is in direct proportion to the perceived damage that was inflicted prior to those measures being enacted. In short, the worse the industry scandals were, the more draconian the new regulations seemed to be.

Entrenching Key Elements of Professionalism in Legislation

In 2009, the regulatory authority in the–U.K., the Financial

Services Authority (FSA), issued rules that codified and established a fee model for British FSPs. These rules took effect in January of 2012.

As a jurisdiction that had been using what is known as a 'principles based' regulatory regime, the U.K. decided it would be desirable to establish new, clear-cut standards that would effectively raise the bar for FSPs. Sound familiar? Their clear intent was to remove the incentive trade-off between commissions and suitability in the hope that it would increase the suitability of products being sold to investors. The new rules require FSPs to set their own fees (just as lawyers and accountants do). As such, there is now a requirement to disclose the cost of advice and the cost of investment products separately. In addition, the British regulator raised the minimum qualification level for FSPs, instituted a Code of Ethics and boosted requirements for continuing education. Once again, doesn't this sound eerily familiar?

The comment letters that the FSA received were particularly telling. Some stakeholders warned (as if the outcome would be unambiguously negative) that a number of FSPs would be forced to leave the business if the reforms that were ultimately enacted came to pass. Again, I recall that in the first edition, I likened the industry to a 'killer course' in first-year university where a prof would ask students to look to their left and look to their right, because statistically, one of them would be gone before the year was out.

The U.K. is not alone. In April of 2010, the Rudd government in Australia announced forthcoming reforms with similar objectives and consequences. In a press release announcing the initiative, the Minister responsible, Chris Bowen, said: "Access to quality advice remains an important part of planning for the future... These reforms will see Australians receive financial advice that is in their best interests, rather than being directed to products as a result of incentives or commissions offered to the financial adviser."

Australia's "Future of Financial Advice" package included:

- A prospective ban on conflicted remuneration structures
- The introduction of a statutory fiduciary duty
- Increased transparency and flexibility of payments, including 'adviser charging'
- Percentage-based fees were to be charged only on ungeared (unbundled) products—and only with investor consent
- The expanded availability of low-cost simple advice

The majority of these reforms were to come into effect on July 1, 2012, but had been delayed temporarily as of our publication date. In the first half of 2012, Australian FSPs were transitioning in earnest in order to be prepared for the new reality that awaited them. One part of the new Australian practices is the concept of a 'Centralized Investment Proposition' (CIP). When making investment recommendations to clients, Australian FSPs are now required to disclose all associated expenses and fees associated with not only the products being recommended but also the alternatives that were not recommended. The onus is now on the FSP to demonstrate why they believe the client will be better off as a result of their preferred course of action.

All of these things are touchstones of what was mentioned in the first edition of this book in 2003. I sometimes feel like Cassandra, who was granted the gift of prophecy but cursed with the knowledge that no one would believe her. People thought my message was unduly alarmist. Meanwhile, nearly half of all FSPs in Australia and the U.K. have recently left the industry because they could not (or would not) comply with the requirements of a more professional paradigm.

Looking at the context provided by other English-speaking jurisdictions, I don't believe CRM represents the destiny of the Canadian financial services industry by any means. Change continues. Indeed, it seems to be accelerating. As with the U.K., people in the developed English-speaking world are watching and waiting to see what comes of all these changes abroad. No one doubts that there will be some amount of confusion, dislocation and trouble. While CRM represents a sea change in Canada, it is more likely a mere drop in the bucket when viewed through a broader international lens. The more substantive changes abroad might actually pave the way for more domestic changes, which might not look that radical when viewed in comparison to what is going on elsewhere.

The Fiduciary Question

One area where there's a lively debate has been regarding the question of whether or not Canada should adopt a fiduciary standard. To date, FSPs in Canada have only been required to make recommendations that are suitable for their clients and not necessarily in their best interests (the fiduciary obligation). At issue here are a number of related matters: the standard of care that FSPs (and their firms) are to be held to, the degree to which investors should rely on FSPs and the liability/consequences associated with inappropriate advice. Should the standard of care in Canada be raised? There are two schools of thought.

Ellen Bessner is a prominent securities lawyer who consistently acts on behalf of FSPs in court proceedings and has written the definitive book on FSP risk management, entitled *Advisor at Risk*. In her opinion, owing to the development of the Canadian legal system, a move to the fiduciary standard in Canada would be largely redundant. Her position is that:

> Canadian law is well settled and already protects
> clients who can prove that their advisors (doctors,
> lawyers, accountants and FSPs) were negligent or
> breached their contract. However, if a client can
> prove that the relationship was elevated to a fiduciary
> level by proving that they reposed their trust and
> confidence in the advisor and were vulnerable, a fi-
> duciary duty will exist (Hodgkinson v. Simms, (1994)
> 3 S.C.R. 377 (S.C.C.)). Not all client/advisor relation-
> ships are fiduciary because clients may be quite so-
> phisticated and involved in decisions made on the ac-
> count—those clients should not be entitled to an ele-
> vated level of protection, particularly when those
> clients are often the author of their own misfortune
> by insisting on aggressive strategies that are against
> the FSP's advice (see Parent v. Leach (2008) O.J. No.
> 2155).[2]

Meanwhile, Paul Bates is a former Commissioner of the
Ontario Securities Commission, a former CEO of a couple of
IIROC member firms and a current member of the OSC's
Investor Advisory Panel. Bates' view is that the fiduciary
standard couldn't come more quickly. He says:

> We should look closely at a proposal put forward by
> the U.K. Financial Services Consumer Panel that ar-
> ticulates specific conditions for engagement when in
> a fiduciary relationship: no conflict of interest; no
> profit at the expense of the customer without their
> knowledge or consent; undivided loyalty to the con-
> sumer; and a duty of confidentiality. By becoming

specific in terms of one's commitment to the client, perhaps in the form of a mutually signed agreement, the nature of exactly what kind of relationship exists would serve both provider and customer well.[3]

As it stands, there are already some FSPs who are undeniably fiduciaries and others who clearly are not. Anyone who is a Portfolio Manager or Associate Portfolio Manager is a fiduciary, for instance. Part of why I elected to become an Associate Portfolio Manager in 2011 is because I actually wanted to be held to a higher standard. The test is one of trust and discretion. There is a trust relationship in place where the FSP has the discretion to place trades without having consulted the client beforehand.

Certain organizations, such as the Financial Planning Standards Council (FPSC) have gone right up to the line without having crossed it. In other words, the FPSC has gone on record to say that CFPs are held to the same standard that fiduciaries are—even if a traditional trust relationship is not formally in place. The FPSC's insistence that CFPs use letters of engagement for all client relationships is an example of the mandatory codification of the relationship that the organization feels is an important part of true professionalism.

This strategic move to require all CFPs to put their clients' interests first seems like a motherhood position at first. Beneath the surface, however, something far more contentious lurks. The interplay between the considerations of transparency, client interest, informed consent and evidence-based research is coming to the surface. One example that could be cited involves the impact of product costs on an investor's long-term retirement projections and ultimate returns. To what extent should that correlation be disclosed?

I've met many FSPs who have been so bold as to suggest

that product cost doesn't matter much, because planning is much more important. To me, that's like saying a person can live a lot longer without water than without food, so having food doesn't matter much. In instances like these, the thoughtful consideration of factual evidence is minimized by making an unnecessary comparison—and often dismissed entirely because it was deemed to be relatively less important.

At issue here is the concern for consumer protection. Polls consistently show that most Canadians think their FSP has a fiduciary obligation toward them. When things go wrong, as they sometimes do, these same people are often shocked to learn that all their FSP had to do was to recommend products and strategies that were deemed to be 'suitable' for their circumstances. To my mind, this is not about revenue compression. This is about managing liability, pure and simple.

"Fiduciaries should strongly consider index funds as an alternative to actively managed funds. Index funds incur about 80% less in transaction costs than actively managed funds...long-term returns for actively managed funds trail their respective indexes."[4] Keenan is not alone in his viewpoint. Prominent American advisors such as money manager and author Larry Swedroe have suggested the same thing. In the *Journal of Financial Planning* 2012, Stewart Neufeld, PhD, also suggests this standard for pension plan fiduciaries in the U.S.

In essence, sometimes change might not come the way we expect it. If Canada were to adopt a fiduciary standard and it then became generally accepted that anyone who is held to a fiduciary standard needs to recommend low-cost products, some of the elements of STANDUP advice would be legislated into existence through the back door.

From a consumer perspective, there's some degree of comfort. It comes from knowing that your FSP *must* act in your *best* interests at all times. It should go without saying that if you're a consumer and you want that standard of care, you should seek out an FSP who provides it. For the large majority of clients, it's not a deal breaker, but it is another valid way of determining whether an FSP is right for you.

There is no doubt that FSPs are already being held to higher standards than ever before. Although the fiduciary standard might seem far off, other related changes have already come into effect. For instance, a few years ago, the primary test of suitability was summarized by the letters 'KYC'—for 'Know Your Client.' These days, there is a parallel obligation called 'KYP,' or 'Know Your Product.' The KYP standard has developed because many FSPs have been deemed liable for making unsuitable product recommendations once it was discovered that they really didn't understand the products they were recommending to their clients. It has been established that a mere reliance on a firm's compliance department is insufficient for an FSP who needs to do proper due diligence on products (especially new concept products) that are being recommended to retail clients. If things go wrong, questionable suitability is often only discovered as being linked to an FSP's inability to grasp the full range of possible outcomes associated with a product's value proposition.

The good news in all this is that the standards associated with giving advice are going up. The question that it begs is whether or not they're going up quickly enough. For those FSPs who want to be ahead of the curve by reflecting the spirit of STANDUP advice even if they are not currently required to do so by regulators, it might be said that a premium could be realized by doing things that go above and beyond what the industry currently requires. Advisory firms should be happy to have leading-edge and highly compliant FSPs. Meanwhile, FSPs could feel good about the work they do and the services they offer by being the professionalism trailblazers. Finally, retail clients would likely also be a fair bit happier if they worked with someone who was going beyond industry norms regarding transparency and alignment.

Just what sorts of activities are we talking about?

Be a STANDUP FSP

Hold yourself responsible for a higher standard than anyone else expects of you.

—Henry Ward Beecher

There's absolutely nothing stopping FSPs from continuing to do business the way they have throughout their entire lives, and no one has to change anything if they don't want to (yet). That's the funny thing about change—it will occur whether you want it to or not. Resisting it usually only makes things more difficult down the road.

For years now, FSPs and the firms they work for have been talking about professionalism in financial services. To hear them tell it, virtually everyone who offers financial advice is a "professional." However, unlike the more established professions, many of the generally accepted attributes of professionalism are not yet consistently present.

There are many FSPs who are true professionals in every sense and a few that are clearly unprofessional—with most FSPs falling somewhere in the middle. In my view, there are three factors to be considered—both for FSPs and for people who are looking to hire an FSP:

1. What evidence is the product or strategy recommendation based on?
2. Is disclosure being made regarding the pros and cons of the recommendation?

3. What is the impact as it pertains to professionalism?

The Professionalism Payoff

By diverting energy from sales pitches toward those activities that are viewed by society as being truly representative of professionalism, we could get to a clear win/win situation for both clients and FSPs. Imagine that—a world where the STANDUP FSPs win out precisely because they are conspicuously good.

The payment method compensating an FSP doesn't indicate either the existence of ethics or a lack of ethics in and of itself. The real issues are in regard to questions of perception, opportunity, evidence-based recommendations and informed consent. Compensation considerations could obviously skew the recommendations being given—and bias, including the perception of bias, obviously still exists. But to the extent that that perception could be altered, why wouldn't we all band together to do it?

If there is one thing that has come across loud and clear in my conversations with most consumers over the years, it is that they are quite open to working with an FSP they can trust to look out for their best interests. As it stands now, most are skeptical. A cynic might even say that the few consumers of financial products and advice who are not skeptical are merely naive. Wouldn't it be great if consumers were neither of those things and justifiably content with that status? Wouldn't it be absolutely fantastic if consumers trusted FSPs implicitly because the way they went about doing their work was transparent, aligned with the clients' highest values and of the highest quality in terms of both competence and ethics?

Clearly, FSPs want to be thought of as professionals. Unfortunately, most consumers think of most FSPs as rather less than that. Imagine if it were different. Imagine if there were a level of trust that existed between a client and an FSP that was comparable to the trust between a patient and a surgeon. It would be implicit. It would be absolute. It would be marvellous!

Trusted professionals should recommend products based not on compensation considerations but on what works best. Of course, everything worth explaining could also be disclosed in writing and in advance of any work being done. FSPs could offer professional and independent advice irrespective of the products used to implement that advice. This eventuality is coming whether we like it or not. To be clear, I believe that most FSPs try to help clients obtain a meaningful understanding of capital markets. Most try to make reasonably suitable recommendations. These FSPs will diversify between equity and income, value and growth, small cap and large cap and a number of other ways, too.

What I see less of though is a meaningful level of willingness to use both active and passive strategies, as well as meaningful disclosure regarding the pros and cons of both strategies. This, of course, could be an all-or-nothing proposition or a mix-and-match (core and satellite) combination. Most FSPs recommend an all active approach all the time. These same FSPs often insist they have no bias at all and that they go out of their way to help their clients make informed decisions about the products and strategies being pursued.

I beg to differ. My sense is there are FSPs who are deliberately silent on the matter of cost impacts when discussing options with their clients. Why not show clients both options? Don't direct them one way or another to start. Simply explain that both options are on the table and that over the course of their lifetime, both would likely be reasonable depictions of their overall investment experience.

I propose that a 'Disclosure of Investment Philosophy' be employed by FSPs when new accounts are opened. Most FSPs would be hard-pressed to offer a succinct expression of their values and beliefs if called upon to do so. Many would likely be hard-pressed to incorporate evidence-based research into their advice, as well. This sort of document could easily do both in a few short paragraphs. Here's an example:

Disclosure of Investment Philosophy

This is to acknowledge that Joe Brilliant, FSP, has advised me that he believes capital markets are sufficiently efficient to justify the exclusive use of passive and/or asset class products. Joe believes this approach features relative predictability and relatively lower volatility. As such, he has advised that I consider building my portfolio entirely using these investment options, except where no such options exist.

Joe has further advised me that by using actively managed investment products, I may be compromising the asset allocation set out in my Investment Policy Statement (as some Investment Managers modify their asset allocations on an ongoing basis), and that I may incur higher tax liabilities as a result of higher portfolio turnover. Moreover, these potential shortcomings do not offer any evident or reliably predictable quid pro quo, as there is no study evidence to indicate that one can identify, in advance, that those actively managed investment products will reliably outperform passive or asset class alternatives. As such, Joe's view is that neither fund picking nor stock picking should be attempted.

In essence, Joe believes that the role of FSPs involves identifying tax minimization strategies, ensuring that clients have the right amount and right kind of insurance, setting and maintaining suitable asset mixes, extending time horizons and maintaining discipline. The one thing that he does not believe advisors should attempt is to identify securities or securities pickers that will 'outperform' after fees over meaningful time horizons.

While there can be no assurances that the

recommended approach will outperform an active alternative, Joe has advised me that in the very long run (twenty years or more), it is highly probable that a passive or asset class approach will offer satisfactory long-term, client-specific, risk-adjusted, after-tax returns and may out-perform active alternatives.

_____   _____   _____

Client   Joe Brilliant, FSP   Date

This sort of disclosure could also be accomplished in another way. Clients could be given a simple visual depiction of alternatives to help them focus on what the science of investing says. For instance, the depictions below show that both historically and logically, an average investor's expected return is the return of the asset class minus the cost of the product used to get exposure to that asset class—plus or minus a degree of variance. In my illustrations, Option A features a 9.5% average expected return with a relatively modest variance (tracking error), while Option B features an 8.5% average expected return, but with a fair bit of additional variance (positive or negative 'Alpha').

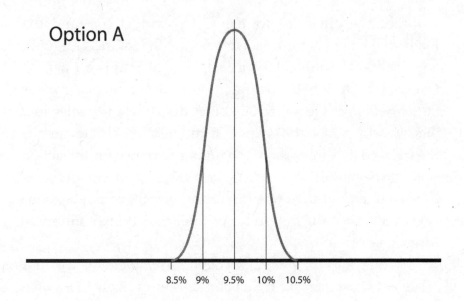

Option A

8.5%   9%   9.5%   10%   10.5%

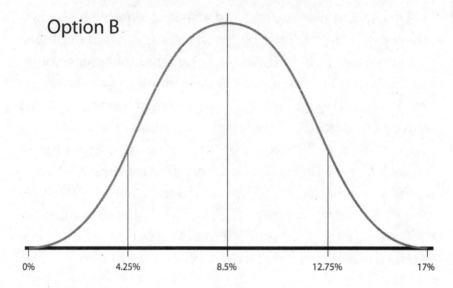

Option B

| 0% | 4.25% | 8.5% | 12.75% | 17% |

Since the differences are due to product cost and the likely dispersion of returns, we're left with Option A hugging a benchmark minus a lower cost, plus or minus a tracking error, and Option B costing more and having a greater variance of possible return outcomes due to security selection. One would reasonably expect a modest tracking error for the passive option and a much higher variance for the active option. If markets return 10% and the passive option costs 0.5%, while the active one (featuring no FSP compensation) costs 1.5%, then the long-term difference is 1% per annum— forever.

My question for potential clients is simple: is it worth a certain 1% cost increase if that choice is most likely to involve a similar reduction in long-term returns with a wider dispersion of outcomes? Remember that for every person on the right side of the centre line in either option, there's another on the left side. There are pros and cons to both approaches, but which option is a typical investor more likely to choose if asked? Both options have a constituency. In this instance, my concern is not so much whether the client chooses one option or another, but rather in ensuring that the client understands the trade-offs involved with the choices. This could be demonstrated through a client signature on an illustration depicting the options. Getting this would show that a reasonable degree of informed consent was solicited regarding the strategy ultimately being pursued.

Investors should clearly understand their options. Here's a value proposition that FSPs may wish to consider taking to them. They could ask, "If I could show you how to save tens or even hundreds of thousands of dollars over the course of your lifetime by simply replacing your current investment products with products that have a similar expected pre-cost risk and return profile but which cost 1% less and have less expected volatility, is that something that would interest you?" All I know is that every time I ask that question, I get a resounding "yes!"

Just about the only people I've ever met who don't give such a response are the people who would never ask the question in the first place. While regulators have finally made meaningful and transparent disclosure a precondition of all account opening procedures, many feel that more needs to be done. As always, FSPs should give serious consideration to being ahead of the curve. Strategically, there could be an 'early mover advantage' to capture in so doing. Now that CRM has been introduced, most of the benefit of what might have been accomplished with a voluntary move to increased transparency and professionalism has evaporated.

In my opinion, these are the sorts of things that a STANDUP FSP could do voluntarily and immediately to improve professionalism, trust and understanding. Since, as the saying goes, "sunshine is the best disinfectant," more disclosure might be preferred to less. This disclosure would likely need to be written in terms any competent layperson could understand. It might include the use of letters of engagement, compensation disclosure letters with transparent fees, written investment policy statements (IPSs) and so forth—many of which are still not mandatory for most FSPs. With client sign-off, clients cannot say these details were not set out clearly at the beginning. This has potential benefits for everyone. Firms appear to like it because sign-off can make it awfully hard to sue compliant FSPs. Consumers and FSPs should like it, too, because setting out the terms of any engagement ought to enhance the level of accountability for both parties—and both consumers and FSPs have an obligation to do better.

The Limits of Research and Associated FSP Obligations

The performance of capital markets is not like physics or mathematics, where specific circumstances lead to the exact same answer every time. Rather, capital markets are more like research done regarding diseases or in the social sciences. There are many things that are generally true, but not necessarily absolutely true. Education and open-mindedness correlate positively, but not exactly. Cigarette smoking and incidence of cancer tend to correlate positively, but not exactly...and there are exceptions in both directions: chain smokers who don't get cancer and lifelong abstainers who do.

But just because there are exceptions does not absolve professional intermediaries from drawing attention to the broad generalities of causation. There are many who feel that professionalism would only be enhanced if FSPs did more than was required of them at the outset.

This sort of improved professionalism is taking place on a macro level, too. Certain industry associations are now raising the bar in areas where regulators have been relatively silent. For instance, those FSPs who hold widely accepted designations such as the CFP will have a huge professional advantage over competitors doing the same work but without the designations, due to their obligations as set out in their Codes of Conduct and Standards of Professional Responsibility. Quebec has already done this.

It strikes me as being entirely possible (and nearly inevitable) that the rest of the country will follow in due course. More than ever, the time has come for FSPs to STANDUP for professionalism. We're well on our way to creating a real profession. It's coming, and everyone knows it.

Presently, FSPs suffer as the 'ham in the sandwich' between their firms and their clients. We're finally getting an explicit recognition of the inherent conflict of interest associated with that position. It should be noted, however, that FSPs needn't necessarily be in conflict with their clients. I know of one vertically integrated financial services company that has gone so far as to request that their FSPs change the disclaimers in their newspaper articles to include the sentence: "The views expressed are the personal views and opinions of the author and not those of [the company] and are not endorsed in any way by [the company]." The firm that took this unusual step did not allow the FSP to make a reciprocal disclaimer to his own clients. It should be obvious that if companies are going to insist on a disclaimer like the one above, FSPs using a disclaimer could also write to their clients saying something like: "Please be advised that the views expressed by [the company] are the personal views and opinions of the people expressing them and not mine." After all, liability and the need for clarity should cut both ways. True professionals will always respect those who have a different view and encourage their clients to invest accordingly. If they disagree, however, they also have a duty to say so.

Most people would agree that limits are a good thing.

Whether the subject is speed limits on highways, spending limits on credit cards, age limits on alcohol consumption or a salary cap on hockey payrolls, society has found lots of useful applications for limits. The very first section of the *Constitution Act* of 1982 makes it clear that the rights and privileges set out in our *Charter of Rights and Freedoms* are guaranteed only to such "reasonable limits prescribed by law in a free and democratic society."

In the financial services industry, the libertarian viewpoint of hard-core capitalism does indeed seem to have limits. For instance, some mutual fund firms avidly recommend their products and are opposed to having legislation enacted that would limit the fees they can charge. They argue that a vigorous free market should set those prices. However, when FSPs want to charge whatever the market will bear for their advice, product distributors and advisory firms have no problem in setting both maximum and minimum fee limits. The manufacturing and distribution sides of the financial advice business need to get their stories straight. Either both sides of the cost equation should be limited—or neither of them.

There are many people who believe cost limits have a role to play in financial services, but how can companies justify putting a limit on FSP fees when there's no limit on manufacturer fees? Shouldn't it be both or neither? The industry is rife with double standards.

Notwithstanding the fact that basic tenets of capitalism call for an unfettered market, there's a good case to be made for putting limits on both. No matter how libertarian one's views are about elements of social welfare, it seems there's a consensus that sometimes limits are necessary simply because of the abuse that would likely occur if there were none.

Another way that one might look at disclosure is to

apply the Golden Rule as it relates to the financial services industry. Essentially, that means FSPs should disclose unto others as they would like others to disclose unto them. That might well mean that their disclosure involves not only (for instance) what a product costs but also what the impact of that cost would be on a portfolio of a certain size over a certain time frame, all else being equal.

The question of meaningful, professional disclosure can be addressed in a number of ways. The most obvious way is to comply with the letter of the regulation. As such, product manufacturers need to make clear disclosures in their prospectuses and offering memoranda, including what their products cost and any associated permutations, such as taxes, performance bonuses and additional service fees. At issue here might be the notion of materiality.

The industry regulator for securities in Canada is the Investment Industry Regulatory Organization of Canada (IIROC). As a self-regulating organization (SRO), IIROC sets rules (including terms and limits) for FSPs to abide by. One of the most all-encompassing rules is found in section 29.7 (1) of the IIROC rulebook. It says that industry participants are to disclose all material facts pertaining to products and services. When I asked an IIROC manager of Business Conduct Compliance to define the standard more precisely, she said: "Materiality is well defined in several places. We expect members to be professionals, able to apply rules reasonably."

Given this response—every answer is a response, but not every response is an answer—it seems our esteemed securities SRO is quite happy to offer general guidance regarding where the line might be drawn on industry matters without ever specifically drawing a line at all. Different firms, in turn, take it upon themselves to draw different lines regarding disclosures, disclaimers and such. The perspective they bring to the table will inform their individual corporate policies and procedures regarding product disclosures and practice disclaimers, among other things. In short, the same marketing piece might involve different disclosures at different firms governed by the same regulatory framework.

Prior to age thirty-five, most people have relatively small portfolios; now, accepting that most people pay more for advice when their portfolios are smaller (either due to a larger proportion of equity or a higher percentage fee or both), we can use this as the start of our 'cost clock.' The kind of money a typical good client might pay over a lifetime, for both financial products and financial advice, assumes that an average good client couple will have invested about $100,000 in assets by thirty-five. This cost is the blended total cost of both products and advice.

My sense is that most clients don't think of it that way. Furthermore, my sense is that the reason most clients don't think of it that way is because most FSPs don't encourage them to think of it that way. The simple truth of the matter is that cost is important. In fact, cost is perhaps the most reliable indicator of likely long-term outcomes that one could use.

Obviously, there are exceptions. There are cheap products that still perform poorly and expensive ones that do very well in spite of their cost. In fact, there are exceptions to virtually anything in life. Still, the existence of exceptions does not disprove a general causal relationship. To say to a client that "it doesn't matter what the product costs as long as you get good performance" is rather like having a physician say "it doesn't matter how much you smoke so long as you don't get cancer." In theory this may be true, but no one has come up with a reliable way to put the theory into practice. Whether or not a person ultimately avoids a more likely outcome does nothing to either prove or disprove a more general causation. Sometimes, individual outcomes can seem random.

The Politics of Cost Considerations

There's an intriguing attribute about the financial services industry that is seldom discussed. Unlike other businesses that provide either goods or services, the business of providing financial services seems to have remained somewhat immune to price competition. This seems to be the case for both products (those manufactured in Canada are consistently among the most expensive in the world) and services (Canadian FSPs generally charge more than American FSPs that offer similar services). There's a real benefit to people if they make a concerted effort to lower their costs—a tactic that is self-evident in most circles.

Your grandmother was right when she offered her home-spun wisdom: "A penny saved is a penny earned." It never ceases to amaze me how so many people miss something so basic. An investment that earns 9% before fees with fees at 2.5% leaves the investor with 6.5% in his pocket. An investment that earns only 8% but costs only 0.5% leaves the investor with 7.5% in his pocket. Anyone who thinks a fraction of a percent isn't worth considering should take a look at their financial independence projections and run them again using a return assumption that is 1% higher—while keeping all other factors (asset allocation, risk and expected pre-cost return) constant.

The savings would be far greater still when you consider that most clients add considerably to their portfolios while they are working. A simple $22,000 annual RRSP contribution added to the original portfolio would make for an astronomical amount of additional savings. Bear in mind that even that severely underestimates the total cost savings when you consider the fact that savings may well continue for ten, twenty or more years in retirement, too. Cost matters. It is a compelling value proposition that too few FSPs are prepared to acknowledge.

It seems to me, therefore, that cost (for both products and services) is a highly material consideration when contemplating portfolio management. Perhaps it's no big deal in your eyes. What if the same firm required different disclosures for different FSPs? After all, if there's no uniformity between firms (a macro question), is it a big deal if there's no uniformity within firms (a micro question)? The question of materiality morphs into an even bigger question involving matters of both consistency and fairness.

If you're buying an appliance, you'll see it comes with a sticker that shows not only how much energy it consumes in an absolute sense but also how much it consumes relative to other appliances one might purchase. As such, government bodies have decided that it is important that consumers can determine not only the absolute quantum of usage but also the comparative quantum of usage. It seems giving consumers only absolute (but not comparative) information might inhibit them from making a responsible self-interested choice. To date, disclosure has revolved around what costs are rather than what they mean for investors.

I think it would be constructive to have the industry include comparative data: how much does this Canadian equity mutual fund cost compared to the universe of Canadian equity mutual funds? I also think an impact disclosure is clearly material, even if the industry's SROs don't force the industry to disclose impact considerations. For instance, $10,000 invested at 10% over ten years yields a total value of $25,937.43. That same product would generate a final value of $20,610.32 after accounting for a 2.5% MER (assuming no difference in pre-cost performance). In my view, that kind of 'impact disclosure' of fact is not only material, it is also something that can be easily applied in a reasonable manner. That's the kind of detail that would help consumers make a truly informed decision.

A major problem is that most FSPs haven't yet managed to connect the dots for the clients they serve. Some understand the considerations and evidence involved, but many don't. Some understand behavioural economics, but many don't. Very few FSPs, however, have combined the two. The difference in cost between active products and strategies and passive ones could easily exceed a quarter of a million dollars for an upper middle class investor over the course of a lifetime. How many people earning in the low six-digit range have been sat down by their FSP and made to understand that, on a balance of probabilities, they would likely be better off to the tune of $250,000 if they simply elected to use low-cost passive products to construct their portfolios?

Pulling It All Together

Earlier in this book, we discussed the various accoutrements of professionalism, along with a few of the larger national and international trends. To the best of my knowledge, while much has been written about the elements of professionalism, the pros and cons of both active and passive management, the fiduciary standard and behavioural economics independently, no one has ever tried to combine the salient elements of all these concepts into one single prescriptive direction.

So far, we've determined that the business of providing financial advice is an emerging global profession, one that could only emerge once there was a large enough middle and upper middle class to support it. We've also learned that while the relative merits of both active and passive approaches are not universally agreed upon, although there is a developing consensus among evidence-based participants that a passive approach is more likely to provide a superior investment outcome over one's lifetime. We've learned that it is becoming increasingly onerous for FSPs, too. It is often no longer sufficient to merely recommend what is suitable to clients.

A higher standard is taking shape, one where FSPs must actively recommend what is in their clients' best interests. But clients are not homogeneous. What is best for one might not be best for another, given the randomness of potential outcomes, based not only on a balance of probabilities but also on some very personal decisions involving mental accounting, biases and trade-offs. In short, there may very well not be a traditional, universal best practice regarding prescriptions, neither for products nor for strategies.

All of these are based on the elements of factual data (Scientific Testing) and how it ought to be interpreted. If informed consent is to be viewed as a hallmark of professional conduct in a world where reasonable people may differ and outcomes are uncertain, then it seems to me that transparency (Necessary Disclosure) is the best solution to this vexing problem. To summarize:

- FSPs are increasingly being asked to put their clients' interests first; but
- Most clients are oblivious to what their choices (read: best interests) are; and
- In particular, most clients are unaware of the considerations between active and passive strategies because their FSP has never discussed those considerations with them explicitly; so

- Most clients end up investing using the strategies recommended by their FSP as a default, where competing options are often never on the table in the first place; even though
- Behavioural economics shows us that most investors are risk averse and would likely choose the option that has a lower downside (even if that means forgoing the possibility of a higher upside).

Disclosure allows FSPs to be a light, not a judge. To be absolutely clear, I have no quarrel with FSPs who work collaboratively with clients—regardless of whether the dominant player in the relationship is the FSP or the client. No matter who's driving the bus, if the decision is made after a full and frank discussion involving the pros and cons of competing value propositions, I'm fine with it.

My concern is with FSPs who are overly presumptive and who think they know what's best for their clients even as they fail to ask those same clients for input on questions that are by definition highly personal and otherwise unpredictable. Stated only somewhat differently, I don't care if people invest using option A or option B or any combination thereof, as long as they were given the pros and cons of each in advance and in a way that they could understand what the choice involved. What I believe is unconscionable is when what is supposed to be professional, educated, impartial advice ends up being compromised and thereby becomes something less than professional.

The issue here is not cut and dried. Financial advice comes in many forms and can encompass a truly mind-boggling array of considerations. Some people end up doing better through active management, but most do worse. A lot of the best advice has little or nothing to do with investing at all. Still, the concepts of comparing and contrasting both products and strategies may very well come down to simple matters of meaningful disclosure and informed consent.

The question, therefore, is: how professional is it to counsel someone to do something that is unlikely to provide a favourable outcome when other alternatives exist, especially when it is done without even acknowledging the existence of those alternatives? Again, just because something is improbable does not make it impossible. However, if FSPs have a mandate to protect the best interests of their clients, why do they consistently encourage them to do things that are likely to leave them worse off?

Part of the answer to this conundrum lies in compensation models. All FSPs want to be paid, which is no surprise. Since product providers don't generally manufacture embedded compensation passive products (there are exceptions), a large number of otherwise well-intentioned FSPs have taken the easy way out and decided not to fight the system. By avoiding the conversation about compensation, they necessarily also avoid the conversation about the relative merits of passive and active alternatives. Now why do you suppose that might be?

Compensation Reconsideration

Let's consider what an appropriate compensation structure for a professional FSP of the future might look like. Would it involve commissions? Certainly not. Doctors don't earn commissions. Would you respect a doctor's opinion if one treatment paid him 20% more than another? Whatever the compensation format is, it should leave the FSP beyond reproach regarding potential ulterior motives. As soon as the client can call the FSP's rationale into question, professionalism is compromised and credibility lost.

There are two ways the problem can be solved. The first is to do what lawyers, accountants and other professionals do: charge a transparent hourly fee. The good news for an FSP who charges $200 an hour is that anyone who pays that fee is most likely to pay attention to what is proposed or written. Furthermore, the likelihood of acting on the advice is also high. Who in their right mind would pay that kind of money for recommendations that were merely interesting? The second and more common way that qualified FSPs charge for their services is through an annual fee linked to the client's account size. An FSP should have no interest in recommending anything other than what is best for clients. If clients become unhappy for any reason whatsoever, they can simply pick up their marbles and go home.

In simple terms, the more the account rises, the more money the FSP makes; the more it declines, the less the FSP makes. This represents a clear performance linkage that more closely aligns the interests of clients with those of the FSP. The FSP, in turn, can go to a client and honestly say, "I succeed when you succeed"—a hallmark of true professionalism.

Meanwhile, some product-manufacturer companies offer to subsidize the marketing efforts of those FSPs who recommend their products in their ads and letters. Is it truly professional to accept money from 'partners' while other companies with comparable products offer no such assistance? What does this say about independence? Obviously, FSPs are not the only people facing these questions. It should be noted that other professionals could also clean up their acts, too. Think of the relationship between physicians and pharmaceutical companies, for instance. The point here is that certain elements of the status quo undermine the principles of professionalism. However, other, more established professions engaging in the same sort of behaviour is hardly evidence that the behaviour is acceptable.

For now, it might be best to examine the attributes one might associate with a professional: if you accept the premise that the world is becoming more complex and interconnected all the time, then the people who are offering advice in light of these changes should also be keeping abreast of them. Membership organizations have made it mandatory for their members to maintain a minimum level of continuing education. Thirty hours of continuing education work is the annual benchmark. This usually includes course work on ethics and is verified with questionnaires that are signed off by members and audited throughout the year.

Sadly, most FSPs still rely on sales tactics to get new business. Most still honestly believe that top performing managers can be reliably identified (and spend an enormous amount of time trying to do so).

I looked up the word 'charlatan' recently. The definition I found was: "n: One who makes a claim to skill and knowledge he does not possess." Since it is doubtful that anyone can reliably pick stocks in a way that adds value on a risk-adjusted basis net of fees, one could reasonably conclude that those FSPs that purport to 'add value' through that activity may simply be charlatans.

Helping people achieve their financial goals is fulfilling and important. Many people have been known to make unduly emotional decisions with their money. STANDUP FSPs need to shoulder their fair share of the burden in ensuring the system offers a reasonable degree of balanced commercialism.

Ethics, Professionalism and Change

The only rational way of educating is to be an example.
—Albert Einstein

Grappling with change is never easy. Change is especially difficult when powerful corporations resist it because it undermines their own interests. We've all heard the cliché: the more things change, the more they stay the same. There are justifiable reasons for people to harbour this kind of cynicism. Inertia often seems like the safest route.

For nearly a generation now, consultants have been earnestly telling FSPs to change their business model from commissions to fees and to get the credentials necessary to have true legitimacy with consumers as bona fide professionals. Many STANDUP FSPs have done precisely these things. Many others have chosen not to. No matter how logically and compellingly applied, moral suasion can seldom overcome human nature. Some believe that leading by example only allows for modest progress. To date, progress in Canada has been both less significant and less disruptive than it has been in other parts of the world. Depending on the urgency one feels ought to be applied to the situation, that turn of events could be either good or a bad.

We expect many things from our professionals, including a dedication to clients' best interests, real independence, professional training and ethical integrity. In spite of generally high standards, these expectations have often not been met in the financial services industry.

We see the signs of societal wear and tear in the other professions already. Doctors have been hit with malpractice suits. The Governor of New Hampshire recently banned tied selling because physicians were getting free trips tied to their prescriptions and calling them due diligence trips. Lawyers have been sued for a number of reasons. Accountants are currently held in wide disrepute due to a recent string of corporate malfeasance scandals. Lawyers are dealing with increased divorce rates. Doctors are treating more people due to stress brought on by financial concerns. Clergy all over the world have to deal with stresses, many of which are financial in nature. Newspapers are full of stories of seniors getting bilked out of their life savings. Those with large sums are even bigger targets, yet regulators continue to equate the possession of capital with the possession of a sophisticated investment mind.

As with any ailment, prevention is the best prescription. In Canada, no one has replaced the policy of buyer beware with one of full and necessary disclosure—yet. No one has changed suitability requirements to require that recommendations be made in consumers' best interests—yet. Many observers, me included, think it is merely a matter of when, not if, these sorts of reforms will take place. It may take another generation, but the global trend toward true transparency and professionalism cannot be denied.

Being a professional means being held to a higher standard than other members of society. Virtually every MBA program and professional school has courses on ethics and many have become mandatory for graduation. Still, the temptation to fudge the rules in order to pad the bottom line remains as attractive as ever.

That's the thing about ethics: they cannot really be

imposed. A reputation for integrity is either earned through years of diligence or not earned at all. Every industry and profession has some bad apples. The intent of this book is to offer clear examples of what the more established professions practice and to uncover some of the inherent inconsistencies in the field of financial advice. This way, the most appropriate concepts can be applied in the hope that a new profession might be born.

The truly professional STANDUP FSPs of the nation have already transformed themselves, but virtually no one has noticed. At the corporate level, profit margins continue to drive conduct, so the focus has been placed squarely on the bottom line, sometimes at the expense of conduct and best practices.

The rationale behind all financial advice needs to be re-considered. In the current environment, it is important for clients to have some choice regarding FSP compensation and absolutely vital that proper disclosure is made before transacting business. Consumers should also have the right to both understand the differences in various compensation models that exist today and to choose which one best meets their needs. All models have some degree of merit, but some are simply more consistent with the generally accepted principles of professionalism than others.

The industry is evolving—perhaps more rapidly than ever. The primary disagreement seems to revolve around how to get to where virtually everyone agrees we are heading. But if everyone pretty much agrees on the state and shape of the industry at present and the approximate shape of the industry in the future, isn't this the ideal time to get all stakeholders involved in a purposeful dialogue?

Disclosure is a difficult thing to do with verifiable evidence when people don't want to acknowledge what you are trying desperately to tell them. FSPs are often guilty of not correcting obvious misconceptions and misunderstandings. Industry players could do more to disclose exactly how and how much they are paid. Until now, the financial services industry has resisted transparency because it was convinced it would cost dearly in terms of forgone income. The real danger now may well be one of reputational risk. In other words, the trend toward transparency might even be seen by cynics as an act of desperate self-preservation more than one of consumer protection.

What FSPs Can Do

Any FSP who is serious about being a STANDUP FSP needs to get with the program as soon as is practical. This means implementing as many as you can of the best practices employed by other professionals as soon as possible. It means getting credentials that demonstrate a capacity to offer advice and no longer making do with merely having licences to sell products. It means talking to clients frankly to explain how the industry is changing and that positive, necessary and long-overdue reforms are coming. Most of all, it means that FSPs will need to put consumer interests ahead of corporate interests in a way that is clear, persuasive and unimpeachable.

Up to now, it has seemed that almost no one has had the courage to stand up and categorically do the right thing voluntarily. Some who have tried have been labelled heretics and have been made to suffer financially and emotionally for their efforts. As other stakeholders become more comfortable with how the industry works and what needs to change, these FSPs will be rewarded. Newly informed consumers of financial services will gravitate toward those FSPs who demonstrate true professionalism.

What Consumers Can Do

More than ever, an informed consumer is a good consumer. This ancient wisdom is more appropriate today than ever before: tell me and I forget; show me and I remember; involve me and I understand. Consumers need to get involved. They need to force the other stakeholders to give them more meaningful information for decision-making. This information also needs to be presented in a more understandable and accessible manner. Consumers need to look closely and to know in advance what it is they should hope to see. There are already enough FSPs in the marketplace who espouse professional principles that finding one shouldn't be difficult. This is particularly important for people who are dissatisfied with their current FSP.

As everyone knows, the business of offering financial advice is predicated primarily on relationships. Relationships, in turn, are predicated on the usual hallmarks of professionalism: honesty, integrity, experience and a genuine concern for the welfare of the client. If the FSP you're working with today possesses these qualities, you would probably be well advised to stick with that person. Of course, constructively encouraging that FSP to get credentials, unbundle and disclose fees and implement a number of professional best practices wouldn't hurt either.

Perhaps most important, consumers need to understand that any FSP who begins a conversation by talking about professionalism will likely be making a huge financial sacrifice that might take many years to overcome. How many consumers would be willing to take a similar pay cut themselves?

Since an ounce of prevention is worth a pound of cure, disclosure at the point-of-sale needs to be overhauled and augmented considerably. This is especially true with regard to so-called 'manufactured' investment products: mutual funds, segregated funds, structured notes and universal life insurance policies.

Consumers need to address the industry's tarnished reputation head on. Concerned stakeholders including the Small Investor Protection Association, the Consumers Council of Canada and the Canadian Association for the Fifty-Plus have been making helpful suggestions for some time now. These groups use their resources to ensure that consumer interests are heard. A number of prominent consumer advocates are also lending a hand.

What Regulators Can Do

It should be noted that IIROC has always insisted that the bar has been set appropriately for matters of disclosure, competency and investor protection. Perhaps we should revisit and ultimately redefine the question of requisite disclosure of material facts. Imagine if a provincial industry association representing physicians were to suggest that getting an 'A' in your final year of high-school biology was considered sufficient training to practice as a qualified physician. No one would doubt that there's a standard, it's just that few would believe that the chosen standard was adequate. Presently, there is no financial services industry requirement to:

- Disclose that product manufacturers make more money on actively managed funds (i.e. through mutual funds) than on passively managed ones,
- Disclose that it is improbable that an active approach (i.e. through individual security selection) will lead to more favourable outcomes, or
- Disclose that frequently trading securities often results in higher annual tax liabilities.

The financial services industry depends on maintaining the trust of the people who hope that the industry is transparent and ethical enough to conduct itself in a matter deserving of that ongoing trust. In my view, many of the industry's non-disclosures pertain to material factors that could very well cause investors to make different decisions if these disclosures were made.

I wonder what the industry fears. If more upfront disclosures were not material, they would not cause people to alter their choices. Accordingly, why not make them in the name of completeness? On the other hand, if, in making the disclosures, investors altered their decision-making, it would essentially prove the materiality of the things that were being withheld in the first place. Making this kind of disclosure should have two primary aims: to maximize consumers' understanding of what it is they are buying and to ensure its suitability. The only way we'll know for sure if it works is to make more meaningful disclosure mandatory.

What You Can Do

In the end, change will come. If we ('we' being all the stakeholders in this discussion) sit back, it will continue to evolve slowly. However, if we take action, it may well come more quickly. It only seems reasonable to choose the second path since the finality of the outcome seems so inevitable.

There is a popular saying that suggests that knowledge is power. I disagree somewhat. I believe knowledge only becomes truly powerful when combined with deliberate, purposeful action. The time has come for everyone involved to put their knowledge into action and come to terms with the changes that will be necessary to move the rendering of financial advice forward and into the realm of a true profession.

There are many who believe that various forms of

malfeasance will not go away and that meaningful dispute resolution is still unavailable. Most FSPs are still unaware of the existence of their own arbitration rights, alternative dispute resolution options and potential recourse offered by the Ombudsman for Banking Services and Investments (OBSI). There are a number of consumer advocates who would suggest that the pursuit of justice through these means is effectively useless anyway, given how few complaints result in rulings that favour consumers. The industry is not seen as being responsive to repeated pleas for increased and improved consumer protection, and any industry that fancies itself as a profession but has dispute resolution mechanisms that are viewed as tantamount to kangaroo courts clearly has a credibility problem.

A related matter regarding both disclosure and the improvement of the FSP-client relationship is performance reporting. The industry has long resisted giving clients a personal annualized rate of return on statements. The stated reason for the resistance is that the mathematics required is cumbersome. This difficulty is why performance reporting will be the last element of the Client Relationship Model to be implemented. There are more than a few skeptics who fear that the real reason behind this suppression of individualized performance reporting is that most companies and FSPs do not want to be held accountable for performance that lags benchmarks. I am one of those skeptics. Conversely, I am confident that trust and understanding would both be greatly enhanced if performance reporting became mandatory.

In the meantime, the website run by the Investor Education Fund, www.getsmarteraboutmoney.com, not only offers people a chance to plug in real-world data to derive customized return data, it also features a wide range of useful tools and calculators to help people help themselves.

We're all in this together. Consumers should demand more. Product manufacturers and distributors can do more. Politicians can do more. Regulators can do more. Enforcement officials can do more. It's time for all stakeholders to step up to the plate and show a real commitment to converting this sales-cultured business into a real profession.

This is a call to action. If you are involved in the financial services industry in any way—as a consumer, FSP, industry executive, legislator, regulator or journalist—do not simply put this book down and move on with your life. Instead, do something to encourage meaningful change in an industry that desperately needs to continue to embrace substantive change in order to become a true profession. If you really care about the future of financial advice in Canada, here are a few groups you might wish to contact in order to effect positive change:

Provincial Regulators

Alberta Securities Commission 403-297-6454
   www.albertasecurities.com
Alberta Insurance Council 780-421-4148
   www.abcouncil.ab.ca
British Columbia Securities Commission 604-899-6500
   www.bcsc.bc.ca
Insurance Council of B.C. 604-688-0321
   www.insurancecouncilofbc.com
Manitoba Securities Commission 204-945-2548
   www.msc.gov.mb.ca
Manitoba Consumer and Corporate Affairs 204-945-2542
   www.gov.mb.ca/cca/
Insurance Council of Manitoba 204-988-6800
   www.icm.mb.ca
NB Office of the Administrator 506-658-3060

www.gov.nb.ca

NB Superintendent of Insurance 506-453-2541

Nfld. and Labrador Securities Division 709-729-4189
www.gov.nf.ca

Nfld. and Labrador Insurance Division 709-729-2571

Nova Scotia Securities Commission 902-424-7768
www.gov.ns.ca/nssc

Nova Scotia Superintendent of Insurance 902-424-6331
www.gov.ns.ca/enla/fin/super.htm

Ontario Securities Commission 416-593-8314
www.osc.gov.on.ca

Financial Services Commission of Ontario 416-590-7000
www.fsco.gov.on.ca

NWT Securities Registry 867-873-0243

NWT Superintendent of Insurance 403-873-7308

Nunavut Legal Registries 867-873-0586
www.nunavutlegalregistries.ca

Quebec Securities Division 514-940-2150
www.gov.qc.ca

Quebec Insurance Division 418-528-9140

PEI Registrar of Securities 902-368-4551
www.gov.pe.ca/securities/

PEI Superintendent of Insurance 902-368-4550

Saskatchewan Financial Services Commission 306-787-5645
www.sfsc.gov.sk.ca

Saskatchewan Superintendent of Insurance 306-787-5550

Yukon Registrar of Securities 867-393-6251
www.gov.yk.ca

Yukon Superintendent of Insurance 867-667-5940

Miscellaneous Financial Services Contacts

Advocis 416-444-5251, 1-800-563-5822
www.advocis.ca

Canadian Banking Ombudsman 416-287-2877, 888-451-4519
www.bankingombudsman.com

Canadian Institute of Financial Planners 1-866-933-0233
www.cifps.ca

Canadian Securities Institute 416-681-2215, 1-866-866-2601
www.csi.ca

Canadian Venture Exchange / Toronto Stock Exchange
416-947-4670, 1-888-873-8392 www.tsx.com

Certified General Accountants Assoc. of Canada
www.cga-canada.org

Canadian Life and Health Insurance Assoc. 800-268-8099
(English) 416-777-2221, 800-361-8070
(French) 514-845-9004, 613-230-0031 www.clhia.ca

Canada Deposit Insurance Corp. 800-461-2342
www.cdic.ca

Certified Management Accountants 905-949-4200,
1-800-263-7622 www.cma-canada.org

Chartered Accountants of Canada 416-977-3222
www.cica.ca

Credit Union Institute of Canada 800-267-CUIC (2842)
www.cuic.com

Financial Planning Standards Council (FPSC) 416-593-8587,
1-800-305-9886 www.fpsc.ca

Institute of Canadian Bankers 800-361-7339
www.icb.org

Investment Counsel Assoc. of Canada 416-504-1118
www.investmentcounsel.org

Investment Industry Regulatory Organization of Canada
(IIROC) 416-364-6133
www.iiroc.ca

Investment Funds Institute of Canada 888-865-4342, 416-363-2158
www.ific.ca

Investor Learning Centre 888-452-5566
  www.investorlearning.ca
Montreal Exchange 800-361-5353
  www.me.org
Mutual Fund Dealers Association of Canada 416-943-5827
  www.mfda.ca
Office of the Superintendent of Financial Institutions
  800-385-8647, 416-973-6662 www.osfi-bsif.gc.ca
Portfolio Management Association of Canada 416-
  367-1831, 613-232-7393 www.ibac.ca
Quebec Deposit Insurance Board 418-643-3625, 1-888-
291-4443

For their part, FSPs should show some initiative and start using letters of engagement and compensation disclosure documents now—before being required to do so by their clients and/or employers. Furthermore, FSPs can set a good example by showing real leadership on matters of discretionary disclosure so that confidence can be re-established with honour and integrity. If you're an FSP, why not press your company's management to put meaningful professional standards in place?

Consumers should stop reading and watching investment pornography. Instead, they ought to focus more on those elements of their financial lives where they have direct control—things such as cost, taxes, planning and personal behaviour. Ask more and better questions when meeting FSPs and contemplating investment products. Never buy a product that you don't totally understand. Above all, Canadians need to realize that no one will ever care more about their finances than themselves. Furthermore, anyone can write letters to branch managers (and ultimately the editor of the local paper) when they are made to endure services that are less than professional.

No matter who you are and what your role in this story has been in the past, it wouldn't hurt to take action by contacting your local MP, MPP, MLA or MNA to request immediate action on regulatory matters such as competency, transparency and materialism. Contacting premiers, ministers of finance and the Prime Minister's Office works even better. Bringing about the continued constructive reform of the financial services industry and reinventing it as a genuine profession is everyone's business. The transformation is well under way and will continue with or without your input. Why not take this opportunity to weigh in on enacting purposeful reforms that could literally have life-altering consequences?

Notes

Part One: Preparing FSPs
Becoming an Advisor
1. Personal interview with Tom Hamza.
2. Personal interview with John Heinzl.
3. Personal interview with Glorianne Stromberg.

Efficient Markets
1. William F. Sharpe, "The Parable of Money Managers," *The Financial Analysts Journal* 32, no. 4, (July/August 1976): 4.
2. P. A. Samuelson, "Proof That Properly Anticipated Prices Fluctuate Randomly," *Industrial Management Review* (Spring (6) 1965): 41–49.
3. *Barron's*, 2 April 1990, 15.
4. *The Financial Analysts' Journal* Vol. 47, No. 1, January/February 1991. pp. 7-9

Education or Indoctrination?
1. Personal interview with Moshe Milevsky.
2. Michael Nairne, interview by the author, Toronto, Ontario, 25 April 2006.

Part Two: Scientific Testing
Fact or Opinion?

1. "The Relation Between Price and Performance in the Mutual Fund Industry," Javier Gil-Bazo and Pablo Ruiz-Verdu, 2009.

Behavioural Finance

1. Daniel Kahneman, *Thinking, Fast and Slow*, (Toronto: Doubleday, 2011): 212.

Part Three
Necessary Disclosure

2. "Ontario Minister Wants Cigarettes Banned," *24 hours*, 10 April 2006: 8.

Part Four: Professionalism
What Do STANDUP FSPs Do?

1. Dan Wheeler, interview by Brad Steiman, 3 May 2006.

The Inexorable Global March to a STANDUP Paradigm

1. A. Rosen, "The OSC simply isn't doing enough," *Financial Post*, March 15, 2007, pg. FP11
2. Interview with Ellen Bessner
3. Interview with Paul Bates
4. Michael C. Keenan, "The Elephant in the Living Room," *Financial Advisor Magazine*, May 2008.

What Adds Value?

1. "Your Fund Manager Likely Is Overpaid," 2 April 2006 [cited 14 August 2006]. Available from *www.fund-manager.org*
2. Kenneth R. French, "The Cost of Active Investing", *Journal of Finance*, 2008
3. Interview with Moshe Milevsky

Get an Investment Policy Statement

1. Gary P. Brinson, L. Randolph Hood, and Gilbert L. Beebower, "Determinants of Portfolio Performance," *Financial Analysts Journal* (July / August 1986): 39–44.
2. James Daw, "OSC Avoids Debate on Asset Allocation Report," *Toronto Star*, 24 September 2005: D2.

Acronyms

BPS   Basis Points: there are 100 basis points in 1%.

CAPM   The Capital Asset Pricing Model: an early empirical framework for describing risk and reward. The three factor model has since overtaken it as the best way to explain risk and reward in securities markets.

CFA   Chartered Financial Analyst: a designation devoted to rigorous security analysis.

CFP   Certified Financial Planner: the premier designation for financial planning.

CI   Critical Illness: insurance that pays a lump sum if you get sick, but live.

CRA   Canada Revenue Agency: the Canadian tax department.

DFA   Dimensional Fund Advisors: a mutual fund company dedicated to developing products based on academic research and empirical evidence.

DIY   Do-It-Yourself: a term used to describe people who prefer to forgo advisors and do their investing using discount brokerages.

DSC   Deferred Sales Charge: also known as 'back-end load,' it is a compensation structure that pays an FSP upfront but locks the investor into a redemption schedule lasting six or seven years. It also features annual trailing commissions.

EMH	Efficient Market Hypothesis: an academic theory put forward by Eugene Fama that posits security prices as always providing a highly accurate depiction of all available public information.
ETF	Exchange Traded Fund: a security that tracks an index at a low cost.
FCSO	Financial Services Commission of Ontario
FSP	Financial Service Provider: a term created to capture the myriad forms that can be taken by people who offer financial advice.
FSPC	Financial Standards Planning Council: a Canadian organization dedicated to the promotion and acceptance of the CFP designation.
GIC	Guaranteed Investment Certificate: a bank product that offers a set interest rate over a prescribed time frame.
GST	Goods and Services Tax: Canada's federal consumption tax.
HST	Harmonized Sales Tax: for those provinces that combine their provincial sales taxes with the GST.
IIROC	Investment Industry Regulatory Organization of Canada: an SRO dedicated to the policing of the securities industry.
IFIC	Investment Funds Institute of Canada: the trade association for Canadian mutual funds.
IIAC	Investment Industry Association of Canada: the new name for the regulatory portion of what was formerly known as the IDA. The new promotional trade association has had no name confirmed at the time of this book's printing.
IPS	Investment Policy Statement: a written document that sets out the primary details of a client's portfolio, including the strategic asset allocation.

KYC Know Your Client: a common advisory industry phrase that entrenches suitability as the 'cardinal rule' of investment advice.

KYP Know Your Product: a recent industry development that puts more of an onus on FSPs to better understand the products they recommend

LTC Long-Term Care: insurance for people needing personal care, typically when they become elderly.

MER Management Expense Ratio: the total annualized cost of owning a mutual fund, expressed as a percentage. An MER of 2.5% costs a $1,000 client $25 per year.

MFDA Mutual Fund Dealers Association: an SRO that is the mutual fund counterpart to IIROC.

MPT Modern Portfolio Theory: Nobel Prize–winning research originally done by Harry Markowitz that shows how risk-adjusted returns can be improved by combining weakly or negatively correlated assets.

OSC Ontario Securities Commission: the most prominent of Canada's provincial and territorial securities administrators.

RRSP Registered Retirement Savings Plan: a federal government retirement program that provides deductions for contributions and tax deferral for as long as the money remains invested.

SPANDEX Sales Pitches And Non-Disclosure Eliminate Excellence: a phrase concocted to characterize FSPs with a sales orientation.

SRO Self-Regulatory Organization: an industry association with a mandate of self-regulation.

STANDUP Scientific Testing And Necessary Disclosure

Underpin Professionalism: a phrase concocted to characterize FSPs with a professional orientation.

UL   Universal Life: a form of permanent life insurance that has an investment component added.

YRT   Yearly Renewable Term: a form of simple life insurance that features annual premium increases as one gets older.

Recommended Reading

Part One: Preparing Financial Service Providers

The Prudent Investor's Guide to Beating Wall Street at Its Own Game by John J. Bowen with Daniel C. Goldie

The Investment Answer by Daniel C. Goldie and Gordon S. Murray

The Power of Index Funds by Ted Cadsby

The New Investment Frontier III by Howard Atkinson with Donna Green

A Random Walk Down Wall Street by Burton G. Malkiel

Innumeracy by John Allen Paulos

Common Sense on Mutual Funds by John C. Bogle

"The Arithmetic of Active Management" William F. Sharpe, *Financial Analysts Journal* Vol 47, No. 1, Jan/Feb 1991, (7-9)

"On Persistence in Mutual Fund Performance" Mark M. Carhart, *The Journal of Finance*, Vol. LII, No. 1, March, 1997

www.ibbotson.com is the site for Ibbotson Associates in Chicago

www.dfaca.com is the Canadian site for Dimensional Fund Advisors

www.globeinvestor.com and www.globeinvestorgold.com are useful sites if you enjoy research on securities and mutual funds

Part Two: Scientific Testing

Global Investing by Roger Ibbotson and Gary Brinson

Asset Allocation by Roger Gibson

The Intelligent Asset Allocator by William J. Bernstein

Winning the Loser's Game by Charles D. Ellis

The Big Investment Lie by Michael Edesess

The Elements of Investing by Burton G. Malkiel and Charles
    D. Ellis

Fooled by Randomness by Nicholas Nassim Taleb

Thinking, Fast and Slow by Daniel Kahneman

Your Money and Your Brain by Jason Zweig

Predictably Irrational by Dan Ariely

Why Smart People Make Big Money Mistakes by Gary Belsky
    and Thomas Gilovich

The Ten Biggest Mistakes Canadians Make by Ted Cadsby

Beyond Greed and Fear by Hersh Shefrin

What Investors Really Want by Meir Statman

The Empowered Investor by Keith Matthews

The Quest for Alpha by Larry E. Swedroe

"Determinants of Portfolio Performance," Gary P. Brinson,
    L. Randolph Hood and Gilbert L. Beebower, *Financial
    Analysts Journal*, July / August, 1986, (39-44)

"Determinants of Portfolio Performance II: An Update,"
    Gary P. Brinson, Brian D. Singer and Gilbert L. Beebower,
    Financial Analysts Journal, May / June, 1991, (40-48)

"Does Asset Allocation Policy Explain 40, 90 or 100 Percent
    of Performance?" Rober G. Ibbotson and Paul D. Kaplan,
    Association for Investment Management Research, Janu-
    ary / February 2000, (26-32)

Part Three: Necessary Disclosure

Who's Minding Your Money? by Sandra E. Foster

The Corporation by Joel Bakan

Winning with Integrity by Leigh Steinberg

Enough by John C. Bogle

The Little Book of Common Sense Investing by John C. Bogle

How Good People Make Tough Choices by Rushworth Kidder

Part Four: Professionalism

True Professionalism by David H. Maister

The Trusted Advisor by David H. Maister, Charles H. Green and Robert M. Galford

Saving the Corporate Soul by David Batstone

Leading Change by John P. Kotter

The Heart of Change by John P. Kotter

Pensionize Your Nest Egg by Moshe A. Milevsky and Alexandra C. Macqueen

The Facts of Life by Paul Grimes

Nudge by Richard H. Thaler and Cass R. Sunstein

www.insurance-canada.ca is the federal government site on insurance

www.ccir-ccrra.org is the Canadian Council of Insurance Regulators' site

www.osc.gov.on.ca is the site run by the Ontario Securities Commission and features good background regarding regulatory principles and procedures.

www.getsmarteraboutmoney.com is run by the Investor Education Fund, a part of the OSC

Acknowledgements

There are always people to thank when a project like this comes together. For years, I've been collecting vignettes about professionalism and commenting on them in national publications in an attempt to be a 'bridge' between everyday Canadians and industry players. The first people I want to thank, therefore, are Dale Ennis at *Canadian Moneysaver*, Phil Porado at *Advisor's Edge Report* and Scot Blythe at www.advisor.ca. I'm humbled to have been able to use their collective soapboxes.

In many ways, more comprehensive undertakings couldn't be properly completed if the constituent parts hadn't already been synthesized and organized. Having written mostly in 800-word segments over the past decade or so has allowed me to bring order to this book a little more easily. Writing regular columns allowed me to delve into the issues of the day, but once that was done, I could look for trends and unifying themes. These were then cobbled together to make up the substance of the book.

In looking over the second edition of *The Professional Financial Advisor*, it struck me that there have been a number of fairly substantial changes—even though I sometimes lament that change has been too slow within the industry. Having a philosophical soulmate like Michael Nairne and an even-handed CEO like Mario Frankovich makes it easier for an advisor to both chronicle and cope with changes in an industry that is often less than eager to examine itself. To borrow a passage from the beginning of Kipling's "If":

If you can keep your head when all about you
Are losing theirs and blaming it on you;
If you can trust yourself when all men doubt you,
But make allowance for their doubting too...

I believe that over the past nineteen years, I have been extremely fortunate to be able to lean on Michael and Mario for guidance, balance and overall perspective. Even if others in the business doubt me and try to blame things on me, these two have always kept me moving forward. After all, criticism is really only effective if it is mixed with a reasonable degree of optimism and positive alternatives.

I'd like to thank the people who offered their kind input regarding the content of this book, including: Cheri Eklund, Lino Magagna and Colin Kirby. Of particular note, my two main proofreaders, John "Jazz" Szabo and Marina Magagna (also my partner in life), have gone above and beyond the call of duty in helping me to remain focused and purposeful. I believe this third edition of *TPFA* is substantially more readable because they cared enough to recommend removing original material that served only to cloud matters. I sincerely appreciate their helping me to keep things 'tidy' and in focus.

Finally, I'd like to offer my gratitude to those people who, over the years, have worked so hard on causes that align with the notion of STANDUP advice. There are too many to name, but suffice it to say that the list includes journalists, investor advocates, enlightened product suppliers, volunteers and lobbyists from industry associations. Our cause is a noble one and I remain convinced that professional status is something that can and will be achieved before long. In the meantime, I am proud to work arm in arm with people who are inspired by the promise of positive change. Transparency and integrity are indeed coming first.

Index

About the Author

John J. De Goey, CFP is a Vice President and Associate Portfolio Manager with Burgeonvest Bick Securities Limited. John enjoys a national reputation as an authority on professional, transparent financial advice in Canada. A frequent commentator on financial matters, he has written for a number of media sources including *Advisor's Edge Report*, *Canadian MoneySaver*, the *Globe and Mail* and the *National Post* and has also made numerous appearances on a variety of television programs, including CBC's *Marketplace*, *Newsworld* and *The National*, BNN's *Market Call*, and CTV's *Canada AM*. In 2003, John released his groundbreaking book, "The Professional Financial Advisor", which was later updated and re-released in a second edition in 2006. John is a recipient of the National Multi-Media Award conferred by the Canadian Association of Financial Planners and the Past President of the CAFP's Toronto Chapter and was recently one the first group of only 33 Canadian CFPs to be recognized as a Fellow of FPSC™. He has spoken at numerous conferences throughout Canada as well as in Ireland, the United States, and the Caribbean and has lectured on behalf of the Canadian Securities Institute. His personal website is: www.johndegoey.com.